FICTION & PHYSICIANS

About the Author

Stephen McWilliams graduated from the Royal College of Surgeons in Ireland in 2000 and is currently a consultant psychiatrist at St John of God Hospital in Dublin. Since April 2001, his articles have appeared regularly in the *Irish Medical Times*, the *Irish Medical News*, *Medicine Weekly*, the *Irish Psychiatrist*, *Scope*, *Forum* and several other publications. His topics have included medicine, psychiatry, literature, history, biography and the arts. He also contributed Forewords to the recently-published compilations, *The Book of Weather Eye* and *Weather Eye: The Final Year* by his father, the late Brendan McWilliams. For more information, see www.stephenmcwilliams.net.

FICTION & PHYSICIANS

Medicine through the Eyes of Writers

Stephen McWilliams

The Liffey Press

Published by
The Liffey Press Ltd
Raheny Shopping Centre, Second Floor
Raheny, Dublin 5, Ireland
www.theliffeypress.com

A catalogue record of this book is
available from the British Library.

ISBN 978-1-908308-26-9

Printed in the UK by TJ International.

Contents

PART TWO: FICTION ABOUT DOCTORS

Contents

Acknowledgements

Thank you to my publisher David Givens for his belief in the idea of *Fiction & Physicians*, and for his practical help throughout the process of finishing this book. Thank you to Jonathan Williams for his generous support, helpful advice and attention to detail. Thank you to the various editors (in particular Kennas Fitzsimons) who have repeatedly accepted my written submissions over the past twelve years. Thank you to my late father, Brendan, who taught me from an early age what to read and how to write. Thank you to my mother, Anne, who suggested to me from an early age that medicine is a noble profession. Thank you to my two young daughters, Claire and Emma, for persistently pulling the books down from the bottom shelf in my study while I try to write. Most of all, thank you to my wife, Dolores, for gently shooing said daughters out, and for her patience and support in everything I attempt to do.

Prologue

The Ghosts of Bewley's Café

I F EVERY STUDENT HAS A FAVOURITE CAFÉ, then mine was Bewley's of Grafton Street. Inspired by the grand Parisian, Viennese and oriental emporia of the nineteenth century, it opened its doors to the public amid the chaotic aftermath of the Irish civil war. As the flagship of the Bewley's empire, the café was certainly an ambitious project; its renovation alone cost some £60,000, a fortune in 1927. Almost immediately, it became enmeshed in Irish popular culture, frequented by iconic writers and artists from Patrick Kavanagh, to Samuel Beckett, to Sean O'Casey, to Bob Geldof. Even James Joyce has referred to it once or twice in his books. But then, how easy it is to picture Irish literary giants sipping coffee as they gazed across a crowded hall at Harry Clarke's half dozen or so brilliant stained glass windows, so much a part of the architecture they are often taken for granted.

The café still stands today, of course, but a further refurbishment several years ago has lent it a more upmarket feel. It continues to sell coffee but, to many Dubliners, its upgrade has marked the end if an era. Gone are the days when a penniless student like my former self could parsimoniously purchase a beverage and nurse it over the course of hours while reading some cheap paperback novel or simply watching the world go by. But then, perhaps small spenders like me were the very reason the place had to reconsider its *modus operandi* at all or, at the very least, its clientele.

I usually sat in the smokers' section, a large balcony protruding like a shelf over the cavernous eating emporium. Like any shelf cluttered with unique objects, it was here (in the little nook farthest from the self-service area) where a cluster of singular characters seemed to congregate. The atmosphere was rich with every walk of life. Fed by wispy columns rising from a few cigarette ends, a diffuse eye level cloud was pierced here and there by beams from spotlights embedded like bullet holes in the low red ceiling. A few imposing, leafy plants stood in strategic places around the balcony. They didn't seem to mind the air any more than I did, although by now these creatures would probably have counted themselves among the smokers. I am a non-smoker, but the aroma of burnt tobacco was not altogether unpleasant; it was the small price I paid (apart from that of my cup of coffee) for the privilege of watching interesting people.

Bewley's was, in short, a good place to sit and think. It was here, you could say, that the ideas for this book first germinated, and here that I conceived of the earlier passages contained within these pages. As I sat reading, my mind would begin cross-referencing authors, characters, themes and perspectives – half-baked ideas I captured in a notebook I soon learned to keep at hand. If the location was important, perhaps it was simply the inspiration provided by ghosts of the literary icons to whom I have already referred.

The final result is *Fiction & Physicians*, a collection of essays, short biographies, opinion pieces and literary reviews that relate to the central theme of medicine from the viewpoint of Irish, European and American literature. The first half of the book covers the lives, works and motivations of doctors – physicians, surgeons and psychiatrists alike – who wrote fiction in the form of poetry, plays, fictionalised case histories, short stories or novels. The second half concerns non-medical authors who, in the course of their commentary on universal themes, described fictional doctors, patients or medical illnesses vividly and memorably.

Much of this book has appeared in one form or another between the covers of the *Irish Medical Times*, the *Irish Medical News*, *Medicine Weekly*, *Scope* or the *Irish Psychiatrist*. These periodicals are principally aimed at a medical readership, but rest assured that only the most accessible pieces feature here, and all unnecessary esoteric jargon has been removed (or at least explained) in the editing process. Many of the passages, moreover, have never been previously published.

The emphasis is specifically upon fiction rather than cinema, television, art or music per se. Indeed, to cross reference medicine with all forms of art would undoubtedly result in a far, far larger volume. Some digressions do occur, but generally in a well-meaning effort to provide the reader with the bigger picture. Beyond this, *Fiction & Physicians* hopefully provides something for anyone with an interest in medicine and literature, and the curious manner in which both are intertwined. From François Rabelais to Thomas Ripley, it is a modicum of medical miscellany to enjoy over coffee.

Part One

DOCTORS WRITING FICTION

Chapter One

The Write Prescription for Success

BY THE TIME ANTON CHEKHOV WAS twenty-six, he had published over four hundred short stories. He was also a novelist, while his achievements as an accomplished playwright are beyond doubt. Less well known – and more surprising, perhaps – is that he was a fully-fledged member of the medical profession. "Medicine is my lawful wife but literature is my mistress," he was once noted to say. "When I'm bored with one, I spend the night with the other. Though it is irregular, it is less boring this way and besides, neither of them loses anything through my infidelity."

Chekhov was not the only doctor to put pen to paper. To begin with, many eminent literary and scientific figures were once medical students who ultimately did not qualify. Most noteworthy is James Joyce, who studied at St Cecilia's Medical School in Dublin and – for a short period – at the Sorbonne in Paris. Others who subsequently applied their intellect to non-medical matters include the writer Bertolt Brecht (medicine at Munich University), the revolutionary Jean Paul Marat (medicine at the University of Toulouse), and the astronomer Nicolaus Copernicus (medicine at the University of Padua). Some writers, as we shall see, qualified in medicine but never practiced, while others practiced initially and then abandoned one calling in favour of the other. And then, occasionally, we come across examples of individuals who successfully juggled two careers as artfully as they approached either one of them.

François Rabelais, Oliver Goldsmith, John Keats, Sir Arthur Conan Doyle, William Somerset Maugham, Oliver St John Gogarty, William Carlos Williams, A.J. Cronin, Michael Crichton, Khaled Hosseini, Paul Carson and many others shared a passion for both disciplines in a list that is seemingly endless. Such physician-writers hail from across the globe, with the Unites States, Canada, Ireland, England, Scotland, Wales, France, Germany, Austria, Russia and Afghanistan represented among their number. Some focused primarily on medical matters in their fiction, utilising their clinical experience and observations to synthesise dilemmas involving fictional physicians. Others – particularly those who are perhaps better known – strayed beyond medical themes to comment on the general workings of the world and the challenges faced by the people within it. What they held in common was a yearning to write and the skills and experience to make it happen.

Four Types of Writer

Although most physician-writers dabbled in more than one form of writing, their work could broadly be divided into four categories, with most specialising principally in one form or another. Writers of poetry include, most notably, John Keats, R.D. Laing, Oliver St John Gogarty and William Carlos Williams. Writers of plays include Oliver Goldsmith, Anton Chekhov and Mikhail Bulgakov, among others. The third category of writing (and first of prose) is the expanded case history. An obvious example here is Sigmund Freud, who penned numerous case histories to exemplify his newly established field of psychoanalysis, a breakaway branch of neurology. Many – such as "Anna O", "Dora" and "Little Hans" – were written under pseudonyms to preserve patient confidentiality but others – "Gustav Maher", "Emma Eckstein" and "Princess Marie Bonaparte", for example – were not.

The twentieth-century Russian neuropsychologist Aleksandr Luria also wrote up subjective case histories in works such as *The Mind and the Mnemonist: A Little Book about a Vast Memory*, while Oliver Sacks writes neurologically based essays and is most famously known as the author of *Awakenings* and *The Man Who Mistook His Wife for a Hat*. Although Luria's case histories were longer than those of Sacks, both men were part of a writing movement that sought to view the person behind the illness and transfer that unique experience onto paper.

Some writers took this process a step further and added the spice of speculation to cases they could not otherwise explain. Such writers include the eminent nineteenth-century American neurologist Silas Weir Mitchell, who wrote poetry, short stories and novels. Sometimes these fictionalisations were born of necessity, where there was no scientific explanation for a phenomenon witnessed in his surgery. An example is "The Case of George Dedlow", the succinct tale of an American Civil War surgeon's assistant who becomes wounded in battle and ultimately requires amputation of all four limbs. Dedlow attempts to understand the phenomenon known as "phantom limb", where pain and other sensations continue to be experienced long after the offending appendage has been removed.

"In other words, the nerve is like a bell wire," Dedlow suggests. "You may pull it at any part of its course, and thus ring the bell as well as if you pulled at the end of the wire; but, in any case, the intelligent servant will refer the pull to the front door, and obey it accordingly." Although Mitchell went to considerable lengths to convey to the reader the subjective experience of amputation (and used quite a bit of medical jargon in the process), he was limited to explanations allowed by the scientific progress of the day. Dedlow outlines the pain, weight loss, poor appetite, insomnia and slow heart rate one might reasonably expect in such circumstances; but he also describes "psychical changes" and how "I was less conscious of myself, of my own existence". Dedlow adds that "all the great central ganglia, which give rise to the movements in the limbs, were also eternally at rest. Thus one half of me was absent or functionally dead". Despite his initial efforts to be scientific, Mitchell was compelled to use his imagination in applying a psychological explanation of the symptoms experienced by his protagonist. Later, he went back to edit the piece with a physiological explanation based on advancements in understanding.

Finally, among physicians, there is the writer of fully-fictional short stories, novellas and novels. Most of the physicians in this book fall into this category, with many establishing themselves as writers of fiction only after they had first done so as doctors. Tobias Smollett's literary reputation was established quite independently of his medical career. His novels were satirical, a reaction to the Age of Reason perhaps, with a tongue-in-cheek approach to recounting the adventures of quixotic rogues who travelled widely. He also gave more than a nod to the epistolary styles of Samuel Richardson and Henry Fielding. His major works of fiction include *The Adventures of Roderick Random* (1748), *The Regicide* (1749) and *The Adventures of Peregrine Pickle* (1751).

Anton Chekhov might also be considered such an example although, as we have said, he was prolific even in his early twenties. Chekhov tried his hand at several freelance occupations, including journalism and the penning of brief comic sketches, but it is his later works – mostly plays and short stories – that are considered worthy of his legacy. Although most of his subject matter strayed far beyond his principal profession, some of his stories had distinct medical themes, for example "An Attack of Nerves" and "The Name-Day Party".

In "Ward Number Six" (1892) Chekhov discusses the fragile, respective roles of the doctor and the patient by curiously juxtaposing them. The story begins with Dr Andrew Ragin as the principal physician at a decrepit rural hospital. Alas, Ragin is disillusioned with his lot in life and complains of the "monotony and palpable futility of his job". He does not enjoy seeing patients; instead he prefers to sit in his study, sipping vodka as he reads the numerous books and magazines upon which he spends half his salary. His only friend is the local postmaster, a former wealthy landowner and cavalry officer who has fallen upon hard times. The two men discuss abstract topics while expressing despair at the dearth of intellect, education and refinement in their small Russian town.

It is only when Ragin develops an opportunistic friendship with Ivan Gromov that the randomness of life's fortunes truly strikes home. Gromov, a psychiatric patient in the neglected Ward Number Six, represents a fine literary example of paranoid schizophrenia. Despite Gromov's "persecution complex", he is clearly a man of Ragin's intellectual equal. Among Gromov's many assertions is the view that a doctor can never fully understand the manner in which a patient suffers if he has never experienced such exquisite pain himself.

There is an element of ironic prophesy in Gromov's musings because it is at this point that Ragin's carefully ordered existence begins to unravel. The local townsfolk note the doctor's sudden inclination to spend hours on the psychiatric ward with his patient, and assume the doctor must be experiencing a mental breakdown of his own. Ragin is compelled to resign and move into more modest lodgings. Alas, his replacement – Dr Eugene Khobotov – is not satisfied with this arrangement; he lures the unfortunate Ragin to the hospital with a spurious request for a second opinion. Ragin takes the bait and thus finds himself detained in the psychiatric ward of which he was once so neglectful.

The travesty of the story lies in Ragin's complete and unquestionable sanity. Indeed, the only manner in which he truly differs from his fellow townspeople is in his advanced intellect. Ragin, himself, asserts that, "There is only one thing wrong with me: it has taken me twenty years to find a single intelligent man in the whole town, and he is insane". Ironically, when Ragin's incarceration with Gromov finally provides him with an infinite opportunity for deep thought and intellectual conversation, the doctor quickly grows bored and yearns for something practical to do.

Chekhov, in many of his short stories, implies that he does not hold doctors in particularly high regard. Many of his medical characters are inherently flawed and thus bring about their own downfall. In the short story "The Butterfly" he makes it clear through narration that he believes artists and writers to be of a much higher status in society. Perhaps this underpinned Chekhov's literary ambitions, yet he still drew heavily upon his medical knowledge in his writing. Many of his short stories describe the daily routines of doctors while, in "Ward Number Six", his central character goes to great lengths to list recent medical and psychiatric advancements:

> *Ordinary general practitioners venture on resections of the knee-joint, abdominal surgery produces only one fatality per hundred operations. . . . There is a radical treatment for syphilis. And there is the theory of heredity, isn't there, and hypnotism? There are Pasteur's and Koch's discoveries, there are hygiene statistics, there's our Russian rural medical welfare service. Psychiatry with its modern methods of classifying disorders, its techniques of diagnosis and treatment . . . a gigantic stride forward, all that! The insane no longer have cold water poured over their heads, they are not put in straitjackets, they are treated decently . . .*

Moreover, in providing a confident, competent and detailed description of Gromov's "persecution complex", Chekhov makes it clear that he understands the nature of what we now call paranoid schizophrenia. Gromov has a fervent belief that he is being spied upon by the police and the judiciary and is convinced that he is on the verge of arrest for crimes he has not committed. Conversely, Ragin shows no signs of mental illness whatsoever and, because the reader has learned to trust Chekhov's judgement in this regard, there is outrage at the protagonist's unjust incarceration.

Although Chekhov's setting is a medical one, his themes are universal. They include the impoverished moral values of society, the effects of mindless bureaucracy and the cruelty of professional indifference. Much of Chekhov's writing, indeed, is holistic and informed by a wide perspective on life. In 1888, Chekhov famously wrote to his editor that, "My holy of holies is the human body, health, intelligence, talent, inspiration, love, and absolute freedom, freedom from force and falseness in whatever form they express themselves. That's the platform I'd subscribe to if I were a great artist."

What Rhyme or Reason to Write?

But the question still remains as to why one might bother writing at all. One obvious answer lies in the fame theory. Let's admit it, most doctors are reasonably ambitious, or – to put it more plainly – most doctors have big egos. Why *not* take a shot at becoming a bestselling novelist? But if ego is the only reason, we have not explained why physicians choose fiction over music, television or acting. Surely, there must be a more deeply rooted reason why any poor soul with a perfectly good day job would strive to scribble his thoughts, secrets and opinions on paper, let alone have them published.

Do both callings have something specific in common? Are they both, perhaps, meaningful ways of addressing human suffering? Do writers take up medicine simply to put food on the table? Is there something unique in the skills required to practise medicine that lends itself to writing? Or, is there something about the extraordinary experiences of a doctor that result in a compelling desire for communication, expression or catharsis?

If a few writers studied medicine only after they had first established themselves in the literary world, they generally did so for financial security. The American novelist Ethan Canin, for example, decided to enrol in medicine after graduating with a degree in arts. He suddenly realised how poorly paid most writers were and concluded that a sensible day job was the only option. The Canadian author Vincent Lam, winner of the 2006 Giller Prize for *Bloodletting and Miraculous Cures* (2006), has cited a similar reason for wielding a stethoscope as well as a pen, while Michael Crichton, author of *Jurassic Park* and the television series *ER*, also began writing primarily with a financial incentive in mind. During his impecunious days at Harvard Medical School, he would allow debts to accumulate during semesters and then use every spare moment of his holidays to deliver spy thrillers under a pseudonym. He confessed to having made little effort at the time to achieve originality or skill at his craft; it simply paid his medical fees and living expenses.

Sir Arthur Conan Doyle initially wrote short stories professionally to supplement the income he earned at his Southsea practice, and also to fill the lull periods between consultations with patients. Personally, I'd like to see my own GP find the time for that, but then perhaps Doyle lived in a less hectic era. His writing was certainly influenced by his medical background, but it is principally for his descriptions of the logical, precise and cocaine-addicted Sherlock Holmes that he is known. The detective was famously modelled in part on Doyle's old university professor, Joseph Bell, and to some degree on a former criminal called Eugène François Vidocq. More about that later, but it is certainly interesting to note that Doyle himself was not an especially logical individual. Towards the end of his life, he was deeply involved in the occult that had become fashionable in the early twentieth century. Even more remarkably, perhaps, Doyle believed in fairies.

Whatever about Doyle, it is certainly true that a handful of personal attributes and skills required to practise medicine lend themselves to writing. Doctors are generally busy; they are often good at time management and can work under the pressure of a deadline. Doctors have stamina; a six-year period of basic training, with many more spent climbing the slippery pole thereafter, helps doctors to develop the kind of thick skin that might be helpful in coping with the inevitable rejection and uncertainty that writers must endure before finally meeting with success. Doctors are observant; they focus upon aesthetics when they learn to describe empirically specific signs and symptoms as though encountered for the first time. This is something Imagist poets like William Carlos Williams, for example, learned to do. And while the skills acquired in medicine might produce a better writer, those required to write can help produce a better doctor.

Writing fiction has even been compared to surgery. The surgeon and author Richard Selzer once asserted that, "The thing I liked best about both surgery and writing, in the beginning, was the craft. Similarly, when I first began to learn to write, it was the suturing together of words into sentences, the selection of these words, the scattering of them on the page, that delighted me."

Either way, all practising doctors write prolifically on a daily basis. Published research has become increasingly important in a medical career and can lead to wider contacts in the publishing field. Writing fiction may simply be a natural progression from writing scientific papers. But on a more fundamental level, the art of composing succinct medical notes hinges upon learning how to tell a story by first listening to the patient, making relevant observations, deciding what to include and what to omit, and finally conveying the finished piece to colleagues for their considered opinions. The concept of the narrative voice comes in here. Both doctor and writer alike must be able to remain empathic and humane while also objectively detached from the object of their scrutiny. Further to this, they must be able to simulate a sequence of relevant events upon which they then place their own brand of meaning and interpretation in order to reach a formulation or central thesis.

And in the end, it is this meaning and interpretation that are important. The story must have a broader application, something universal, be it the clinical relevance of a case or piece of research presented at a medical conference, or the central theme of a novel painstakingly constructed through the use of character, plot and language. Alas, such a technique exists in both medicine and literature; all that differs is the style.

There is, however, a far more convincing reason why doctors write fiction. Doctors possess relevant specialist knowledge that lends itself to public curiosity. The study of medicine exposes the medical student or doctor to many strange and singular situations. From the tender age of seventeen, he or she is not only expected to assimilate large volumes of science, but also to grapple with the philosophical concepts of life and death, health and disease, ethics and psychology on a first-hand, day-to-day basis. It is a privileged position in which they are allowed to observe close up – even participate in – daily events to which other writers (and, indeed, most people) do not have access. The typical doctor in an average working week will observe more joy, suffering, pain and general human experience than they might otherwise see in a month or even a year. The doctor witnesses countless births and pronounces countless deaths. They are invited to be privy to the most intimate, vulnerable, challenging moments of a patient's life, to examine them up close with a stethoscope, to prescribe medication and monitor its effects, to scrutinise their very bones on x-ray, to perform surgery. What other profession offers such a raw and frank view of humanity?

Add to this the statistical evidence that doctors themselves endure more stress, hide more alcoholism and experience more suicidal ideation than most other workers, professional or otherwise. But there is more. The Irish medical workforce is culturally diverse, while many Irish doctors travel widely to work in the hospitals of America, Africa or the Far East. Even in the local context, the doctor knows the extremes of power; contrast, for example, the vulnerable patient or relative with whom they come into contact daily, with the traditionally – and ridiculously – god-like consultant under whom they might have trained. As if these circumstances weren't sufficiently eye opening, the medical student dissects dead bodies, while the surgeon dissects live ones. In short, any doctor with a remotely philosophical disposition has ample opportunity to observe and contemplate many aspects of the raw and fragile truth.

Edmund Pellegrino summed up nicely the similarities in a paper published in 1982 in the journal *Literature and Medicine*. "For both are ways of looking at man and both are, at heart, moral enterprises," he wrote. "Both must start by seeing life bare, without averting their gaze." The latter perhaps refers to "clinical gaze", a term coined by philosopher Michel Foucault referring to the art of viewing medicine holistically with the patient at its centre. Neither medicine nor literature, Pellegrino continues, "can rest in mere looking. To be authentic they must look with compassion. Medicine without compassion is mere technology, curing without healing; literature without feeling is mere reporting, experience without meaning."

One particular graduate of St Thomas's Medical School in London is a fitting example of a writer who based much of his prose on his professional experience. William Somerset Maugham's first novel *Liza of Lambeth* draws heavily on the author's experiences of attending women in childbirth, while his semi-autobiographical masterpiece, *Of Human Bondage*, is based largely on his life as a medical student. Indeed, Philip

Carey (the clubfooted protagonist of this novel) tries to forge a career in both medicine and the arts, much as Maugham himself did. Maugham once said, "You don't just get a story . . . you have to wait for it to come to you. I've never written a story in my life. The story has come to me and demanded to be written." As such, he acknowledged that his craft was a direct result of his experiences.

A.J. Cronin also relied on his medical memoirs to provide him with material. A graduate of Glasgow University Medical School, he served as a ship's surgeon in the Royal Navy during World War I and as a doctor in various Indian hospitals. Examples of his writings include the popular Doctor Finlay stories and his novel *The Citadel*, which was based on his investigation of occupational diseases in the coal mining industry of the 1920s. Cronin wrote in the Realist genre and spared us none of the harsh detail. To him, both medicine and creative writing were about communicating the results of a close scrutiny of human nature. Not buildings, not machines, not law and not money, but people.

These doctors were diverse in their experience, but similar in their hunger to write and to be published. And this might not always have been so easy, given the time constraints to which we have already alluded. Even if Sir Arthur Conan Doyle had time to spare between his infrequent patients, it is unlikely the same can be said for most of his peers. Perhaps this was why many physician-writers chose short stories as an alternative to novels. Anton Chekhov, Sir Arthur Conan Doyle, Arthur Schnitzler and William Somerset Maugham all used this form of storytelling, which allowed for a franker, more documentary style of prose. Few tools were needed for this endeavour; indeed, William Carlos Williams is thought to have penned much of his material on disused prescription pads.

As we can see, therefore, Rabelais, Goldsmith, Keats, Doyle, Maugham, Gogarty, Cronin, Crichton and Carson – and a long, long list of others – all did what Chekhov purported to do. They spent night upon night with both medicine and literature. Income from the latter supplemented that of the former, the former compelled engagement in the latter, and a similar process was used in both endeavours. Each physician-writer, in turn, earned his share of celebrity. So, perhaps that is why physicians, surgeons and psychiatrists so often put pen to paper.

But to tell the story properly, we must go back to the very beginning.

Chapter Two

Old Medical Masters

S O, WHERE SHOULD WE BEGIN? If we wanted to, we could go back as far as Hippocrates and Galen but neither of these remarkable men, as far as we know, wrote fiction. As such, we need really go back only five hundred or so years to find doctors first conceiving characters, settings and plots as they scratched them onto parchment. Obvious pre-nineteenth century examples include François Rabelais, Oliver Goldsmith, Tobias Smollett and Erasmus Darwin. One might also include Nostradamus, although the jury remains out as to whether his *Centuries* are fiction at all.

Rabelais without a Cause

The book is a very old invention indeed. The Romans had hand-written scrolls, but even subsequent printing has existed for quite some time. As early as the seventh century, the Chinese were using ink on carved wooden blocks to print images onto paper; by the fourteenth century, the earliest paper mills were springing up around Europe and, by 1423, the Europeans were using block printing to manufacture books. This allowed the subsequent manufacture of a mass-produced bible by Johannes Gutenberg, using a printing press of the scribe's own invention. From then, it was only a matter of time before people began writing novels.

One of the first to do so was François Rabelais. He wrote a series of five novels, collectively entitled *The Life of Gargantua and the Heroic Deeds of Pantagruel*. Recounting the epic adventures and chaotic mishaps of two grotesque giants, the novels were written in a famously crude, satirical and occasionally violent manner, with several chapters displaying lengthy, coarse narratives clearly designed to offend.

The first in the series was *Pantagruel* (1533), published under the pseudonym Alcofribas Nasier (an anagram of the author's real name), and this debut was followed a year later by its sequel, *Gargantua*. The protagonists were son and father respectively, and the former was thought to be a thinly veiled satire of King Henry II of France. Unsurprisingly, the controversy did not stop there; *Gargantua* was equally noteworthy for its social commentary, such as its call for educational reform and the provision of free schooling for all.

Despite their weighty substance, the novels were criticised for having poor literary structure. There were also notable inconsistencies in the plot, most obviously the inexplicable manner in which the two giants seemed to vary in size. Pantagruel, for example, spends significant periods of the novel in a courtroom to which he gains access via the doorway. Conversely, one of the final chapters sees the narrator living inside Pantagruel's mouth for six months. Indeed, this orifice is so vast that it houses "Larynx and Pharynx, which are two great cities, such as Rouen and Nantes, rich and of great trading" and "great rocks, like the mountains of Denmark – I believe they were his teeth".

Notwithstanding these shortcomings, both novels were enormously successful. Indeed, they were reprinted nearly one hundred times during the sixteenth century, although it is thought that Rabelais made little money personally from his writing. The subsequent works – perhaps less well known – were simply entitled *Tiers Livre* (1546), *Quart Livre* (1552) and *Cinquième* (1564), literally the third, fourth and fifth volumes respectively. There are some claims by notable academics that the last, published more than a decade posthumously, may have been edited or even written by other authors. Either way, Rabelais influenced numerous subsequent writers, including Jean de La Fontaine, Victor Hugo, Voltaire, Honoré de Balzac, Jonathan Swift and Laurence Sterne.

So, what is known about Rabelais? It seems he was a man of principle; he lived around the time of King Henry VIII of England and, at one point, he petitioned the Pope to revoke the king's excommunication from the Catholic Church. Destined to become a timely example of the Renaissance man, he was born (as far as we know) in 1494 near Touraine, France and was the youngest son (with two brothers and a sister) of a local lawyer and landowner. A pious man, he became a Franciscan monk at the age of twenty-seven but, soon after, acquired special dispensation from Pope Clement VII to switch to the Benedictine monastery of Saint-Pierre near Poiters instead, where he was secretary to Geoffrey d'Estessac, Bishop of Maillezais.

After spending some time studying law at the University of Poiters, he set his mind instead upon medicine, acquiring a degree from the University of Montpellier at the ripe old age of thirty-six. At this point he moved to Lyons, where he worked initially as a proof-reader for Sebastian Gryphius, a German printer of some repute. His medical career continued in parallel and, in 1532, he was made Chief Physician at the most prestigious hospital in Lyons. In 1537 – at the age of forty-two – he was made Doctor of Medicine and began lecturing at the University of Montpellier on various subjects that included anatomy, Galen and Hippocrates. Indeed, he was among the first doctors to teach anatomy using the dissection of corpses.

As his reputation grew, he became personal physician to Cardinal Jean du Bellay of Paris. This, in turn, led to Rabelais working for the Cardinal's brother, Guillaume du Bellay, Lord of Langley; subsequently, the renowned doctor became Master of the King's Requests, the king in question being Henry II of France whom he had once satirised in fiction. Rabelais was soon appointed Canon of St Maur and finally, by 1550, he was the non-resident curé of Meudon, a position from which he resigned in 1553, shortly before his death.

During all this, of course, Rabelais was a prolific writer. Following his early work as a proof-reader, he acquired a position editing medical textbooks. He published in his own name from 1532 onwards, and began with a translation of Dr Jean Manardi's *Medical Letters* and one of Hippocrates's Aphorisms. He also wrote extensively on archaeology. Although a distinguished man of letters, Rabelais was nevertheless considered gregarious and even cunning, while his works of satirical fiction were thought rather unbecoming of a man of the cloth. Indeed, Rabelais gave rise to the term *Rabelaisian*, meaning exuberantly imaginative with coarse humour.

Rabelais died on 9 April 1553 and was buried in St Paul's Cathedral, Paris. History shows him as the archetypal Renaissance man, with a pious nature, an interest in law and ethics, a pioneering influence over the teaching of medicine and a flair for creative writing. Mischievous and bold in his literary endeavours, he set the standard for novelists almost from the point at which technology allowed this medium to exist. And, as we have established, the book is a very old invention indeed.

The Talented Prognosticator

Nostradamus has never been more popular. With every world shattering current event, his prophecies are subjected to a frenzy of retrospective scrutiny. Some have claimed he predicted the French Revolution, Hitler, Napoleon, and even the desecration of his own tomb. His *Centuries* are among the most published documents in history and have inspired countless subsequent novels, plays and theses. Nostradamus, indeed, is a name so synonymous with prophecy that it conjures up images of some superstitious medieval sorcerer. It is perhaps surprising therefore, that he was very much a child of the Renaissance. A prosperous, well travelled and liberally educated physician, he was both highly intelligent and – most notably – sane. Whereas his prophetic abilities are controversial, his talent as a doctor is beyond doubt.

Michel de Nostredame was born in Saint-Rémy de Provence, France, on 14 December 1503. The Nostredames, originally Jewish, had converted to Catholicism two generations previously to escape the unwanted attentions of the Inquisition. The latter was at the height of its power during the sixteenth century, and frequently blamed those of Jewish faith for crop failure and plague to such a degree that those who refused to convert faced exile or execution. The Nostredames' sagacity was matched by their education, many of them practicing medicine or law. Young Michel, who showed intelligence from an early age, was tutored by his maternal grandfather, Jean de St. Rémy, and educated in the fields of ancient history, Greek, Latin, astrology, chemistry and anatomy.

Nostradamus was subsequently sent to study medicine at Avignon. He spent just three years at the university before an outbreak of plague cut short his studies and claimed the lives of many fellow students. In order to allow him to assist with the epidemic, he was granted an immediate licence to practice. Nostradamus was an innovative physician, employing many techniques of his own invention. For example, he refused to bleed the sick, a common remedy for most diseases at the time. It was believed that draining the body of its warm blood could cure fever; Nostradamus was apparently one of the few physicians to notice that the patient usually died as a result.

He was also an early advocate of keeping patients in well ventilated, sunlit rooms. This principle was quite revolutionary, as most sixteenth-century physicians believed that sickness was spread through air-vapour and that the windows and doors of patients' chambers should therefore be kept firmly shut. Furthermore, Nostradamus insisted that his patients take a daily bath in an epoch when even aristocrats would take the plunge only once per year.

As Nostradamus's reputation grew, he was invited to lend his expertise to many of France's plague stricken regions. Indeed, for several years he practiced as a travelling doctor between cities such as Bordeaux, Toulouse and Narbonne and thus, in a sense, plague became his specialty. In 1529, he enrolled in Montpellier, one of the most distinguished medical schools in sixteenth-century Europe. Four years later, he received his medical degree and although he was invited to teach at the university, some hostility towards his unorthodox ideas led him to decline the offer. Instead, he worked on his first publication, a translation of *The Book of Orus Opollo, Son of Osiris, King of Egypt*.

He travelled for a further year before settling in the cosmopolitan town of Agen, Aquitaine. This was the home of another sixteenth-century scholar, Julius Caesar Scaliger, who first introduced Nostradamus to the occult, with its forbidden books and methods of prediction. Around this time, Nostradamus married a local girl of "high estate" and fathered two children. In an ironic twist of fate, however, the 1538 outbreak of plague in Agen claimed the lives of his young family. He resumed his travels and spent the next decade moving through France, Italy and Sicily. While in Lorraine, he became an initiate of the Priory of Sion, a heretical Rosicrucian order, which taught that Jesus survived on the crucifix, married Mary Magdalene and moved to France (a story familiar to readers of Dan Brown's *The Da Vinci Code*).

His success in ameliorating plague was ongoing, most notably in the Marseilles outbreak of 1544 and the Aix-en-Provence outbreak of 1546. The latter resulted in his being granted a full pension by the city fathers, while his efforts in Lyon earned him a sack of gold that he subsequently gave to charity. In 1547, he settled in the town of Salon-en-Craux and married a rich and well connected widow. His wife's wealth allowed them both to move into a new house, where he could devote much of his time to astrology and writing. From 1550, he began to promulgate his numerous precognitions by publishing annual almanacs, month-by-month astrological predictions of the year's forthcoming events. In 1552, he published a book of medicine, which included many useful drugs, feminine cosmetics and even jam recipes. At the time, many of his medicinal theories were quite novel – for example, the concept of boiling water before drinking. As the popularity of printed works grew with the Renaissance, so too did the seer's celebrity.

Around this time Nostradamus, now in his early fifties, engaged a pupil, Jean Aimes de Chavigny, who later became his biographer. He described the seer as "little less than middle height, robust, cheerful and vigorous. His brow was high and open, the nose straight, the grey eyes gentle, though in wrath they would flame . . . a severe but laughing face, so one saw allied with this severity a great humanity."

Alas, Nostradamus is so noted in history for his prophesies that his immense medical talent goes largely ignored. Many do not even realise he was a doctor. Yet while his ability to predict the future is controversial, few could doubt his skill for healing. Indeed, had Nostradamus not expounded his predictions so successfully, history would have noted him as one of the great physicians of the Renaissance. But although he began publishing his predictions relatively late in his life, it is for these that he is chiefly remembered. History, which has named many magnificent doctors, can record only a handful of seers, of whom Nostradamus is easily the most famous. His *Centuries* are extensively published, his name is almost synonymous with prophecy, and his character is a source of fascination to many. So, was his prescience due to supernatural insight, sound political judgement or mere good luck?

There is one famous story, which tells of Nostradamus riding alone on a dusty road near Ancona, Italy, in 1548. When he happened upon a line of mendicant friars, he dismounted and knelt before the youngest member of the group, Felice Peretti, claiming that he must "kneel before His Holiness". The young friar, who remembered the incident well, became Pope Sixtus V in 1585.

On another occasion, Nostradamus's powers were put to the test while he was a guest at the Château de Fains, Lorraine. His host, the Seigneur de Florinville, produced two piglets and asked the prophet to predict their fate. Nostradamus replied that the black piglet would be cooked for dinner, while the white one would be eaten by a wolf. In order to prove the seer wrong, Florinville surreptitiously instructed his cook to prepare the white piglet for dinner. A little later, having regaled his guests with food and wine, Florinville boasted that the seer's prophecy was incorrect and summoned his cook to prove it. However, when questioned, the cook reluctantly admitted that a wolf cub had indeed stolen the white piglet from the kitchen and that black one had been cooked for dinner after all.

A prolific writer, Nostradamus's prophecies were not confined to mere anecdotes. During the last decade of his life, he produced his series of *Centuries*, so-called not because they were in any chronological order but because each contained one hundred prophesies in quatrain format. With numerous references to astronomy, most verses were extremely esoteric, perhaps to avoid the unwanted attention of the Inquisition. To this day, they remain difficult to interpret, but there are one or two exceptions:

> *In the kingdom of the great one, reigning well*
> *The king and duke, allied together*
> *Will force the brass gates open, by strength of arms*
> *The port is demolished, the ship sunk, the day is serene.*

A prediction of the sinking of the *Titanic* in 1912, this is one of the few quatrains with a universally accepted explanation. The "great one" referred to is Cronus, king of the twelve Titans, who ruled the universe until dethroned by his son Zeus, referred to here as the "duke". The allegedly unsinkable flagship of the White Star Line, named in honour of the Titans, struck an iceberg in the north Atlantic in a manner remarkably similar to that mentioned in the verse. Shearing of iron rivets on the port side of the vessel allowed the steel plates of the hull to be ripped apart at the waterline. The "brass gates" (bulkheads) were forced open and the *Titanic* sunk within hours on a night that, as Nostradamus had predicted, was "serene".

Nostradamus wrote over a thousand such quatrains, making predictions as varied in their chronicity as in their content. Such was his celebrity that, on 15 August 1555, he was summoned to the court of Henry II and Catherine de' Medici, where he was invited to predict the king's fate. The latter died agonisingly on 10 July 1559, following a jousting accident in which a competitor's weapon pierced his helmet and mortally wounded him in the eye. The event had been ominously predicted four years earlier by the seer, who wrote:

> *The younger lion will overcome the older*
> *In single combat on the field of war*
> *His eyes will be pierced in their golden helm*
> *Two breaks made one. He subsequently dies a cruel death.*

Catherine de' Medici, who was impressed by the prophet's accuracy, continued her patronage and even consulted Nostradamus regarding the future of her children. The queen's interest was naturally advantageous to the seer; there were many calls for his arrest as a sorcerer but the queen ordered that he be left alone. Nostradamus died on 2 July 1566, at the age of sixty-two, crippled with arthritis.

He was entombed in the wall of the Church of the Cordeliers, Salon, a resting place that soon became a pilgrimage site.

Before long, a rumour circulated that the seer's tomb contained a secret document that could be used to decipher his quatrains. This rumour remained alive until 1700, when city officials decided to move his body to a more prominent area of the church. While the tomb was open, they indulged themselves by peeking inside the coffin and, although they found no papers, they did find a medallion around the skeleton's neck, inscribed with the number 1700. Nostradamus enjoyed the last laugh by predicting, in 1566, the exact year of the desecration of his own tomb.

Although most people treat Nostradamus's predictions with scepticism, fascination with the seer is as strong today as it ever was. One can see the attraction; the future is an unknown entity to us all and the very idea of successful precognition brings into question the concepts of fate, chance, destiny and freedom of choice. Indeed, if something can be predicted to happen, what power do we have to stop it?

In the end, Nostradamus was a clever man indeed. He consorted with many influential people and, as such, much of his short term prescience, at least, could be put down to shrewd political judgment. Yet, a few of his longer term predictions appear to have transpired, even if one takes subjective interpretation into account. So, could he see into the future? This, we will never know for sure, but we will certainly never prove that he could not.

More Flamboyant than Physician

In his eighteenth century classic *The Vicar of Wakefield* (1766), Oliver Goldsmith writes of his eponymous protagonist's love of the written word. Dr Primrose – a vicar who has had the misfortune to lose most of his inherited estate, thus forcing him to take up residence in a humbler parish – recounts to his daughter an explanation of the purpose of literature:

I armed against the censures of the world, showed her that
books were sweet unreproaching companions to the miserable,
and that, if they could not bring us to enjoy life, they would at
least teach us to endure it.

These days, *The Vicar of Wakefield* seems to have been reduced to little more than a rumour – at least if my own recent
piece of extensive and rigorous research is to be believed. Without mentioning the author in question, I asked among friends,
who had heard of the book, let alone read it; for the most part,
I was greeted with mumblings, head-scratching or blank stares.
Hard to believe, therefore, that it was one of the most popular
eighteenth-century novels among Victorians. It was certainly
widely cited; George Eliot mentioned it in *Middlemarch*, Charles
Dickens in *A Tale of Two Cities* and *David Copperfield*, Jane
Austen in *Emma*, Mary Shelley in *Frankenstein* and Louisa May
Alcott in *Little Women*. But then, Goldsmith was also noted to
opine that, "As writers become more numerous, it is natural for
readers to become more indolent."

Goldsmith, if not widely read today, remains influential at
the very least. An audacious man in his time, he spent some
years working informally as a doctor and referring to himself
by the same title. Although he studied medicine at the University of Edinburgh and then anatomy at Leiden University, he
did not qualify. Nevertheless, he gained some medical experience – if you like – by working as the assistant to a chemist;
from there, somewhere along the line, he made the transition
to physician without acquiring the letters first. But then, Goldsmith was perhaps the Oscar Wilde of the Georgian era; flam-
boyance was his trademark. Although not noted for his sport-
ing physique, he liked to dress in bright clothing and a scarlet
cloak. Indeed, he was even reputed to have worn purple silk
underwear, although exactly who verified this is not clear.

Goldsmith was born in County Longford on 10 November
1728, the fifth of eight children. His father, Charles, was a lo-

cal farmer and the rector of the Kilkenny West parish. Surprisingly, Goldsmith was not considered particularly clever at school; nonetheless, he went on to study classics at Trinity College, Dublin before his unsuccessful sojourn to Edinburgh. He tried his hand at several different occupations as a young man and, indeed, was imprisoned for a brief period of time, accused of having enlisted in the French army while securing passage to the continent. Eventually, he became a freelance journalist, writing for such periodicals as *The Critical Review*, *The Monthly Review*, *Lady's Magazine*, *Public Ledger* and *Busy Body*.

Before long, he established his own magazine, *The Bee*, but it is his novel *The Vicar of Wakefield* and his play *She Stoops to Conquer* (1773) that have proven his legacy. Notwithstanding this success, he was relatively poor for much of his life and supported himself largely by compiling histories for publication. Eventually, he was appointed Professor of Ancient History at the Royal Academy of Art. Quite the Renaissance man moreover, Goldsmith was a talented flautist and is thought to have used his musical proficiency to fund his travels around Europe. A founding member of Dr Samuel Johnson's Club in Soho, Goldsmith reputedly consumed a lot of alcohol and enjoyed gambling. Dr Johnson, it is said, assisted Goldsmith in publishing *The Vicar of Wakefield*, but the book did not sell especially well during Goldsmith's lifetime.

She Stoops to Conquer was supposedly based on real events. To illustrate further Goldsmith's proneness to inadvertent buffoonery, he is once reputed to have arrived auspiciously in the Longford town of Ardagh following a long and arduous journey. Seeking an inn or hotel in which to rest his weary bones, he asked a passing stranger for directions to "the best house in town". A misunderstanding must have ensued, because Goldsmith made his way to the grand domicile of Sir Ralph Featherstone, where he proceeded to stay the night. Sir Ralph, it is said, understood the error at an early stage and – for his own entertainment – played along. Indeed, it was only as Goldsmith attempted to pay the bill next day that the playwright realised his mistake. Little wonder that Horace Walpole once referred to Goldsmith as "an inspired idiot".

In spite of his quasi-professional status, Goldsmith did not enjoy particularly good health during his short lifetime. He was afflicted with smallpox at the age of nine and was badly disfigured with pockmarks as a result; during later life, he endured painful difficulties with his kidneys and bladder. Following violent convulsions, he died at home in London on 4 April 1774. Before his burial at Temple Church in London, his coffin was reopened for a moment so that Mary Horneck (the woman with whom Goldsmith was in love but never married) might receive a lock of his hair.

In the end, Oliver Goldsmith is a writer well worth a revival. Having tried his hand at many endeavours – including medicine – he settled upon the written word and influenced greatly many of the novelists who followed. Indeed, if the words of Goldsmith could not bring us to enjoy life, they might at least teach us to endure it.

The Adventures of Tobias Smollett

Around the same time, Tobias Smollett was also busy writing novels. He was born in Dalqahurn, near Dunbarton in Scotland, shortly before 19 March 1721 – the recorded date of his baptism. His father was a landowner who died when the young Tobias was just two. His grandfather, Sir James Smollett, was a member of parliament, a judge and a commissioner who assisted in the Union of Scotland and England. The youngest of three children, Tobias was educated at Dunbarton Grammar School and subsequently went on to study medicine at the University of Glasgow.

In 1736, he was apprenticed to the surgeon Mr John Gordon, but decided within three years that literature was his major calling and moved to London to work in the theatre. When this initial endeavour failed, he joined the Royal Navy and spent some time as a surgeon on both the *HMS Chichester* and the *HMS Cumberland*. In 1741, he travelled to the West Indies and took part in a failed assault on the Spanish occupied port of Cartagena. He resided in Jamaica for a number of years before returning to London in the late 1740s to set up practice as a surgeon in Downing Street. In 1750, he was awarded his Doctorate of Medicine (MD) by the University of Aberdeen.

Smollett's first major novel, *The Adventures of Roderick Random*, was published anonymously in 1748. An argument broke out, however, when the book was later translated into French; Henry Fielding was erroneously credited with the work and arguments over plagiarism ensued, so much so that Smollett is thought to have satirised Fielding as Mr Spondy in *The Adventures of Peregrine Pickle* (1751). Such animosity did not end until long after Fielding's death.

Smollett's early works also include *The Regicide* (1749) and *The Adventures of Ferdinand Count Fathom* (1753). Smollett was intricately involved in the literary society of his day, was appointed editor of *The Critical Review* in 1756, and was a friend and peer of Oliver Goldsmith among other prominent writers. Smollett was considered a man of robust temperament, stubborn and argumentative at times to such a degree that he was inclined to get himself into trouble. For example, he wrote *The Life and Adventures of Sir Launcelot Greaves* (1760) while serving a three month prison sentence for libelling Admiral Charles Knowles. Laurence Sterne satirised Smollett as the fictional character Smelfungus in his work *Sentimental Journey* (1768), and referred to him as a "choleric philistine". Horace Walpole, moreover, considered Smollett a "profligate hireling".

If Smollett was not always popular, it was not because of any desire not to socialise. He was fond of a drink and liked to frequent taverns when not busy mingling with high society.

Viewed to be a handsome man, he married Nancy Lassells at a young age while still living in Jamaica. Nancy was of English descent and heiress to a profitable plantation. The pair had one daughter, Elizabeth, but sadly she died in 1763 at the tender age of fifteen. Notwithstanding Nancy's inheritance, Smollett was a spendthrift by nature and fell heavily into debt on account of his lavish lifestyle and the expense incurred in maintaining an opulent residence in fashionable Chelsea. Indeed, much of his later literary endeavours were a direct attempt to generate much needed income.

Smollett's reputation as a writer of fiction was established quite independently of his medical career. Like Rabelais, his novels were satirical, picaresque even, with realistic portrayals of, for example, naval life, often in humorous detail. He also gave more than a nod to the epistolary styles of his old adversary Henry Fielding and the writer Samuel Richardson. Smollett's characters tended to be adventurous rogues who travelled far and wide. Not unsurprisingly, therefore, Smollett's noteworthy publications include a translation of Cervantes's *Don Quixote* (1755) and *A Complete History of England* (1765).

Having travelled throughout his life, Smollett eventually settled in Italy. As he advanced through middle age, his health began to deteriorate insofar as he had ever enjoyed rude health at all. Indeed, not only is he thought to have suffered from stomach ulcers, chronic rheumatism, asthma and various skin conditions, but it has been suggested he may have had tuberculosis. In 1771, he developed diarrhoea, fever and convulsions and was diagnosed with a severe intestinal infection. He died on 17 September of that year, aged just fifty. His final novel, *The Expedition of Humphry Clinker*, was published posthumously.

On the Origin of Charles Darwin

When we think of evolution, the name that immediately springs to mind is that of Charles Darwin. Born in 1809, he began studying medicine at Edinburgh University when he was sixteen but left just two years later to pursue, instead, a vocation as a clergyman at Christ's College, Cambridge. In the end, he left that too, in favour of a five year tour on the *HMS Beagle*. Travelling the world as an unpaid naturalist under the command of Captain Robert Fitzroy, Darwin acquired two legacies of note: *chagas disease*, which left him permanently prone to lethargy, an irregular heartbeat and attacks of fainting; and a theory of evolution that was destined to have a similar effect on most of his fellow God-fearing Victorians. And all this because of a visit to the Galápagos Islands.

Darwin waited twenty years or more before he published his theory of evolution. In the meantime, Alfred Russel Wallace arrived at the same conclusions and wrote to Darwin in the 1850s for advice on the subject; in the end, they published an article jointly in the *Journal of the Linnaean Society* (1858). *On the Origin of Species: By Means of Natural Selection* (to give Darwin's subsequent book its full length title) was sold out on the day of its publication and required half a dozen reprints to satisfy demand. In short, it made his reputation (perhaps as surely as it stole the limelight from Wallace) and placed Darwin forever in the annals of history. He died on 19 April 1882, at the age of seventy-three.

But Charles Darwin was not the first to consider matters of evolution; indeed, he was not even the first in his own family to do so. His grandfather, Erasmus Darwin, was a figure so eminent in his day that it is rumoured he once turned down an opportunity to be the physician to King George III. But then Erasmus Darwin had many other strings to his bow. A key thinker of eighteenth-century England, he was a naturalist (and a founder of the Lunar Society of Birmingham, a gathering of natural philosophers and pioneering industrialists), a physiologist, an abolitionist, an inventor and a poet. His poetry was largely about natural history, with particular reference to evolution, the topic that would become a family favourite.

On 12 December 1731, Erasmus Darwin was born into a family of six older siblings at Elston Hall in Nottinghamshire. His father was a former barrister at Lincoln's Inn and thus naturally valued education; the young Erasmus was enrolled at Chesterfield Grammar School and subsequently at St John's College, Cambridge. Although he acquired his Bachelor of Medicine degree there in 1755, and went on to submit a doctoral thesis at the University of Edinburgh, it is not known whether he was actually conferred his MD per se.

At the age of twenty-five, he began practicing in Nottingham; when this initial enterprise turned out to be financially unrewarding, he moved instead to Lichfield where a novel course of therapy administered to one of his patients (a well connected gentleman from Staffordshire) enhanced his local reputation sufficiently to ensure that he could earn a living. He practiced successfully as a physician in the English midlands for almost half a century, but he was by no means restricted to this endeavour. While in Lichfield, he wrote poetry, philosophised about evolution and tinkered with various amateur inventions that most-notably included a machine supposedly capable of reciting basic language.

Darwin had a somewhat turbulent love life. His first wife was Mary Howard, whom he married in 1757; she bore him five children but sadly two died during infancy. Among those surviving was Robert Waring Darwin, the father of the famous Charles. In 1770, Mrs Darwin passed away and the services of a governess named Mary Parker were engaged in order to care for the children. Within a year, it is said, Erasmus and Mary had an affair that resulted in two illegitimate daughters.

In 1775, Erasmus made the acquaintance of Elizabeth Pole, daughter of the second Earl of Portmere and wife of the distinguished Colonel Edward Pole. Naturally, it behoved Erasmus to be somewhat discreet about his amorous feelings towards Mrs Pole and he was forced initially to confine such yearnings to the lines of his poetry. But, in 1870, Edward Pole died and the situation naturally changed. Erasmus and Elizabeth were soon married and he moved into her home at Radbourne Hall near Derby. They went on to have four sons and three daughters. In all, therefore, Erasmus had fourteen children.

After a long and useful life, Erasmus died suddenly on 18 April 1802, just weeks after moving into a new home at Breadsall Priory near Derby. He was buried at All Saints Church in Breadsall and is, moreover, featured on one of a series of famous Birmingham monuments called the Moonstones.

So, for what is the older Darwin most remembered? As well as a physician, he was a devoted naturalist who founded – among other organisations – the Lichfield Botanical Society whose primary aim was to translate into English the Latin writings of the Swedish botanist Carolus Linnaeus. Two publications ensued from this project: A *System of Vegetables* (1785) and *The Families of Plants* (1787). Indeed it was Erasmus Darwin who originally devised many of the commonly used plant names of today. Further to this, Erasmus wrote a poem entitled "The Loves of the Plants", again based on the work of Linnaeus; it was published in *The Botanic Garden* (1791). Most important among his publications, however, is a dual-volume medical work entitled *Zoonomia* (1794). A scholar of the evolutionary ideas of James Burnett, whom he cited in *Temple of Nature* (1803), Erasmus also anticipated the theories of Jean-Baptiste Lamarck and, in doing so, his own grandson's more modern theory of evolution.

As we can see, therefore, the original thinker in the Darwin family was Erasmus rather than Charles. Physician, naturalist, inventor and poet, he might easily have sown the seed of his grandson's theory of evolution. Perhaps here lies the true origin of *On the Origin of Species*.

Chapter Three

Nineteenth Century Physician-Writers

B Y THE NINETEENTH CENTURY, THE ART of writing fiction was well established. For the paltry price of a small volume, the reader could be educated, entertained and seduced into parallel worlds populated by heroes, detectives, spies, villains, doctors, patients and various others with whom they might not get the chance to acquaint themselves in real life. The book was also a lucrative sideline for any well educated professional who already had a perfectly good day job (or, at least, the wherewithal to avail of one if they so wished). John Keats and Arthur Schnitzel ultimately left medicine in favour of writing, while Georg Büchner technically did not qualify at all. Oliver Wendell Holmes Sr, Silas Weir Mitchell and Anton Chekhov successfully combined writing with serious medical careers. But perhaps the finest example of all is Sir Arthur Conan Doyle, creator of the archetypal fictional detective.

Torn between Two Loves

When John Keats falls in love with Fanny Brawne, his amorous intentions are, for the most part, met with disapproval. Mrs Brawne – Fanny's mother and Keats's landlady – is quick to point out the poet's paucity of income and even poorer prospects. Although she clearly likes the young poet, finding him both witty and kind, she is a widow who knows all too well the social limitations of late Georgian England. A good husband must have the means to provide. As a result, the engagement is kept largely secret while Keats continues to write.

Thus begins Jane Campion's delicate and sensitive 2009 film *Bright Star*, which tells of the romance between John Keats (played by Ben Whishaw) and Fanny Brawne (played by Abbie Cornish). Campion won an Academy Award for *The Piano* in 1994 and this subsequent offering is no less impressive. Like the poet's work itself, each scene is timed to delicate perfection, relying on few of the conventions of popular cinema to move the audience. For example, the film is virtually devoid of music, relying instead upon carefully chosen verse recited against the backdrop of an unfolding love story.

But a story is only such if the protagonists face their share of challenges. Keats and his fiancée each live in separate halves of a narrowly partitioned Hampstead cottage owned by Fanny's mother. At times, the young couple might easily live one hundred miles apart, particularly in view of the aforementioned parental disapproval. Moreover, there are other detractors, not least Charles Armitage Brown, Keats's friend, mentor and sponsor.

Brown's reasons for fervent disapproval are different. In *Bright Star* he despairs at the manner in which the all-consuming love affair threatens the fluency of Keats's poetry. "You'll lose your freedom permanently," he warns. "You'll be slaving at medicine fifteen hours a day and for what? To keep Mrs Keats in French ribbon!" Thus the poet is presented with a choice: the abstract life of the artist or the harsh practicalities of family life. He is torn between two loves, neither of which, for the record, is medicine.

Ironically, it is ill health that ultimately deprives the young poet of both. The early part of the film makes reference to Keats's younger brother Tom, who died of tuberculosis at the tender age of nineteen. Tom's death is an ominous overture to the film's climax; we all know what is destined to happen.

Keats was somewhat of a hypochondriac. This is understandable in view of his years spent studying medicine. In the end, his fears were justified, perhaps even prophetic; by his early twenties he had acquired tuberculosis and a range of venereal diseases. Indeed, it is thought that he took laudanum for pain relief and mercury for syphilis. Some of his concerns about health and mortality are reflected in his poetry, not least in "Ode to a Nightingale", written when he was twenty-three and deeply in love:

> Darkling I listen; and, for many a time
>   I have been half in love with easeful Death,
> Call'd him soft names in many a mused rhyme,
>   To take into the air my quiet breath;
> Now more than ever seems it rich to die,
>   To cease upon the midnight with no pain,
> While thou art pouring forth thy soul abroad
>   In such an ecstasy!
> Still wouldst thou sing, and I have ears in vain –
>   To thy high requiem become a sod.

Composed in May 1819 beneath a plum tree in his Hampstead garden, the poem describes the sound of a nightingale building its nest in a nearby tree. Supposedly written in just one day, a few months after he met and fell in love with Fanny Brawne, it was subsequently published in the *Annals of the Fine Arts* (1820). It was more pessimistic, perhaps, than much of Keats's previous work, the tone seeming to reject the frivolous hedonistic tendencies of his earlier poetry and exploring, instead, the themes of nature and how life is truly ephemeral. Perhaps the young man was grappling with the idea of having to settle down and earn a living.

Although the nightingale in the poem is described as experiencing a kind of death, it does not actually die; rather, it is described as living through its song, something of which Keats considers humans incapable. In the end, Keats seems to accept that pleasure cannot last forever, nor can, indeed, life itself. Again, rather prophetically, the poet foresees his own death, with the physical world absent as he lies beneath the ground unable to hear the nightingale that sings over his grave.

The young poet portrayed in the film clearly has some difficulty coming to terms with love as being anything other than abstract. Quite apart from the longer term implications of love, namely the need for commitment and compromise, the affair itself seems virtually platonic. But then Keats experienced a lot besides love in his tragically short life. Born in Moorgate, London in October 1795, he was the eldest son of an innkeeper who met his with own untimely demise by falling from a horse when the young poet was just eight years old.

Keats's mother, Frances, soon remarried a bank clerk but this moratorium on family turbulence was short lived. The death of Frances's own father, shortly after, yielded a legal dispute over the inheritance of his livery stables that essentially rendered her penniless. Faced with destitution, she disappeared into the underworld and left Keats – and his three surviving younger siblings – in the care of their maternal grandmother in Edmonton, north London. Frances eventually succumbed to tuberculosis – the illness that would eventually claim two of her sons – and died in 1810, leaving her children in the care of guardians.

Keats was educated initially at the Reverend John Clarke's School in Enfield, and left at the age of fourteen to become apprenticed to a surgeon-apothecary in Edmonton. He remained in this role for some five years before acquiring a post as a surgeons' assistant at Guy's Hospital in London. In 1816 – at the age of twenty – he qualified as a licensed apothecary and, a year later, became a member of the Royal College of Surgeons.

But, of course, it is his poetry that matters. Keats first displayed his literary talents while still at school, his teachers taking some pride in showing his work to Leigh Hunt, who later became his publisher. Keats was also friends with fellow romantic poet Percy Shelley. In due course, Keats wrote drama reviews for the *Champion*, while his own most notable works included the poems "Endymion" (1818), "Lamia" (1820) and "The Eve of St Agnes" (1820). When it came to the discipline of writing, Keats was not renowned for his organisational capacity. Apparently, he wrote lines and stanzas on scraps of paper, only later retrieving them to weave into some semblance of a complete verse. Indeed, it is thought the mythical poem "Lamia" required considerable editing because of the manner in which Keats mispronounced Greek names, affecting rhyme and rhythm alike.

Keats's work was not universally well received either. *Blackwood's Magazine* more or less advised him not to give up the day job, while John Gibson Lockhart regarded "Endymion" as "calm, settled, imperturbable drivelling idiocy". Keats, upon his deathbed, believed himself a failure. Only since then has he been truly appreciated as one of the greatest Romantic poets.

In 1820, with rapidly deteriorating health owing to tuberculosis (and in vain the hope of clearing his lungs), Keats travelled by sea to Italy with the painter and diplomat Joseph Severn. Faced with a painful descent into oblivion, he made several attempts at suicide, overdosing on laudanum and requiring friends to rally round to prevent his premature demise. His peaceful passing soon followed, however, in Rome on 23 February 1821 when he was just twenty-five. Buried in the Protestant Cemetery of that city, along with letters by Fanny Brawne and a lock of her hair, Keats was subsequently the dedicatee of Shelley's poem "Adonis". Indeed, when Shelley drowned a year later, he was said to have had a volume of Keats's poems in his possession.

Bright Star paints a portrait of a man torn between poetry and love. But he was claimed by neither, taken instead by an illness that killed so many of his generation. In the end, he almost seemed to welcome his own passing, having been, in his own words, "half in love with easeful Death".

The Casebook of Oliver Wendell Holmes

Matthew Pearl's novel *The Dante Club*, tells the tale of a collection of brutal and bizarre killings. A Supreme Court judge is badly assaulted and then left in his garden to be eaten alive by strategically placed maggots. A minister is buried upside-down while his feet are set on fire. A third victim meets a similarly gruesome end as he is sliced open exactly down the middle. Something sinister, it seems, is afoot.

When members of the Dante Club (a small gathering of poets in the process of translating *The Divine Comedy* from Italian to English) notice similarities between these murders and the various punishments divvied out in Dante's *Inferno*, they set about solving the crimes in an effort to salvage Dante's reputation. Thus the unlikely sleuthing skills of Henry Wadsworth Longfellow and James Russell Lowell are put to the test, along with those of their peer, Oliver Wendell Holmes.

When we think of Oliver Wendell Holmes, it is easy to forget that there were two of them. Holmes Junior (1841–1935) was famous for his eminent position as US chief justice, while his father – the man described in Pearl's novel – was a physician, a scientist, a writer and a member of the Fireside Poets, along with Longfellow and Lowell among others. Holmes Senior was, indeed, a household name in the United States at the time, actively sought out by distinguished visitors to American shores including Oscar Wilde, William Makepeace Thackeray and Charles Dickens. He epitomised the American nineteenth century enlightenment and was a skilled conversationalist much in demand on the lecture circuit and for after-dinner speeches. It is no exaggeration to refer to him as a father figure of both modern medicine and the American Literary Renaissance.

He was born on 29 August 1809 in Cambridge, Massachusetts to Abdiel Holmes (a minister of the First Congregational Church) and his second wife Sarah Wendell. A precocious child who, it is said, suffered from asthma, the young Holmes was an avid reader from an early age and had at his disposal his father's extensive library. Here, he encountered the works of Oliver Goldsmith and Alexander Pope, poets who would, in turn, influence Holmes's own verse. He penned his first poem at the tender age of thirteen.

Holmes was educated initially at the private Port School in Cambridge, where his teachers felt obliged to remind him repeatedly to stop talking or cease reading novels in class. At the age of fifteen, he attended the Phillips Academy, Andover, a Calvinist establishment intended to instil in the young Holmes a vocation in theology. He spent just one year at Phillips, where he was elected to the literary Social Fraternity and where his teachers, having noted his penchant for poetry, duly encouraged him to pursue it. He subsequently attended Harvard University from where he graduated in 1829.

With little interest in sports at college (he was a slight man of a little over five feet), Holmes found allegiance in a gathering of scholarly students referred to as the Aristocrats. He excelled in several European languages, was awarded the Deturs (an honour for academic achievement that yielded the more tangible prize of a volume of poetry by James Graham, John Logan and William Falconer), and continued to write throughout his time at Harvard. Indeed, he collaborated with two friends in writing the *Poetical Illustrations of the Athenaeum Gallery of Painting*, a collection of satirical poems about Boston's newly established art museum.

Perhaps sensing the requirement to earn a living, Holmes applied for and was accepted into Dane Law School after his graduation. Alas, by 1830, he was somewhat disenchanted with law, and began pursuing poetry with even greater alacrity. He published numerous verses anonymously in the *Collegian*, an ill-fated periodical established by peers from Harvard. These contributions included some of his best known early work, such as "The Dorchester Giant", "Reflections of a Proud Pedestrian" and "The Height of the Ridiculous".

The same year, Holmes penned "Old Ironsides", a poem expressing opposition to the dismantling of the eighteenth century frigate *USS Constitution*. Initially appearing in the *Advertiser*, the poem was soon republished by higher profile periodicals in New York and Washington. As a result, not only was the ship preserved, but Holmes garnered himself some celebrity in the process. He went on to publish "The Last Leaf", which Edgar Allan Poe commended as "one of the finest works in the English language".

In 1830, Holmes enrolled in medicine in Boston and began studying anatomy and surgery, medicine, obstetrics, chemistry and *material medica* – the only subjects medical students were expected to learn in early nineteenth century America. He also became a part-time apothecary at the hospital pharmacy. A student of Dr James Jackson, Holmes learned at an early stage the importance of detailed observation of the patient and a humane approach to treatment. This was in contrast to the bloodletting, blistering and other outmoded practices still in use at the time.

In 1833, he travelled to Paris for two years to study medicine in the more progressive hospital environment on offer owing to a recent overhaul of the city's medical practice. There, he became a student of Pierre Charles Alexandre Louis, a pathologist who, like Jackson, tutored him on the pointlessness of subjecting patients to the practice of bloodletting. When Holmes finally returned to Boston, he carried with him the philosophy of *methode expectante*, whereby it was recognised that the physician should aid natural processes of recovery insofar as this was possible. Holmes was awarded his MD by Harvard Medical School in 1836.

Although Holmes published his first collection of poetry the same year, it was clear to him that medicine was his real vocation. He joined the Massachusetts Medical Society shortly after graduation, along with the Boston Medical Society and the Boston Society for Medical Improvement. Meanwhile, his reputation was further enhanced by his winning the much coveted Boylston Prize on more than one occasion. Soon after, he co-founded Tremont Medical School (which would later merge with that of Harvard) and spent much of the decade that followed teaching. He also maintained a private medical practice.

By 1839, his reputation had grown to such a degree that he was appointed Professor of Anatomy at Dartmouth Medical School. The following year, he wedded Amelia Lee Jackson (niece of the aforementioned James), and fathered three children – Oliver, Amelia and Edward. Holmes continued his research, expounding on such matters as the degree to which puerperal fever was spread from patient to patient via contact with physicians – a milestone in the germ theory of disease. Indeed, two controversial essays of that era, namely "Homeopathy and its Kindred Delusions" (1842) and "The Contagiousness of Puerperal Fever" (1843), were highly progressive in their advocacy of antisepsis. Holmes is also credited with coining the term *anaesthesia* in a letter to the dentist William Morton, who was the first clinician to demonstrate in public the expediency of ether in the art of surgery.

Holmes was appointed Parkman Professor of Anatomy and Physiology at Harvard Medical School in 1847, and was Dean there until 1853. Indeed, he taught at Harvard for thirty-five years and, true to his own training, emphasised the importance of the anatomical and pathological bases of disease. Although a popular professor, he was criticised by the staff and student body alike for considering the application of Harriot Kezia Hunt to the medical school. Eventually, she was persuaded not to pursue her application; indeed, women were not admitted to Harvard Medical School until after World War II.

By 1848, Holmes had abandoned his private practice in favour of teaching. That year, he built a holiday retreat in the fashionable Pittsfield, Massachusetts, using money his wife had inherited. There, he spent time mingling with literary figures such as Herman Melville and Nathaniel Hawthorne. Alas, by 1856 the maintenance of the house had proven too costly and the family decided to sell up and leave.

In 1850, an element of murder mystery found its way into the life of Holmes. Still dean at the time, he was a witness for both defence and prosecution in the infamous murder trial of Parkman and Webster. The victim was George Parkman, a wealthy doctor and a generous benefactor of the medical school; the accused was John Webster, professor of chemistry. Both men were graduates of Harvard. In the end, Webster was found guilty and hanged, while Holmes dedicated his introductory lecture that same semester to the memory of George Parkman.

Holmes spent much of the 1850s lecturing throughout New England. His topics were diverse enough to encompass anything from ethical and scientific advances in medicine to nineteenth century English poets. He continued to publish his own poetry during this period. On a more controversial footing, he was criticised by the press for not being sufficiently abolitionist in his views on slavery. In fact, Holmes did not support slavery; but he did not support the more extreme views of the abolitionists either. More important to him was the Union and its preservation, as he would later write in articles such as "Bread" and "Newspapers". In the end, the controversy led him to give up lecturing.

The Saturday Club was established in 1857 as a supportive advisory panel to *Atlantic Monthly*, edited by Holmes and founded by James Russell Lowell. Contributors to the periodical included Henry Wadsworth Longfellow and Ralph Waldo

Emerson, as well as Holmes himself. In it, he republished *The Autocrat at the Breakfast-Table* (which originally appeared in 1832 as a series of brilliant conversations in *The New England Magazine*) and the success of this endeavour led to a book of the same title in 1857 which sold very well indeed. A sequel, *The Professor at the Breakfast-Table*, found its way onto the shelves two years later.

Holmes published his first novel in 1861. Entitled *Elsie Venner*, it is the strange tale of a woman whose personality is part-serpent on account of her mother having been bitten by a snake while she was pregnant. It was originally serialised in *Atlantic Monthly* and, although well received by some reviewers, the church condemned it as heresy. Thoughts of heaven and hell might indeed have been on Holmes's mind around this time, the period referred to at the outset when he, Henry Wadsworth Longfellow and others began translating Dante's *The Divine Comedy*. It was published in three volumes in 1867, the same year Holmes produced a second novel entitled *The Guardian Angel*.

As Holmes grew older, he continued to write prolifically. In 1872, he published *The Poet at the Breakfast-Table*, a somewhat more forgiving narrative than its predecessors. Subsequent publications include a collection of medical essays entitled *Pages from an Old Volume of Life* and a biography of his friend and contemporary, Ralph Waldo Emerson. In 1885, Holmes published his third and final novel, entitled *A Mortal Antipathy*.

Holmes retired from academia in 1882 and was made a professor emeritus at Harvard. In the wake of his youngest son's untimely passing, he travelled to Europe with his daughter and visited various famous writers, including Henry James and Alfred Lord Tennyson. He was awarded honorary degrees from the universities of Cambridge, Oxford and Edinburgh, but the highlight of his tour seems to have been a meeting with the microbiologist Louis Pasteur, whom he held in high regard.

Holmes recounted his adventures in a book entitled *Our One Hundred Days in Europe*.

Holmes's wife, Amelia, died in 1888, while their daughter followed just a year later, after a short illness. With failing eyesight and a fear of his own demise, the octogenarian continued to write almost until the very end. He died in his sleep on 7 October 1894 at the age of eighty-five, survived only by his eldest son, Oliver Wendell Holmes Jr. He was buried in Mount Auburn Cemetery, Cambridge, Massachusetts, alongside his wife.

Oliver Wendell Holmes's legacy is considerable. A pioneer of medicine from both a scientific and an ethical viewpoint, he was also a philosopher, a conversationalist, an academic, an editor, a poet, a novelist and a family doctor. Throughout all this, he even found time to translate Dante into English. Alas, his ability to solve murders is a figment of Matthew Pearl's imagination. But it was a nice idea.

The Revolutionary Writer

Not all physician-writers were as dedicated to medicine as those we have mentioned. Some, indeed, barely limped past their doctorates. Georg Büchner, for example, was a student of both natural sciences and medicine, but was far more interested in social revolution and writing fiction. But then, perhaps the taste of insurrection makes plays and short stories all the more exciting.

Büchner was born on 17 October 1813 in Goddelau, Germany and grew up in the town of Darmstadt. The first-born son of a doctor, he attended the local Gymnasium before enrolling at the University of Strasbourg and subsequently at the Hessen State University at Giessen. In 1833, an attack of meningitis cut short his studies and confined him to his bed in Darmstadt. It was during his convalescence that he garnered the opportunity to study in more detail the French Revolution. Energised by this, he founded the Society for the Rights of Man and began distributing pamphlets criticising contemporary social conditions. A warrant was soon issued for his arrest and this compelled him to flee to Strasbourg. He never returned to Germany again.

Büchner wrote not simply to expound on his ideas, but also to support himself as a fugitive. His first play, *Danton's Death* (1835), depicted an activist's disillusionment with the French Revolution, and was the only dramatic work Büchner saw published in his lifetime. Within a few months, he penned a short story entitled "Lenz" (1835) and the comedy drama *Leonce and Lena* (1836), but by far his most famous work was *Woyzeck* (1836), a Realist play that he never managed to finish. Büchner did not complete his medical studies either. Indeed, the records show that he received his Doctorate in Philosophy in 1836 from the University of Zurich and went on to become a lecturer in natural sciences. Such success did not last long; he died of typhus on 19 February 1837 aged just twenty-three. Most of his work was not premiered until many decades after his death.

The Regaling Researcher

Occasionally, when facts are not known, fiction can substitute nicely. The American neurologist Silas Weir Mitchell certainly subscribed to this philosophy in his debut short story "The Case of George Dedlow" (1866). Recall it is the tale of an army surgeons' assistant wounded in battle severely enough to require the amputation of all four limbs. Dedlow attempts to understand the phenomenon known as phantom limb, where pain and other sensations continue to be experienced long after surgery. Although Mitchell initially set out to describe it scientifically, he was a man ahead of his time and thus found it necessary to invent a psychological basis for symptoms where he could not pinpoint a physical one. Only later, did he go back and edit the piece with a physiological explanation based on advancements in understanding.

But then, Silas Weir Mitchell was a man of considerable talent. Not only was he one of the most eminent American doctors of the nineteenth century with pioneering research in neurology, neuro-anatomy, pharmacology, toxicology and physiology, but he is credited with discovering the part of the brain known as the *cerebellum*. He was the first to prescribe the *rest cure* consisting of bed, massage, electrotherapy and dietary measures that rapidly became popular across America and Europe. Moreover, there can be few other full time family physicians so accomplished that they have a rare neurovascular disorder named after them. And yet, amid all his contributions to medicine, he still found time to write children's fiction, poetry, short stories and novels.

He was born on 15 February 1829 in Philadelphia and was the son of the physician John Kearsley Mitchell. He enrolled at the University of Pennsylvania at a young age but was barely in his second year when his father became unwell and the young Silas was obliged to withdraw briefly in order to assist at home. Perhaps this inspired in him a vocation because, by 1848, he had become a student at Jefferson Medical College. He was conferred his MD in 1850 and, following a period of study in Paris, he returned home to practice alongside his father. By 1852, he had published his first scientific paper and, by 1853, he was a member of the Academy of Natural Sciences of Philadelphia. When his father died in 1858, Mitchell inherited his medical practice but his research nevertheless continued. Notable early scientific work includes an important paper entitled "Researches upon the Venom of the Rattlesnake" (1860), published in *Smithsonian Contributions to Knowledge*.

Like many physician-writers in this book, Mitchell drew upon both his professional and personal experiences when it came to storytelling. During the American Civil War, he served as a surgeon at Turners Lane Hospital in Philadelphia. With up to four hundred wounded soldiers at any given time, it afforded Mitchell ample opportunity to hear accounts that would influence stories such as "The Case of George Dedlow". It also yielded many research opportunities that led to seminal papers including "Gunshot Wounds and Other Injuries of Nerves" (1864) and "Reflex Paralysis" (1864).

After the war, Mitchell's medical career continued to flourish. From 1870, he spent some forty years working at the Philadelphia Orthopaedic Hospital for Nervous Diseases, and was also a professor at the Philadelphia Polyclinic and College for Graduates of Medicine. During this period he published over one hundred academic articles and books, including *Wear and Tear* (1871), *Injuries of the Nerves and Their Consequences* (1872), *Fat and Blood* (1877) and a paper entitled "On a Rare Vasomotor Neurosis of the Extremities and on the Maladies with Which It May be Confounded" (1878). The last described the illness *erythromelalgia*, which was subsequently re-named Mitchell's disease in his honour. Moreover, he was president of the College of Physicians of Philadelphia, a member of the National Academy of Science, and the recipient of honorary degrees from Jefferson Medical College and the Universities of Harvard, Princeton and Edinburgh.

Clearly Mitchell was a pioneer in the medical field but what about his fiction? His debut was in 1864 in the form of a book entitled *The Children's Hour*, co-written by Elizabeth Stevenson. Although the royalties went entirely to the Sanitary Commission, the greater prize went perhaps to Mitchell in the form of a newfound talent for writing popular fiction. He published his own children's book in 1867 entitled *The Wonderful Stories of Fuz-Buz the Fly and Mother Grabem the Spider* but, by then, *Atlantic Monthly* had already published his first piece of fiction aimed at adults, namely "The Case of George Dedlow".

In 1880, Mitchell released a volume of novellas entitled *Hephzibah Guinness*. Two years later, he published his first book of poems entitled *The Hill of Stones*. His first full-length novel aimed at adults was *In War Time* (1884), initially appearing in serial format in *Atlantic Monthly*. As he advanced in age, he began to write historical and romantic fiction even more prolifically, the most famous of which includes *Hugh Wynne, Free Quaker* (1897), *The Adventures of François* (1898) and *The Red City* (1909). Mitchell was particularly praised for his character sketches and his ability to describe empathically a range of psychological difficulties in his female protagonists. Examples include the bedridden Octopia Darnell in the novel *Roland Blake* (1886) and Sybil Maywood with her dual personality in *Dr North and His Friends* (1905).

Mitchell was married briefly to Mary Middleton Elwyn in 1858; they had two sons before she died from diphtheria in 1862. As if to sum up the two sides of Mitchell's public life, his elder son John grew up to become a family doctor, while his younger son Langdon became a successful playwright and poet. In 1875, Mitchell married for the second time; he and his new wife Mary Cadwalader had one daughter, Maria. Perhaps echoing the tragic death of Mitchell's first wife, she died of diphtheria when she was just twenty-two.

Although he is virtually unread today, Silas Weir Mitchell was a highly successful physician and writer of the nineteenth century. So positively received was "The Case of George Dedlow" that many readers forwarded donations to the hospital in which the fictional Dedlow had been treated. In addition to popular success moreover, Mitchell enjoyed critical acclaim from prominent figures such as William Dean Howells, Oliver Wendell Holmes Sr and James Russell Lowell. In the end, it further proves that occasionally, when facts are not known, fiction can indeed substitute nicely.

The Casebook of Arthur Conan Doyle

Readers familiar with Julian Barnes's novel *Arthur and George* will recall it is the story of two entirely different men. Hail-ing from contrasting environments in late nineteenth century Britain, Arthur is the son of an alcoholic from a run down area of Edinburgh, while George is the son of the Indian born vicar of a small Staffordshire village called Great Wyrley. Arthur grows up to become first a doctor and then one of the most famous writers of his time, while George becomes an obscure Birmingham based solicitor specialising in the intricacies of railway law.

Their paths cross in 1907 when Sir Arthur Conan Doyle intervenes in a miscarriage of justice, campaigning for George Edalji's innocence of the "Great Wyrley Outrages" – a curious case in which horses and livestock are slashed and maimed. The story is based on true events that eventually led to the establishment of a Court of Appeal in English law. Even more interesting are the lengths to which Barnes goes in order to bring to life the two protagonists. Both are described in intricate biographical detail, compared and contrasted with great effect.

Doyle was born in Edinburgh on 22 May 1859, the second eldest of seven children. His father was Charles Altimont Doyle, an illustrator and a clerk in the Scottish Office of Works, while his uncle was Henry Doyle, director of the National Gallery of Ireland. The young Arthur was educated by the Jesuits at the Stonyhurst School in Lancashire until 1875, and then at the Stella Matutina School in Feldkirch, Austria for a further year. He studied medicine at the University of Edinburgh and graduated in 1885. After spending several years as a ship's surgeon, first on an Arctic whaler and then on a steamship off the coast of Africa, he returned home to work as a general practitioner in Plymouth and Southsea. Growing restless of this, he travelled to Paris and Vienna to train as an eye specialist and, upon his return, established an ophthalmology practice near Wimpole Street in London.

As we have noted, Doyle originally wrote short stories professionally in the late 1880s to supplement his income, while also filling the lulls between consultations at his Southsea practice. His first published work, however, was some ten years earlier, a short story entitled "The Mystery of the Sassassa Valley" that was featured in *Chambers Journal* when he was a mere lad of nineteen. Doyle's writing was certainly influenced by his medical background, as in the case of, for example, "The War in South Africa" (1902), based on his experiences as a volunteer field physician during the Boer War. He also spent a brief period in the Sudan as a war correspondent for the *Westminster Gazette*. He was knighted in 1902 for his efforts.

Doyle wrote numerous works of fiction during his career including a historical romance entitled *The White Company* (1890) and a series of novels featuring Professor Challenger, the first of which was entitled *The Lost World* (1912). Without a doubt, however, the hero for whom Doyle will always be remembered is the logical, precise and cocaine addicted Sherlock Holmes, first introduced to the public in 1887 in *A Study in Scarlet*. Its success led to a series of short stories in the *Strand Magazine* running from 1891 to 1927, and subsequently published in book form as *The Adventures of Sherlock Holmes*, among other titles. The detective was famously modelled in part on Doyle's old university professor, Joseph Bell, to some degree on Edgar Allan Poe's Detective Dupin, and finally on a former criminal named Eugène François Vidocq. The last became the first chief of the Sûreté in Paris on the principle that it takes a thief to catch one. Dr John Watson, incidentally, is thought to have been based on Doyle's secretary, Major Alfred Wood.

Doyle was not always pleased with the success of Holmes. He once complained that, "I feel towards him as I do towards pâté de fois gras, of which I once ate too much, so that the name of it gives me a sickly feeling to this day". Doyle's growing boredom with his most successful character finally resulted in that infamous scene at the Reichenbach Falls, in which Holmes grapples with his arch-enemy Professor Moriarty causing the pair plunge to their supposed deaths. This was much to the disappointment of a fanatical readership – so much so that Doyle was obliged some ten years later to bow to public pressure and resurrect his hero in *The Hound of the Baskervilles* (1902).

Doyle was certainly hard working. He was in the habit of writing 3,000 words daily, usually before lunch or in the early evening. He nevertheless enjoyed his leisure time and was a keen sportsman who enjoyed soccer, cricket, boxing, cycling, golf, fishing and billiards. He was married twice, first in 1885 to Louise Hawkins, the sister of one of his patients. Louise died of tuberculosis in 1906 and Doyle married Jean Leckie just a year later. He had five children in all, two in his first marriage and three in his second.

Doyle was a tall, strong and heavily built man who enjoyed rude health for most of his life. Nonetheless, he suffered several mild heart attacks in his later years and died at home in Windlesham Manor, Sussex on 7 July 1930 at the age of 71. The date was coincidentally the seventy-eighth birthday of the fictional Watson.

In Barnes's book, particular attention is paid to Doyle's belief in the supernatural. Although a conservative man by nature, whose most famous fictional character was a very rational thinker, Doyle believed in fairies, was interested in spiritualism and was a member of the Psychical Research Society. What eventually became an intense preoccupation is attributed largely to Doyle's son being killed in World War I and the understandably profound effect this event had upon Doyle. It is little wonder that he provides such an interesting study for a novelist.

From a psychiatric perspective, however, it is George Edalji who might easily hold our attention. Barnes describes an introverted and naïve individual with little imagination and a stringent, precise daily routine from which he rarely strays. The solicitor still lives at home, sleeping each night in the same room as his father until well into his mid twenties and long after his younger brother has left home. His interests are mostly restricted to railway law (about which he seems to know everything), while he is described at various times as clumsy, aloof, reticent and unsociable. Given some contemporary experts' retrospective (and speculative) inclination to diagnose with Asperger's syndrome just about anyone from Darwin to Einstein, couldn't one attribute this condition to Barnes's version of George Edalji?

Asperger's syndrome is a disorder within psychiatry that lies at the milder end of the autistic spectrum. Autism is itself a rare disorder marked by severe difficulties in communicating, forming relationships with other people and appreciating abstract concepts. Well portrayed fictional examples include Christopher Boone in Mark Haddon's *The Curious Incident of the Dog in the Night-time* and Dustin Hoffman's character Raymond in the film *Rain Man*. People on the autistic spectrum develop language later than expected, find it harder to socialise, and tend to resist change with conviction. Characteristically, they are preoccupied with a narrow range of hobbies or interests and display few signs of creativity or fantasy, as is the case with Julian Barnes's description of George Edalji.

So, one could be forgiven for presuming that the author knew more than a little about Asperger's syndrome when he set about bringing his protagonist back to life. Indeed, *Arthur and George* generates food for thought in so many ways, with both its protagonists a clear source of fascination for different reasons, but in equal measure. The skill in unravelling such complexity lies, of course, with Julian Barnes: how he achieves such a feat is far from elementary.

The Secret Mystery Writer

"All the suspects in a classic murder mystery have secrets," according to Kate Summerscale in her account of *The Suspicions of Mr Whicher*, "and to keep them they lie, dissemble, evade the interrogations of the investigator . . . For most of them, though, the secret is not murder. This is the trick on which detective fiction turns."

Her book tells the true story of a prominent investigation into the untimely death of Samuel Kent's three-year-old son at the family home on 30 June 1860. The story is almost archetypal in its set-up as a country house murder mystery with a finite list of suspects, all of whom have something to hide. The case attracted much public attention at the time and was the subject of considerable media speculation, enticing writers as eminent as Charles Dickens to put forth their theories.

The detective novel is a relatively recent addition to the literary menu. Think of early pioneers and names such as Edgar Allan Poe and Raymond Chandler spring to mind. Often their protagonists were based on real detectives, the early examples of whom gained celebrity status through newspaper accounts of their logically driven methodology. Wilkie Collins's *The Moonstone*, for example, is thought to be based on the Road Hill House murder, and was published just eight years later, in 1868. Collins's description of Sergeant Cuff is not unlike that of the real Detective Inspector Jonathan Whicher, while the plot displays a remarkable resemblance to real events. As we know, all these early examples eventually culminated in the ultimate super-sleuth, namely Sir Arthur Conan Doyle's flawed detective genius, Sherlock Holmes.

By the late nineteenth and early twentieth centuries, detective fiction had gripped society. Everybody was having a go, including some writers who ultimately became famous for entirely different genres. In 1922, A. A. Milne published *The Red House Mystery*, a classic Agatha Christie style whodunit, far removed from Winnie the Pooh and the Hundred Acre Wood. But it is Anton Chekhov who provides the biggest surprise in his only novel, *The Shooting Party*.

Published in 1885, the story is that of an aristocrat, a local magistrate and an estate manager, all of whom become embroiled in the murder of a young seductress named Olga while out shooting in the woods. Chekhov's medical expertise is evident in the novel, particularly when he describes in forensic detail the injuries sustained by the victim. For example, he notes that, "On the left side of the head, at the suture of the temporal and parietal bones, was a one-and-a-half inch wound that extended to the bone". Meanwhile, "The edges of the wound were neither smooth nor straight . . . It had been inflicted by a blunt instrument, most probably, as we later decided, by the haft of a dagger". Enough surely, to rival any modern detective story.

Anton Chekhov wrote prolifically. Born in the port of Taganrog, Russia in January 1860, he was the third son of a grocery shop owner. His maternal grandfather was a cloth merchant and his paternal grandfather a serf whose job at a sugar beet refinery had allowed him to pay for his freedom. Chekhov, showing an early flair for writing, founded a newspaper – *The Stammerer* – while still at his Russian grammar school. Shortly after, his father was declared bankrupt; Chekhov was only sixteen at the time and was left at the mercy of a creditor whose son he was obliged to tutor in order to pay his debts. Chekhov was eventually awarded a scholarship to study at the Moscow University Medical School, from where he graduated in 1884. His first job was in the town of Babkino, near Moscow; from there his career took him to Hong Kong, Singapore and various parts of Europe until he finally became the Cholera Superintendent for Melikhovo, near Moscow.

During his college days, Chekhov wrote a series of humorous short stories for various St Petersburg magazines under the *nom de plume* of Antosha Chekhonte. Recall that, by the time he was twenty-five years old, he had more than four hundred publications to his name. Later, he took to writing plays, most notably *The Seagull* (1895), *The Three Sisters* (1901) and *The Cherry Orchard* (1904). His career as a playwright did not get off to an auspicious start, however. An audience in St Petersburg rioted on the opening night of *The Seagull*, critics condemning the work as "intellectual rot". Chekhov, upset by the negative reaction, vowed never again to write for the stage. Notwithstanding this first hurdle, the play was subsequently re-commissioned with great success.

As his fame spread, he became known as "The Russian Maupassant"; indeed George Bernard Shaw was reputed to have declared that reading Chekhov made him want to tear up his own plays. Chekhov was elected a fellow of the Russian Academy of Sciences in 1900 and secretly married Olga Knipper in 1901, his bride a former actress in *The Seagull*. In terms of appearance, Chekhov was a tall man with thick brown hair and a scar on his forehead, who reputedly ate very little and slept even less. Perhaps this style of sustenance took its toll on his health. He died in Germany in July 1904 of tuberculosis which had spread from his lungs to his intestines. On his death bed, in considerable pain and desperately short of breath, he was nonetheless reputed to have drunk champagne. His remains were transported to Moscow for the funeral, but mourners there confused his procession with that of General Fedor Keller of Manchuria, and were led inadvertently to the wrong graveside.

In the end, it seems that few writers were untouched by the detective genre. Anton Chekhov is just one among a distinguished list of such writers who ultimately became better known for entirely different work. Perhaps, deep down, all writers have a hankering to pen the antics of a super-sleuth.

Fin de Siècle

Vienna at the end of the nineteenth century was a decadent place. If you were not involved in gambling, duels or adulterous affairs, you might at least have attended the occasional masked ball or operetta. In any case, this was the *fin de siècle* according to Arthur Schnitzler, physician, playwright, early master of micro-fiction and a contemporary of Sigmund Freud who chronicled Viennese society and its bohemian underworld.

He was born on 15 May 1862 in Vienna, and was the son of an eminent Jewish laryngologist whose interest in the theatre would one day help to shape his son's career. The young Arthur enrolled in medicine at the University of Vienna in 1879 and graduated in 1885. He acquired a two-year post at the General Hospital in Vienna and also served a year in the army before joining his father's practice where he remained until the latter's untimely death in 1893. Schnitzler then went into private practice of his own but ultimately abandoned medicine altogether in favour of writing fiction and plays.

Schnitzler was a member of Vienna's avant-garde set of the 1890s, a group of progressive young artists and writers who swapped ideas regularly at the Café Griensteidl. His contemporaries included playwrights, poets and critics such as Hermann Bahr, Peter Altenberg and Felix Salten, among others. Schnitzler was a prolific writer in his own right and kept a diary from a young age almost until his death. By this time, he had amounted some eight thousand pages of notes that included, most notably, detailed accounts of his sexual conquests. Perhaps unsurprisingly, Schnitzler was a noted womaniser who would often involve himself in several relationships simultaneously.

The commonest themes in Schnitzler's work are sexuality and a strong stance against the anti-Semitism that was evolving in Austria at the time. Often, his work was seen as controversial; his satirical comedy *Reigen* (1900) was much criticised for its depiction of ten couples before and after sexual intercourse, in addition to the clear evidence of partner-swapping among the characters. Adolf Hitler would later brand it as "Jewish filth" and, indeed, much of the play's criticism has been subsequently regarded as more anti-Semitic than culturally conservative. After World War II, it was filmed in French by the German director Max Ophüls under the title *La Ronde* (1950).

Other notable plays by Schnitzler include *Anatol* (1893) and *Countess Mizzie* (1909), yet his short fiction is viewed as equally impressive. Laced with bitter-sweet melancholy, his stories focus on the inner lives of narcissistic soldiers and duallsts, Jewish doctors, reluctant composers and vulnerable young seamstresses and actresses. Schnitzler was interested in hypnosis, a technique expounded on at the time by the French neurologist Jean-Martin Charcot. Clearly influenced by the study of dreams and the human psyche, the narrative in short stories such as "Lieutenant Gustl" (1900) and "Fräulein Else" (1924) resemble a stream of consciousness that would have attracted the admiration of Freud.

Amid the success, the controversy ensued. "Lieutenant Gustl", a critical portrayal of the army's rigid code of honour, resulted in Schnitzler losing his commission as a reserve officer in the medical corps. In the end, he died of a brain haemorrhage in Vienna in 1931 and is buried in the Jewish part of the municipal cemetery of that city. His best known work also includes his play *Professor Bernhardi* (1912) and a full-length novel entitled *The Road into the Open* (1908), while his novella *Dream Story* (1926) inspired Stanley Kubrick's last film *Eyes Wide Shut* (1999). It is little wonder, therefore, that we presume Vienna at the *fin de siècle* to be a very decadent place indeed.

Chapter Four

Twentieth Century Physician-Writers

COUNTLESS TWENTIETH CENTURY doctors wrote fiction. Some churned out good old fashioned thrillers, while others were more literary in their approach. The master of the medical yarn was, of course, Michael Crichton. In contrast, William Somerset Maugham and A. J. Cronin were authors of more character driven novels, while Mikhail Bulgakov wrote satire. Perhaps more literary still, Oliver St John Gogarty and Williams Carlos Williams composed poetry, as did the eminent psychiatrists Emil Kraepelin and R. D. Laing. Sigmund Freud, a prolific writer, was linked to poetry too, although perhaps not in the way we might at first assume. Though their styles of writing differed, all made a meaningful contribution to literature in the twentieth century.

Poets and Psychiatrists

According to the nineteenth century French priest Joseph Roux, "Science is for those who learn; poetry, for those who know". But it should never be assumed that the two are mutually exclusive. Psychiatry, for example, is deeply rooted in the science of medicine, yet it has spawned at least two poets of note and a psychoanalyst who is the unlikely subject of a poem by W. H. Auden. Regarding the last, the elegy in question is *In Memory of Sigmund Freud* (1939), penned in a conversational style at a time when the world was descending into turmoil. Auden makes the inevitable comparison between poetry and psychoanalysis, in that both are liberators of the unconscious that focus upon the individual. But what about psychiatry's two poets?

I once suggested to a medical student under my tutelage that he spare a thought for the work of R. D. Laing. He replied earnestly that he had one or two of her albums yet, had I rolled my eyes to heaven and begun expounding on *The Divided Self* (1960), I doubt he would have ended up any the wiser. Instead, as I sensed in my young protégé an appreciation of the arts, we spent a little time discussing how Laing was a patron of philosophy and literature who would eventually publish volumes of his own poetry, such as *Knots* (1970) and *Sonnets* (1979).

He was born Ronald David Laing in Glasgow on 7 October 1927. An only child, he would one day openly describe his parents as somewhat odd, although his own son later suggested in a biography that this sentiment might have been somewhat of an exaggeration. Either way, Laing was well provided for, educated at Hutcheson's Grammar School before enrolling in medicine at the University of Glasgow. Upon qualification, he joined the Royal Army Medical Corps, although his asthma kept him from active service and he was honourably discharged in 1953. He worked briefly as a consultant at the Gartnavel Royal Hospital in Glasgow before transferring to the Travestock Clinic in London where he began to develop some of his seminal ideas in the field of psychiatry.

Although Laing's early career was unremarkable (he failed his final medical examinations and was obliged to re-sit in order to qualify), he was to have a significant impact upon the conceptualisation of psychiatry in the twentieth century. He challenged the conventional view of psychiatric illness as a group of diagnostic entities, asserting that it overemphasised unproven biological components at the cost of social, intellectual and cultural elements. His name is linked with *antipsychiatry*, although he disliked the term itself. After an illustrious career, he died relatively young on 23 August 1989.

Laing's poetry showcases a unique skill in describing complex human dynamics using very simple language. In Knots, for example, he describes the manner in which "human bondage" is subject to "tangles, fankles, impasses, disjunctions, whirligogs, binds" in a style that reads almost like the stanzas of a children's poem or a kind of psychodynamic allegory. A good example is this passage on Jack and Jill:

> Once upon a time when Jack was little,
> he wanted to be with his mummy all the time
> and was frightened she would go away.
>
> Later, when he was a little bigger,
> he wanted to be away from his mummy
> and was frightened that
> she wanted him to be with her all the time.
>
> When he grew up he fell in love with Jill
> and he wanted to be with her all the time
> and was frightened she would go away . . .

Laing was not the only psychiatrist to have dabbled in verse. Emil Kraepelin, although an intensely private man, wrote poetry that was published posthumously in 1928. Born on 15 February 1856 in Neustrelitz, Germany, he studied medicine in Leipzig and Würzburg and was conferred with his MD in 1878. By 1886, he was professor of psychiatry at the University of Dorpat in what is now Estonia and, by 1890, he was professor of psychiatry at the University of Heidelberg. He was elected to the Royal Swedish Academy of Sciences in 1908. He died on 7 October 1926.

Kraepelin wrote prolifically throughout his career and is widely considered the father of modern biological psychiatry, namely that element involving concepts of neurology, pharmacology and genetics. His views on the matter dominated psychiatry during the early part of the twentieth century and, were

Freud not so eminently charismatic, Kraepelin might well have usurped him as the most famous psychiatrist in history. Kraepelin published hundreds of dreams during his career, many of them his own, but his most important work is perhaps *Compendium der Psychiatrie* (1883), in which he sets out his thesis that psychiatric illness should be investigated for physical causes in the same empirical manner as in any other medical specialty. In addition, he devised a means of classifying mental illness that is still referred to clinically today. Finally, he wrote romantic poetry peppered with references to nature and travel, much of it influenced by his visits to India, Java and America. Through the verse, we see a pensive and rather trapped man who, in another life, might have chosen a different path. Perhaps, like Joseph Roux, he preferred to learn than to know.

It seems poetry is so ubiquitous that even the most famous of psychiatrists have been touched by it. Sigmund Freud is a perfect case in point. He was born on 6 May 1856 in Freiberg, a town in what was then part of the Austro-Hungarian Empire. The eldest of eight children and the son of a wool merchant, the young Sigmund migrated with his family to Leipzig and then to Vienna, all within a year of his birth. From the age of nine, he was educated at the Sperl Gymnasium and in 1873 he enrolled in medicine at the University of Vienna. From there, he went on to study neurophysiology under the German physician Ernst Brücke at the Physiological Institute. He remained there from 1876 to 1882, excluding a brief interlude in 1879 when he was conscripted into the Austro-Hungarian Army.

Upon qualification, Freud practiced briefly at the Vienna General Hospital, but was soon diverted to the Psychiatry Clinic of the eminent Austrian neuropathologist Theodor Meynert. By 1885, Freud had been appointed lecturer in neuropathology at the University of Vienna. From there he travelled to Paris to attend the lectures of Jean-Martin Charcot, professor of anatomical pathology at the Salpêtrière Hospital. Freud became highly respected as his career progressed, and was awarded the Goethe Prize in 1930 and membership of the Royal Society in 1936.

In 1886, he married Martha Bernays and they went on to have five children. Freud was famously neurotic and suffered poor health as he advanced through middle age. With a list of medical complaints that included a fluttering heart, shoulder pain, constipation, indigestion, migraines, agoraphobia and a fear of travelling on trains, many of his symptoms could indeed be attributed to his anxieties. In the end, he succumbed to something far more real in the form of mouth cancer, for which he received no fewer than thirty-three operations from 1923 until his death in Hampstead, London on 23 September 1939.

Freud was a prolific writer throughout his life. As we noted in Chapter One, he penned numerous case histories to exemplify his newly established field of psychoanalysis, a breakaway branch of neurology. Many – such as "Anna O", "Dora" and "Little Hans" – were written under pseudonyms to preserve patient confidentiality but others – "Gustav Maher", "Emma Eckstein" and "Princess Marie Bonaparte", for example – were not. Additional topics upon which he wrote with authority include sexuality, hysteria, dreams, narcissism and his concepts of the *ego* and the *id*. Not all of his books were necessarily bestsellers; his masterpiece, *The Interpretation of Dreams*, was published in 1899 yet its first inventory of just six hundred copies did not sell out for a further eight years.

Undeterred, Freud laboured for twelve hours each day, generally seeing his patients in the mornings and writing notes and essays in the evenings. In a manner perhaps consistent with his *free association* style of tapping into the unconscious, he was a fluent writer who rarely went back to edit what he had written. He is also said to have preferred to write longhand rather than use a typewriter. His many interests included archaeology, languages and poetry, and he enjoyed the work of John Milton,

Sir Walter Scott and Lord Byron. The American poet Hilda Doolittle once wrote of him that "his beautiful mouth seemed always slightly smiling". But did Freud, himself, write poetry?

Alas it seems not, but perhaps the greater accolade lies in his becoming the subject of a long verse by the poet W.H. Auden as alluded to earlier. *In Memory of Sigmund Freud* opens with a reflection on how difficult it is to write an elegy at a time when so many people are dying unnecessarily. Freud passed away barely three weeks after Hitler invaded Poland leading, as we know, to the enormous casualties of World War II. Auden's comparison between poetry and psychoanalysis is remarkably poignant in the context of such tumultuous events:

> *He wasn't clever at all: he merely told*
> *the unhappy Present to recite the Past*
> *like a poetry lesson till sooner*
> *or later it faltered at the line where*
>
> *long ago the accusations had begun,*
> *and suddenly knew by whom it had been judged,*
> *how rich life had been and how silly,*
> *and was life-forgiven and more humble,*
>
> *able to approach the Future as a friend*
> *without a wardrobe of excuses, without*
> *a set mask of rectitude or an*
> *embarrassing over-familiar gesture.*

Auden was familiar with *The Interpretation of Dreams* and understood Freud's admiration of poetry. Indeed, Freud saw similarities between poetry and dreaming, and viewed both as manners of condensing meaningful ideas such that they needed only the correct interpretation to decipher. Similarly, Auden, as we can see, describes psychoanalysis as the "unhappy Present" reciting "the Past like a poetry lesson".

It is not the first time this comparison has been made. We have already noted that Kraepelin was both a prolific scribe of dreams and a published poet. Auden, moreover, makes a direct comparison between art and psychology in general. The purpose of both, he suggests, is not to tell people what they should or shouldn't do, but rather to uncover a common understanding so that individuals may then choose what to do for themselves. So, even though Freud did not write poetry, he was still in a sense a published poet.

Weathered Faces Lined in Pain

According to the singer-songwriter Don McLean, in his song subtitled *Starry Starry Night*, "Weathered faces lined in pain are soothed beneath the artist's loving hand". The artist to whom he refers is the post-Impressionist painter Vincent van Gogh, a man recorded in the annals of history for two quite separate reasons. First is the creation of some of the most beautiful pieces of art the world has ever seen, not least *The Potato Eaters* (1885) and *Sunflowers* (1888). Second is the more infamous impulse to slice off part of his left earlobe.

Unsurprisingly, van Gogh was prone to intense bouts of emotional instability. He was also a close personal friend of fellow post-Impressionist painter Paul Gauguin and it was allegedly following an intense argument (while the latter was staying at the former's yellow house in Arles) that van Gogh perpetrated his signature piece of self-mutilation. It is said that he took the severed appendage to a local house of ill repute, where he thought he might track down Gauguin. Instead, he presented it to a lady of the night (shall we say) named Rachel. It is doubtful she extended any but the coldest thanks.

So, what has any of this to do with fiction? What has it to do with physicians, for that matter, other than the medical assistance van Gogh might have needed once he had finally calmed down? Alas, Gauguin was an artist not shy of controversy in his own right, if Somerset Maugham is to be believed. Like van Gogh, Gauguin was prone to bouts of depression and despair, attributes reflected in Maugham's novel *The Moon and Sixpence* (1919). In the book, Gauguin is presented to the reader in the thinly veiled guise of Charles Strickland, a respectable middle aged Englishman who abandons his wife and children without warning to devote himself to art in Paris. Strickland's subsequent rejection of Western civilisation brings him to Tahiti where he contracts leprosy and, after many painful years of illness and disability, ultimately dies.

Beyond the biographical account of Gauguin, *The Moon and Sixpence* is the universal tale of the tormented artist. In the eyes of Maugham, art cannot exist without suffering and the writer uses leprosy, with its chronic invasion of the totality of being, as an icon to symbolise his point. As we shall see in Chapter Eight, Maugham's Strickland is obliged to suffer his mutilating disease in the same way Gauguin suffered for his art. Although not a visual artist himself, Maugham was a connoisseur of fine art. Fabulously wealthy at the height of his success, he owned paintings not only by Gauguin, but by Pissaro, Renoir and Monet and others. He was even given a Matisse in lieu of payment for the screenplay of his novel *The Razor's Edge* (1944).

Somerset Maugham, the fourth surviving son of English parents, was born in the British embassy of Paris in 1874 in order, it is said, he be born on British soil. When he was a tender lad of just eight, his mother succumbed to tuberculosis; his father, a solicitor, passed away just two years later. In a manner that mirrors events in the writer's autobiographical novel *Of Human Bondage* (1916), the newly orphaned Maugham was dispatched to live in Kent with his uncle, the Rector of Whitstable. At that time, having lived in Paris all his life, Maugham spoke little English, an impediment compounded by a severe stammer (in contrast to Philip Carey, the protagonist in *Of Human Bondage*, who had a club foot instead).

Maugham was educated at King's School, Canterbury until the age of sixteen when, as a result of a lung infection (he suffered from tuberculosis for most of his life), he was sent to Hyeres in southern Provence for some fresh air. Shortly after, he spent a year in Heidelberg. Philip Carey did the same in the novel but, unlike Maugham, he subsequently trained as an artist, while the author returned to England to begin a career as an accountant. When this didn't work out, he turned his eye to medicine, enrolling as a student in St Thomas's Hospital, London in 1892 where he was employed as a clerk in the out-patient department. Using his skills, he spent most of World War I as an ambulance driver, apart from a brief period during the Russian Revolution when he reputedly worked for British intelligence.

Maugham turned to writing at an early age. His most successful work includes his first novel *Liza of Lambeth* (1897), in addition to *Of Human Bondage* (1916), *The Moon and Sixpence*, *Cakes and Ale* (1930) and *The Razor's Edge*. He also wrote popular plays such as *The Circle* (1921) and *The Constant Wife* (1926).

Maugham was considered rather a difficult man to deal with. His acerbic cynicism and acute powers of observation were useful tools in his writing which nonetheless made him many enemies during his long life. It is said that Noel Coward based the homosexual anti-hero of his play *A Song at Twilight* on Maugham; indeed, it was predicted at the time that a libel case could ensue, something that might have transpired had Maugham not died before the play's opening night in 1966. In fact, he passed away at his villa in Cap Ferrat on 16 December 1965 at the age of ninety-one. Upon his death, Coward referred to Maugham as a "Poor, miserable old man, not very sadly mourned, I fear".

The author Selina Hastings recently wrote a well-received biography entitled *The Secret Lives of Somerset Maugham*. In it, Maugham is portrayed as an embittered, selfish and even cruel man whom few held in high regard on a personal level. Despite being married to the gregarious Syrie Wellcome (of pharmaceutical company fame), Maugham conducted a long and open homosexual affair with his personal secretary, Gerald Haxton. Somewhat parsimonious also, Maugham was obsessed with avoiding tax collection and, during World War II, was reputed to carry at all times a briefcase containing $100,000.

Maugham was once quoted in *The Observer* as stating that "I've always been interested in people, but I've never liked them". Perhaps this explains why the novelist was unafraid to base many of his characters on well known figures. Paul Gauguin is not the only case in point; in *Cakes and Ale*, Edward Driffield is widely considered to be a fictional version of Thomas Hardy, while Alroy Kear is thought to be the English novelist Hugh Walpole. For much of the research required to perform this fictionalisation of the famous, Maugham relied heavily upon Gerald Haxton and the latter's sources of gossip.

Strangely, Maugham did not regard himself as particularly creative. In his memoir *The Summing Up* (1938), he wrote, "I am a made writer. I do not write as I want to; I write as I can ... I have had small power of imagination ... no lyrical quality ... little gift of metaphor". He countered, instead, that he possessed "an acute power of observation, and it seemed to me that I could see a great many things that other people missed". It was said of Maugham that, while his capacity to describe the superficial was incisive, his ability to engage the reader on a spiritual level was often clumsy.

Maugham owed much of his success to sheer hard work. A disciplined writer who put pen to paper every morning without fail, he was also a good businessman, adopting the approach of studying his market and then giving readers exactly what they wanted. His decision to write plays at all, indeed, was largely in anticipation of the potential financial rewards that such an endeavour could produce. He went to the theatre often and paid close attention to what was well received by audiences so that he might replicate these qualities in his own work. Indeed, during the 1930s, he was the highest paid writer in England.

Despite his enormous commercial success, many of the more discerning critics of the day (and, indeed, subsequently) refused to acknowledge his talents. Famously, for example, the *New York Review of Books* in 1978 regarded him as "the mahatma of middlebrow culture". Kinder words were written by reviewers such as fellow author L. P. Hartley, who cited Maugham's work as "nearly perfect". Raymond Chandler, also a fan, wrote that, "His plots are cool, and deadly, and his timing is absolutely flawless". Throughout the review process, however, Maugham remained his own harshest critic. On the topic of his own abilities, he could be as vituperative as anyone else and, as a result, paid little attention to what the critics said.

In 1953, the artist Graham Sutherland drew a portrait of Maugham, in which he captured the craggy face of a man in his late seventies for use in a limited edition of *Cakes and Ale*. To return to the haunting words of Don McLean, this might represent a more modern example of the weathered face lined in pain, soothed beneath the loving hand of an artist.

Poetic and Medical Licences

To a few, the name Oliver St John Gogarty conjures up only images of a pub in Temple Bar with a pea green façade. Most, however, will recognise this drinking emporium as the namesake of a poet, playwright, surgeon, champion athlete, aeronaut and senator. Indeed, Gogarty, often scandalous but clearly a man of considerable accomplishment, was the great all-rounder of the Irish literary Renaissance.

He was born in Dublin on 17 August 1878. His upper middle class roots included a strong medical tradition dating back three generations, which was unusual for Catholics in nineteenth century Ireland. Gogarty was a child when his father died, but the family was left well provided for, affording him an education at the prestigious Stonyhurst school in Lancashire and, later, at Clongowes Wood in County Kildare. At eighteen, he embarked upon his medical studies at the Royal University in Dublin.

Unfortunately this seat of learning (by tradition, the preference for educated Catholics at the time) lacked the necessary stimulus for Gogarty, who passed only two of his first ten examinations. He moved to Trinity College in 1898 but, even there, he excelled at everything but medicine. He became a protégé of Professor J. P. Mahaffy, the renowned classicist, philosopher and one-time tutor of Oscar Wilde. Mahaffy must have noted in Gogarty a sharpness of observation and a natural wit in the art of conversation. The young medical student could effortlessly regale a crowd with his stories and limericks and was constantly in demand at college social events. He not only won the vice-chancellor's verse prize on three successive occasions at Trinity, but he was also a champion cyclist and a first rate swimmer (around 1900, he rescued no fewer than three people from drowning in the Liffey). In 1924 he revived the ancient Tailteann Games, coming third in archery, and in 1928 he became a founder of the Irish Aero Club. Here was a true Renaissance man, but one who nevertheless required three years to pass his second-year anatomy examinations and ten in all to finish medical school.

Gogarty and his clique of fellow medical students would frequently skulk around Dublin, indulging in esoteric witticisms and intellectual discussions. By night they would abandon their middle-class respectability to frequent the bars and taverns of the Kips, a bohemian and often dangerous area of Dublin where the artist and criminal alike could drink until sunrise. Indeed, Gogarty saw many similarities between the artistic and felonious fraternity; "Laughter," he wrote, "is the primeval attitude towards life, a mode of living that survives in only artists and criminals."

Yet, Gogarty was also on intimate terms with many influential people, including Arthur Griffith and W. B. Yeats, a poet whom he held in high regard. The feeling was mutual, with Yeats referring to Gogarty as "One of the great lyric poets of our age". It is little wonder that Gogarty's own ballads and limericks were popular and widely praised among Dubliners. He became a close friend of James Joyce, with whom he stayed very briefly in the Martello tower in Sandycove; he even supported the impecunious Joyce financially until the two young men disagreed and parted company.

The Martello towers, which were built to defend Ireland's coastline during the Napoleonic era, had become fashionable domiciles by 1904. One such tower features in Joyce's *Ulysses* (1922) as the abode of "stately plump Buck Mulligan", a character modelled upon Gogarty. Since the latter was, by 1922, a successful surgeon with a reputation to uphold, he was furious with Joyce over the portrayal. "That bloody Joyce whom I kept in my youth," he complained loudly, "has written a book you can read on all the lavatory walls in Dublin!"

In contrast to his less than brilliant record as a medical student, Gogarty's postgraduate career was impressive. He passed his final exams in 1907, the same year in which he married Martha Duane, and proceeded to undertake an apprenticeship with Sir Robert Woods, an eminent ear, nose and throat surgeon. Although Woods had an instant affinity for his protégé (and would eventually refer many patients to him), Lady Woods was too wary of the gregarious poet to allow him attend any of her dinner parties. Following a short period of study in Vienna, the young surgeon returned home to the Richmond Hospital, where he enjoyed considerable success. Gogarty was said to possess a burning compassion beneath his cynical exterior and also, more importantly perhaps, great dexterity as a surgeon. Only thirty-three when he performed Ireland's second ever laryngectomy (an operation that involves the removal of the larynx), he continued to practice very successfully throughout his career.

As a writer, Gogarty was very critical of the British occupation of Ireland and tended to satirise colonial rule in his plays and poems. His political interests did not end there. Unsympathetic to Eamon de Valera, he provided a safe house for Michael Collins during the War of Independence, and subsequently became a senator of the Irish Free State. His affiliations were so prominent that he was kidnapped by republicans in 1923 and escaped only by courageously swimming across the Liffey. Later, in a characteristically flamboyant gesture in recognition of his good fortune, he published a volume of poetry entitled *Offering of Swans* and presented the river with two fine avian examples.

In 1937, Gogarty published a controversial memoir entitled *As I Was Going Down Sackville Street*. Although much anticipated, the book was subsequently the subject of a libel action that Gogarty lost. Embittered by this and by the Irish political situation in general, Gogarty moved to New York where he lectured, wrote articles, and ultimately died on 22 September 1957. During his lifetime he published numerous plays, poems and novels, but it is for his charm and chivalry that he will always be remembered. His enduring witticisms complemented his daring escapades and fervent political views. Oliver St John Gogarty: no finer name to grace the door of a Dublin pub.

Forfeiting Pound for the Dollar

Perhaps the most iconic American physician-writer of the twentieth century was the New Jersey paediatrician William Carlos Williams. His most famous pieces are poems such as "The Red Wheelbarrow" (1917), "To Elsie" (1923) and "The Sea" (1923). But he was diverse in his literary endeavours, writing short stories like "The Venus" (1932) and "The Zoo "(1950), improvisations such as *Kora in Hell* (1920) and *The Great American Novel*

(1923), the stage play *A Dream of Love* (1948), and non-fictional pieces that include most notably *The Autobiography* (1951).

With a medical rather than a literary background, Williams was initially self-conscious as a writer and struggled to find his voice. He then underwent a kind of literary renaissance during his mid-thirties, perhaps not unlike that of W. B. Yeats. Williams learned to embrace self-awareness and reject the perceived trivialities of youth, emerging as a key figure in the Imagist poetic movement alongside contemporaries such as Hilda Doolittle and Ezra Pound. Williams was known to scribble his verse on the backs of disused prescription pads between consultations. Perhaps it was the immediacy of this process that allowed him to capture "no holds barred" yet empathic snapshots of life. How easy it is to sense the keen eye of the physician in Williams's simple imagery, such as in his masterpiece "The Red Wheelbarrow" (1917):

> so much depends
> upon
>
> a red wheel
> barrow
>
> glazed with rain
> water
>
> beside the white
> chickens.

Departing from the traditional style of European poetry, "The Red Wheelbarrow" shows us Williams focussing upon a vivid image that does not require an idea to affirm its existence. It is simply a matter of looking at something familiar with a fresh eye. Despite – or, perhaps, because of – its simplicity, the poem has still managed to capture generations of imaginations, including those of some who are prominent contemporary artists in their own right. For example, it is recited in Woody Allen's film *You Will Meet a Tall Dark Stranger* (2010), while John

Green's novel *The Fault of Our Stars* (2012) sees one character quote it to another.

But Williams was not without his critics. Hilda Doolittle considered Williams's literature flippant and derivative; she wrote to Williams asserting that "I consider this business of writing a very sacred thing!" In response, Williams asserted that "there is nothing sacred about literature: it is damned from one end to the other". Williams was a close friend of Ezra Pound since their shared days at university around the turn of the century, yet Pound was no more appreciative than Doolittle. In *Kora in Hell* for example, Williams utilised an experimental technique of flowing narrative and free association, exuberantly combining history and autobiography with snippets of opinion. It was something new but Pound dismissed it as "incoherent".

Pound also failed to grasp why Williams was to evidently obsessed with America when most of the avant-garde had long before migrated to Europe in search of higher culture. But Williams did not take lightly his decision to remain in America. His short story "The Venus" (1932) is essentially a conversation between a German woman and an American man about the pros and cons of American culture. As they wander through a garden in Frascati, Italy, she asks him what America is like. He initially attempts to evade the question, but eventually replies that it resembles "something muffled – like a badly trained voice. It is a world where no man dare learn anything that concerns him intimately – but sorrow – for should we learn pleasure, it is instantly and violently torn from us as by a pack of hungry wolves so starved for it are we and so jealous of each of us is our world". Hardly a glowing endorsement of the United States, yet it explained why the character would return there and why the author would never leave. America, despite its alleged primitive nature, was a source of the familiar imagery upon which so much of Williams's poetry depended.

Williams was born on 17 September 1883 in Rutherford, New Jersey and spent his early childhood there. In 1897, his father dispatched him to boarding schools first in Geneva and then in Paris; upon his return, he completed his basic education at the Horace Mann School in New York. Williams enrolled in medicine at the University of Pennsylvania in 1902 and was awarded his degree in 1906. He practiced as a family doctor and ultimately as a paediatrician for most of his working life but found time in the evenings for his writing. His first book of poetry was published in 1909.

Williams married Florence Herman in 1912 after his proposal to her older sister was declined. He and Florence nevertheless enjoyed a supportive and enduring marriage. In M. L. Rosenthal's anthology of Williams's work, he recalls how Williams's youthful letters revealed a difficult man who could be short with people but who, as he grew older, was loved and admired by younger writers for his courtesy and his encouragement of their work. Rosenthal, indeed, describes Williams as "a serious, wonderfully articulate, and good man talking about ordinary life and about poetry with an absolute immediacy of involvement". While Rosenthal does not believe Williams's thinking to have been particularly original or even consistent, he asserts that it was nevertheless "the product of long contemplation of a few principles brought to bear on the accidental issues of the moment".

Throughout Williams's life, medicine had a profound influence upon his writing. In *The Autobiography*, he describes how his vocation as a family doctor provided him with a unique insight into the "secret gardens of the self" to such a degree that he felt compelled to write them down:

> I was permitted by my medical badge to follow the poor, defeated body into those gulfs and grottos. And the astonishing thing is that at such times and in such places – foul as they may be with the stinking ischio-rectal abcesses of our comings and goings – just there, the thing, in all its greatest beauty,

may for a moment be freed to fly . . . about the room. In illness, in the permission I as a physician have had to be present at deaths and births, at the tormented battles between daughter and diabolic mother, shattered by a gone brain – just there – for a split second – from one side to the other, it has fluttered before me for a moment, a phrase which I can quickly write down on anything at hand, any piece of paper I can grab.

Williams describes perfectly the privileged invitation the family physician has into the most intimate aspects of so many different lives. His consequent desire to put pen to paper is no less applicable to any of the physician-writers discussed in this book.

Williams suffered a heart attack in 1948 and from then on his health began to decline. He died on 4 March 1963 at home in Rutherford and is buried in Hillside Cemetery, New Jersey. Just two months posthumously, he was awarded the Pulitzer Prize for *Pictures of the Brueghel and Other Poems* (1962) along with the Gold Medal for Poetry of the National Institute of Arts and Letters. He was clearly much admired among his peers.

The Tale that Wagged the Dog

Anton Chekhov, about whom we have already spoken (twice), was not the only Russian doctor to publish fiction. Less well known but equally impressive was Mikhail Bulgakov, who wrote numerous plays and half a dozen novels or short-story collections. Most famous of these is his novel *The Master and Margarita*, a masterpiece begun in 1928 and repeatedly re-written almost until Bulgakov's untimely death in 1940. But from a medical perspective, it is perhaps *The Heart of a Dog* (1925) that is of more interest to us.

Here, we have the allegorical tale of an experiment gone wrong. A stray dog named Sharik is befriended by two wealthy and successful doctors, Professor Philip Philipovich Preobrazhensky and his assistant Dr Ivan Arnoldovich Bormenthal.

Enticed with sausage meat back to their lavish eight-roomed apartment in Moscow, the dog is allowed to become comfortable with the comings and goings of a busy urban domicile that doubles as a medical practice. Life is good for our young four legged friend.

Although Sharik chews galoshes and chases cats with alacrity, he is more intelligent than we might expect from a dog. He informs us that most dogs can read, yet he also insightfully asks, "Why bother to learn to read when you can smell meat a mile away?" Much of the early part of the story is, indeed, told from the dog's viewpoint, with the narrative switching effortlessly from the first to the third person. It is only upon its transformation that the dog becomes objectified in the mind of the reader.

With such a technique, Bulgakov garners the reader's sympathy for the dog and, in doing so, makes the novel's climax all the more effective. With almost cruel decisiveness (notwithstanding ominous early references to experimentation and taxidermy), the professor receives a sudden phone call and the dog is quickly whisked away to an operating theatre and anaesthetised. Bulgakov proceeds to describe a surgical procedure in gruesome detail. The dog is sliced open and transplanted with the pituitary gland and testicles of a recently deceased twenty-five year old man. So vividly painted is the mental picture, that one is left in no doubt about the author's insider knowledge of anatomy and surgery.

For example, "The dome of Sharik's brain was now laid bare – grey, threaded with bluish veins and spots of red. Philip Philipovich plunged his scissors between the membranes and eased them apart. Once a thin stream of blood spurted up, almost hitting the professor in the eye and splattering his white cap". Later, as the operation progresses, we are told, "He peeled aside the layers of cerebral membrane and penetrated deep between the hemispheres of the brain. It was then that Bormenthal went pale, and seizing Sharik's breast with one hand he said hoarsely: 'Pulse falling sharply . . .'"

In the chapter that follows, we are treated to a series of medical notes by Bormenthal describing the dog's recovery and transmogrification from a canine to a human physique. Within a week, the dog is moulting and his limbs begin to grow. Within two, he is walking on his hind legs, laughing out loud and repeating words to himself. Indeed, so efficient is Sharik in acquiring language that Bormenthal correctly hypothesises he must have "already accumulated a massive quantity of sense-data". He adds that, "All the words which he used initially were the language of the streets which he had picked up and stored in his brain. Now as I walk along the streets I look at every dog I meet with secret horror. God knows what is lurking in their minds".

Eventually, to much comical effect, the dog becomes virtually indistinguishable from his human counterparts. Yet Sharik – or Poligraph Poligraphovich Sharikov, as he now calls himself – is far from refined. His table manners are appalling, he drinks too much vodka, he "barks" his words rudely and he still chases cats, causing much chaos and farce within the household. Rumours abound and the threat of scandal looms for the professor, yet Sharikov is quickly accepted by the proletariat of the apartment block who are eager to punish the professor for his bourgeois ways.

For some time, Sharikov remains idle within the household. On one occasion, the professor asks him, "What makes you think that you're a worker?" Sharikov replies, "I must be – I'm not a capitalist." In true form, Sharikov finally acquires a post in charge of the "sub-department of the Moscow Cleansing Department responsible for eliminating vagrant quadrupeds". In his own words, "it may smell a bit – that's because of my job. I spent all yesterday strangling cats".

The Heart of a Dog is, in many ways, a satirical re-telling of Mary Shelley's *Frankenstein* – a novel we shall discuss in some detail later. Certainly, the central themes are identical, namely the dangers of "creating a monster" through ill advised scientific experimentation. As a cautionary tale, it was a firm favourite among the Gothic novelists of the nineteenth century and would subsequently become popular among modern medical thriller writers. Many such examples will be examined during the course of this book. Like Frankenstein's monster, Sharikov was created to satisfy a greed for knowledge and then regretted almost instantaneously leading to a subsequent rejection of the end product. In this regard, Bulgakov alludes to the ethical issues of consent and paternity. The transmogrified dog asks of the professor, "Why shouldn't I call you 'Dad', anyway? I didn't ask you to do the operation, did I?"

The other major theme in the book is the rise of Bolshevism, something the professor seems to consider tasteless. "If you care about your digestion," he asserts, "my advice is – don't talk about bolshevism or medicine at the table". He famously adds, "And, God forbid – never read Soviet newspapers before dinner". On a more symbolic level, perhaps, Bulgakov demonstrates that if you give a dog a human pituitary gland and testicles it will become human. So, if you give power to the Bolsheviks, will they inevitably become bourgeois? With worse implications still, it is noteworthy that Sharikov acquires a job strangling cats for a living. Will the new Soviet regime invoke a similarly fatal solution for all public nuisances?

In the Soviet Union of the 1920s, such a non-conformist view was not well received and, as censorship acquired some teeth, Bulgakov experienced increasing difficulty publishing his manuscripts. He managed to produce a few plays, yet he and his wife often went hungry. So frustrated was Bulgakov indeed, that he wrote first to Maxim Gorky and the Politburo and eventually, in 1930, to Joseph Stalin himself asking for permission to emigrate if the degree of censorship to which he was subjected was to continue. Stalin made a personal telephone call to Bulgakov and offered him a job as an assistant director at the Moscow Arts Theatre.

It is an example of how Bulgakov's life was peppered with struggle and serendipity in equal measure. He was born in Kiev on 15 May 1891, the son of a lecturer at the city's Theological Academy and a teacher at the aristocratic preparatory school. It was an origin that would mark him down as bourgeois. He studied medicine at the University of Kiev, from where he graduated in 1916, but much of his practice would prove to be in the context of the regional social upheaval of the time. Initially drafted as an army doctor for the Ukrainian Republic, he was subsequently seconded to the White Guard and then finally conscripted into the Red Army.

In many ways, Bulgakov's reality during the civil war was similar to that of Boris Pasternak's *Doctor Zhivago*, also on the agenda for later. Bulgakov had no interest in fighting; indeed he had little interest in a profession that he ultimately abandoned in 1920. Instead, he opted to become a writer and moved to Moscow to work freelance, penning satirical articles and reviews for various periodicals that even included proletarian newspapers such as *Gudok* and *Rabotchiy*. Bulgakov was a dab hand at subtly criticising the Soviet Republic, and did so with alacrity in the early nineteen-twenties.

His first works of fiction include a collection of short stories entitled *The White Guard* (1924), the novel *Diaboliad* (1924) and a novella entitled *The Fatal Eggs* (1924). Alas, with censorship evolving, the bourgeois Bulgakov was being watched and listened to by the authorities and, on one occasion, his apartment was ransacked and his manuscript of *The Heart of a Dog* (1925) was confiscated. Neither it nor *The Master and Margarita* (1938) were published during Bulgakov's lifetime. It would be some fifty years or more before they saw the light of day. Bulgakov managed to produce a dozen or so plays, but none were published until censorship was relaxed, long after Stalin's demise. Perhaps it would have been easier for Bulgakov had he simply remained a doctor.

Approaching the Citadel

Bad tempers do not always suit the mining industry – at least not in fiction. Take Emile Zola's masterpiece *Germinal* (1885) as a case in point. In this epic tale, Etienne Lantlier is an intelligent young man with a penchant for hard work; his Achilles heel lies in the fact that he is rather easily rubbed up the wrong way. As a result, when he takes a mining job at Le Voreux in northern France (the story is set in the late 1860s), and sees first hand the ill health, household debt and sheer famine to which the ordinary miners are subjected, he is incensed and finds himself leading the kind of strike that would make Arthur Scargill's little escapade in the early 1980s look like a minor kerfuffle, if you'll forgive the pun. Needless to say, it all ends in disaster.

Dr Andrew Manson in A. J. Cronin's *The Citadel* has a similarly short fuse. His sense of anger – present throughout the novel – threatens his livelihood, his friendships and, ultimately, his marriage. But his anger is not always misplaced. He begins as a newly qualified doctor, full of idealistic vision of how medicine ought to be practiced, and takes a job in the fictional mining town of Drineffy, south Wales. Although eager to succeed – and the possessor of a first class honours degree – he is unsure of his abilities at first:

> *How often had he envisaged it as, in a crowd of students, he had watched a demonstration in Professor Lamplough's wards. Now there was no sustaining crowd, no easy exposition. He was alone, and confronted by a case which he must diagnose and treat unaided. All at once, with a quick pang, he was conscious of his nervousness, his inexperience, his complete unpreparedness, for such a task.*

Manson soon makes gains, both in confidence and in competence, and finds himself increasingly angered not merely by the manner in which medicine and surgery are poorly practiced by his so-called colleagues. To his dismay, science, it seems, plays little useful role in contemporary treatment; instead, antiquated remedies based on obsolete text books and old wives' tales are what the doctors frequently order. Alas, Manson is too young to exert any real influence over his medical and nursing colleagues and, in some cases, even his patients.

As he moves to a larger town, his troubles deepen as his conviction strengthens that quackery abounds. Jealous of the influence the more senior quacks nonetheless seem to have, Manson channels his anger into the acquisition of membership of the Royal College of Physicians and, subsequently, a Medical Doctorate. Such postgraduate qualifications were not the least bit essential in the 1920s and 1930s. Now highly qualified, Manson moves to London with his long suffering wife Christine and ultimately sets up a private practice in the West End.

The Citadel is, in many ways, the classic cautionary tale. If you value materialism over humanity, you will sacrifice your soul and quite possibly a lot more besides. On a more tangible level perhaps, Cronin's central thesis is that the medical profession (at the time of his novel's publication) is so fundamentally dysfunctional that it actually represents a danger to society. In the author's view, doctors should be required to continue in education long after initial graduation. Science should be brought "to the frontline", while doctors should work in teams and be given "the chance to co-operate in research". The "useless guinea-chasing treatments", the "crowds of worthless pseudo-scientific proprietary preparations we use" and the "unnecessary operations" should be cut out completely, while doctors should never ally themselves with the pharmaceutical industry by recommending tonics with little scientific basis purely for monetary gain.

Such an ethical stance seems quite reasonable – indeed, essential – from a twenty-first century viewpoint but, as Cronin illustrates in painful detail throughout the novel, common practice in the early part of the twentieth century was under the influence of an entirely different zeitgeist. Even Manson – once ethical to the core – progressively loses his youthful idealism as he is seduced and corrupted by the trappings of unethical practice. On a symbolic level, it is Christine who acts as his conscience until even she is eventually silenced by Manson's misdirected anger.

But then, if it were not for the young doctor's tempestuous nature, he might never have won his wife's hand in the first place. Early in the book, upon hearing that a child with measles has been sent to school regardless, he immediately storms up to the young schoolmistress – then known as Miss Christine Barlow – and threatens to report her to the authorities for breaking the law. Calming down, as Manson usually does (and realising, also, that he is developing a crush on the rather fetching Miss Barlow), he finds himself compelled to make an ignominious apology. Miss Barlow is so forgiving that she eventually agrees to marry him.

As Manson's conscience, it is Christine who repeatedly reminds him of his earlier values, inspiring the novel's otherwise cryptic title. "Don't you remember how you used to speak of life," she implores him, "that it was an attack on the unknown, an assault uphill – as though you had to take some castle that you knew was there, but couldn't see, on the top –"

Cronin based much of the material in *The Citadel* on his own medical experiences. He was a man of conviction, whose own journey mirrored that of Manson, beginning with his post as a doctor in the Tredegar Cottage Hospital in south Wales. The novel – Cronin's fifth and a bestseller upon its publication in 1937 – has been credited as one of the key catalysts leading to the eventual formation of the United Kingdom's National

Health Service. It is no coincidence that Aneurin Bevan, the Labour health minister responsible for the Service's inception, was himself the son of a coalminer from Tredegar.

Cronin was, in his own right, a talented and committed doctor. Born on 19 July 1896 in Cardross, Dunbartonshire, Scotland, the young Archibald Joseph spent his early years in Helensburgh and attended the Grant Street School. His father – a salesman – died of tuberculosis when the young Archibald was only seven; mother and son were therefore compelled to return to Dumbarton, where she eventually became Scotland's first female public health inspector.

Cronin attended the Dumbarton Academy where, you might say, he had somewhat of the Midas touch. He won academic prizes and writing competitions, and displayed proficiency in athletics, football, golf and fishing. When the family moved to Glasgow, he became a pupil at St Aloysius's College and, from there, was awarded a scholarship to study medicine at the University of Glasgow.

He enrolled in medicine in 1914, just as Europe was descending into a state of war. Indeed, he interrupted his studies two years later to spend a year in the Royal Navy as a Surgeon Sub-Lieutenant. He graduated from the university in 1919 with first class honours and acquired a post as ship's surgeon on a liner bound for India. His training resumed upon his return; indeed, around this time, he trained at – among other hospitals – the Rotunda in Dublin, before finally taking up a position as a general practitioner in Tredegar. He became a member of the Royal College of Physicians in 1924 and was awarded his Medical Doctorate by the University of Glasgow the following year.

In 1924, Cronin's experience led to an appointment as Medical Inspector of Mines for Great Britain, which required him to tour the country's various collieries, surveying and auditing medical regulations in much the same manner as the fictional Manson is required to do. Based on his findings, Cronin published several scientific reports on the effects of coal dust inhalation and its link to pulmonary disease. Indeed, it was this esoteric knowledge that he would eventually draw upon when writing *The Citadel* and another novel of the same genre entitled *The Stars Look Down*. In time, he moved to London and practiced in Harley Street, before eventually establishing his own successful practice in Notting Hill, where ophthalmology became his special interest.

In 1930, ill health (a duodenal ulcer) forced Cronin to take some time off, affording him the opportunity to fulfil the lifelong ambition of writing his first novel. Entitled *Hatter's Castle*, it was prepared and edited in just three months. The manuscript was accepted by Gollancz – the first and only publisher to which it was submitted – and was an immediate success upon its publication. Indeed, so well received was his debut that, from then on, Cronin wrote prolifically (penning, among other novels, the enormously successful *Doctor Finlay* series) and never felt the need to return to the practice of medicine again.

In 1921, Cronin married Agnes Mary Gibson, formerly a fellow medical student from Glasgow University. They had three sons. As Cronin's novels were adapted for the silver screen, he and his family moved to the United States and lived, at various times, in California, Massachusetts, Connecticut, Maine and New York. Cronin travelled widely, and kept homes in Bermuda and the south of France. Eventually, he returned to Europe permanently, setting up home by Lake Geneva, Switzerland and continued to write well into his eighties. He died in Montreux on 6 January 1981.

Like Emile Zola and other proponents of the nineteenth century Realist movement, Cronin had a strong sense of humanity and social conscience that was evident in his writing. More importantly, perhaps, his prose was always entertaining, with witty dialogue, a hint of romance and colourful characters. It is little wonder his novels were bestsellers. In the end, Cronin, like his protagonist Andrew Manson, was a man of passion and conviction who chipped away at injustice in his own inimitable manner. One hopes he was a little better at remaining calm; but then, perhaps the occurrence of real change requires the fraying of at least a few tempers.

A Timeline on Michael Crichton

Ask anybody who John Lange is and they probably won't be able to tell you. The same could be said of Jeffery Hudson. This is because Michael Crichton wrote about a dozen novels under pseudonyms before he ever became famous under his own name. It was the late sixties and he was still at medical school, no doubt trying to avoid the vituperations of professors and deans who might have preferred that he apply his intellect to his academic studies. But keeping this raw talent under wraps became increasingly difficult for Crichton as he began to garner prestigious prizes, not least an Edgar Award in 1969 for his novel *A Case of Need*.

He was not an especially literary writer; the emphasis in his books was usually upon the plot and its necessary background research, with little attention to characterisation or the subtleties of human dynamics. But when it came to action adventure and science fiction, Crichton was king, spinning the archetypal, old fashioned yarn in the same vein as Sir Arthur Conan Doyle and Sir Henry Rider Haggard some eighty years earlier. Indeed, Crichton borrowed from Doyle the title *The Lost World* (also, as it happens, a book about explorers and dinosaurs), while the novel *Congo* pays more than scant homage to *King Solomon's Mines*. Author, producer, director and doctor, Crichton sold over two hundred million books during his lifetime, a feat unmatched by any other physician-writer to date.

His plots were often based upon quasi-futuristic, not-quite-invented-yet-but-almost technology and the flawed human nature that would inevitably lead to its doom. Recall that this was not a new theme, but rather one that writers from Mary Shelley to Mikhail Bulgakov had already based their novels upon. Notwithstanding, Crichton was among the first to return to this theme in a modern thriller. For example, in *Prey* (2002), bio-nanotechnology intended for medical treatment ends up taking on a mind of its own and threatening the human species. In *Timeline* (1999), DNA errors lead to psychotic symptoms in time-travellers while, in *Jurassic Park* (1990), greed and vanity lead to a cascade of system failures in a supposedly perfect security system meant to incarcerate dangerous dinosaurs. One way or another, Crichton's tales were usually cautionary ones, his thesis being that, if you set up complex order and fail to incorporate the human component, chaos will ultimately ensue.

But Crichton also cautioned against over-caution. In *State of Fear* (2004), he highlights the dangers of biased research, presenting an argument refuting the existence of man made global warming based on a carefully selected minute proportion of the available evidence on climate change. In his ironic take, he demonstrates how science can be used to fabricate almost any argument if one is selective enough with the results.

Crichton was born in Chicago on 23 October 1942 and grew up in New York. An avid writer from a young age, he had a travel column published in the *New York Times* when he was a mere lad of fourteen. He went on to study English literature at Harvard in 1960 but fell out with his professor over grades he alleged were artificially low. Indeed, Crichton famously conducted an experiment (with the permission of another professor) aimed at proving the perceived discrepancy. Deliberately plagiarising George Orwell's work and submitting it in his own name, Crichton was proved correct when he was awarded a B minus. It prompted him to switch allegiance to anthropology, in which he was finally awarded a degree in 1964.

From there, he was appointed Henry Russell Shaw Travelling Fellow for a year and, in 1965, he became a visiting lecturer at the University of Cambridge. It was at this point that his brief career in medicine began, one that was destined to shape much of his literary endeavours over the subsequent forty years. He enrolled in Harvard Medical School and, in parallel with this, began writing novels under his carefully chosen pseudonyms. Crichton was six feet nine inches tall and it is rumoured that his choice of *nom de plume* was often related to his unusual stature. *Lange* means long in German, while Jeffery Hudson – a prominent seventeenth century English courtier – also happened to be a dwarf.

Crichton graduated from Harvard Medical School and was awarded his MD in 1969. No longer fearing the disapproval of academic staff, he was now free to publish in his own name and did so with his debut, *The Andromeda Strain*, a novel about a group of scientists who discover a dangerous extraterrestrial micro-organism that coagulates human blood almost instantaneously. The novel – a bestseller – was made into a film just two years after its publication. Despite this success, Crichton continued to write under a pseudonym until *The Terminal Man* in 1972. Once again, the theme of "science gone wrong" is explored, namely the effects of influencing the human mind with implanted electrodes. The book was also made into a film, although the latter was not as well received by critics as *The Andromeda Strain*.

More novels followed, including *The Great Train Robbery* (1975), *Congo* (1980) and *Sphere* (1987), but it was *Jurassic Park* that catapulted Crichton into a different stratum, particularly when it was filmed by Steven Spielberg and thereby transformed into the summer blockbuster of 1994. Subsequent novels included *Disclosure* (1994), *Airframe* (1996) and *Next* (2006).

Crichton was also the creator and executive producer of *ER*. Originally intended as a film to be directed by Spielberg, it was transformed instead into a television drama that ran for fifteen seasons. As a result of its success, Crichton enjoyed the unique accolade of occupying simultaneously the number one chart position of book sales, television ratings and cinema outings for *Disclosure*, *ER* and *Jurassic Park* respectively.

Crichton had his share of idiosyncrasies. Like Sir Arthur Conan Doyle, he was known to consult psychics and gurus. Famously a workaholic who would lock himself away to write his drafts quickly, he was married five times, the first four matches ending in divorce. He had one daughter and, at the time of his death, one unborn son. Crichton died of throat cancer on 4 November 2008. In the end, there were few thriller writers quite like him. As Steven Spielberg was quoted as saying upon Crichton's death, "there is no one in the wings that will ever take his place."

Chapter Five

Twenty-First Century Physician-Writers

I F THE PHYSICIAN-WRITERS MENTIONED thus far have something in common more fundamental than their shared occupations, it is that they are all sadly deceased. So, what about those who are still writing? The dusty shelves of many a bookshop are stacked with the medical thrillers of Paul Carson, Tess Gerritsen, Michael Palmer and Robin Cook, while the more literary connoisseur is catered for by the likes of Ethan Canin and Khaled Hosseini. Oliver Sacks is in a class of his own, publishing the type of fictionalised case histories alluded to in Chapter One. In all, with around one hundred published novels between them, these authors show the world that physicians have as much to contribute to the world of literature as they ever had.

Would the Real Doctor Sacks Please Stand Up?

Sometimes the mind can play tricks on the listener. Utter the name "Doctor Sacks" for example, and we might well picture the elusive caricature of a 1959 novel by Jack Kerouac. A childhood fantasy of the novelist's protagonist Jackie Duluoz, the eponymous Doctor Sax is described as a dark figure dressed in a black cape and hat, living in the woods outside the nearby town of Dracut. Sax is affable, notwithstanding his sinister demeanour, while his motivations are relatively pure. He is an alchemist by trade, who experiments in brewing potions capable of killing the "Great World Snake" that seemingly threatens to devour us all. Alas, Kerouac's imagination was a famously vivid one.

But there is an altogether more impressive doctor by a similar name. Lovers of reality-based literature will know of Dr Oliver Sacks, Professor of Neurology and Psychiatry at Columbia University Medical Centre and author of countless neurologically inspired essays and fictionalised case histories. Most famous of these is *Awakenings* (1973), yet Sacks has published an additional ten volumes to date on the wonders of neurological phenomenology. With each fictionalised journey, he advances deeper into the as-yet-uncharted frontiers of the human mind, and emerges with articulate and often moving descriptions of what he sees.

Sacks was clearly influenced by the twentieth-century Russian neuropsychologist Aleksandr Luria, author of *The Mind and the Mnemonist: A Little Book about a Vast Memory* (1987). But Sacks, himself, is no stranger to literary success. Among his best known work is *The Man Who Mistook His Wife for a Hat* (1985), a collection of first-hand case histories of patients with unusual neurological presentations. According to Sacks, scientists to date have mapped the left cerebral hemisphere in far greater detail than the right. As a result, some of the rarer abnormalities seen in clinical practice can leave experts scratching their heads in wonderment. A good example is the opening anecdote from which the book borrows its title.

Here, Sacks describes a music teacher with an acquired inability to recognise familiar faces. As one might anticipate from a classically trained musician, the patient compensates for his newfound deficit by gathering clues through what he hears. He also scans features rather than faces as a whole and, in doing so, recognises people with distinctive characteristics such as moustaches or scars. Yet his deficit does not stop there. He cannot name random everyday objects like the flower or the glove; he seems unable to discriminate between his foot and his shoe; and it soon becomes evident that he recognises only one side of his body. He can describe the plot of Leo Tolstoy's *Anna Karenina* but not its visual characteristics. When he does not know, he confabulates, and when he turns to leave, he attempts quite literally to put his wife's head on his own, just like a hat.

Sacks astutely describes an abnormality localised to a specific area of the brain. The patient, he notes, has managed to function perfectly well as a music teacher, indicating that the *temporal lobes* are intact, while his sense of touch and smell are also noted to be normal. What the patient lacks, Sacks surmises, is the ability to place any meaning on the objects he sees. The author compares this deficit to a computer that gathers minute detail but is unable to form any judgement based on what it accumulates. This deterioration has been a gradual one, if one goes by a series of wall paintings completed by the patient over the course of years. The earlier examples are conformist while the later ones, it appear to Sacks, make no sense at all. Alas, when he suggests this to the patient's wife, she accuses him of philistinism and suggests her husband has simply developed his skills as an artist.

We never quite discover the actual disorder, but Sacks gives us the benefit of his expert supposition. He attributes the presentation to some form of *visual agnosia* affecting the *occipital* or *parietal lobes* of the brain, perhaps due to a tumour or degenerative process. In doing so, he writes in the style of a fictional narrator, almost as though his vivid encounters are a figment of his own rich imagination. He uses dialogue in the manner a novelist might, while his storyline is unravelled with all the twists and turns of a good old fashioned yarn. Even his digressions are thought provoking, for example his contemplation of whether pathology colludes with creativity in producing the advanced work of any great artist towards the end of a long and fruitful career.

Sacks certainly showcased his talent as a storyteller in his most famous memoir, *Awakenings*. Readers unfamiliar with the book may have encountered the play it inspired Harold Pinter to write, entitled *A Kind of Alaska* (1982). Others may have seen the Oscar-nominated film *Awakenings* (1990), directed by Penny Marshall and starring Robert De Niro alongside Robin Williams. Here, we have the true and moving account of fifteen or so patients who resided at the Beth Abraham Hospital in the Bronx around the time Sacks first began working there as a neurologist. By then, the patients had already spent several decades in states of *akinetic mutism*, rendered unable to initiate spontaneous movement or even talk. The severity of their *catatonia* was such that they required constant care from staff and relatives.

In his book, Sacks traces the origin of their shared condition to the great pandemic of *encephalitis lethargica* (or "sleepy sickness") that occurred between 1915 and 1927. In the late nineteen-sixties, Sacks was among the first neurologists to experiment with treating such survivors with the then-pioneering medication *L-dopa*, originally intended for patients with Parkinson's disease. Through his novel approach to patient care, Sacks managed to bring his catatonic patients briefly back to life.

In the film version, Sacks is fictionalised as Dr Malcolm Sayer, a shy and introverted research neurologist who lives alone and enjoys botany in his spare time. It is almost with a sense of serendipity that Dr Sayer notices in his patients a response to various stimuli – the throwing of a ball (which they nimbly catch), patterns on the floor, certain kinds of music or the mention of their name. One such patient is Leonard Lowe, a man of around fifty years who has been unwell since the age of ten. Leonard somehow communicates with Dr Sayer by using a Ouija board and thus evokes in the doctor an intense curiosity of what truly lies beneath his patient's blunted façade.

Given the expense of L-dopa and the controversy of the proposed experiment, Dr Sayer is permitted to involve only one patient in his trial. He selects Leonard for the medication and succeeds in rousing his patient almost immediately from his state of dormancy. Leonard walks, Leonard talks, Leonard marvels at the world like the child he was before he fell ill. Leonard even falls in love. As an evident triumph is celebrated, the other patients are revived in the same manner, but their real tragedy lies in the short lived nature of their renaissance. The dosage of L-dopa is difficult to get right; its paucity yields Parkinsonism and its excess leads to paranoia. Eventually, it wears off altogether, leaving only the memory of a beautiful summer and some semblance of hope that it may one day return.

If *Awakenings* gives us a fictionalised version of Oliver Sacks, what can we say about the real man? He was born on 9 July 1933 in London into a family of doctors; his father, Samuel, was an established physician, while his mother was Muriel Elsie Landau, one of England's first female surgeons. Sacks enrolled at Queen's College, Oxford in 1951 and earned his bachelor's degree in physiology and biology three years later. The same college awarded him his medical degree in 1958. After first converting his qualifications to those acceptable for practice in the United States, he went on to complete residencies and research at the Mt Zion Hospital, San Francisco and the University of California, Los Angeles.

Sacks's list of honours is a long one. In addition to his professorial appointment at Columbia, he was named the first Columbia University Artist in 2007. He has been awarded honorary doctorates by around a dozen other universities, including Oxford, Georgetown and Tufts, and he was appointed Commander of the Order of the British Empire (CBE) in the Queen's 2008 Birthday Honours list. As if all this were not enough, a planet is named 84928 Oliversacks in his honour.

Throughout all the accolades, his writing continues. His more recent works include *An Anthropologist on Mars* (1995), *The Island of the Colorblind* (1997) and *The Mind's Eye* (2010). But *Awakenings* remains his masterpiece, the touching story of how one man's passion and curiosity can produce a profound change in a group of encephalitis survivors otherwise forgotten. So, the next time you hear someone enunciate the name "Doctor Sacks", forego the work of Jack Kerouac and contemplate, instead, the talented neurologist who writes about the soul.

The Physician-Writer of Kabul

Few books have captured the public imagination quite like *The Kite Runner*. A universal tale of atonement and redemption, it has been published in some seventy countries and translated into a dozen or more languages. It is such a critically acclaimed bestseller that even its own author Khaled Hosseini must have been daunted by the monumental task of providing readers with an encore.

The story is set largely in Afghanistan and charts, from a young man's perspective, the country's turbulent modern history from the fall of the monarchy in the early nineteen-seventies to the cruelties of the Taliban regime some thirty years later. The central character is Amir, just twelve years old as the story opens. He is eager to impress his father, whose apparent wealth and importance locally gives the young man a lot to live up to. To complicate matters, Amir has a rival for his father's approval in the form of Hassan, the family's low caste servant of Hazaran extraction. While Hassan has natural social disadvantages, a cleft lip and the ignominy of regular ridicule by more privileged children, he is clearly a boy of courage and integrity. Amir cannot help but feel jealous and fears his father sees in Hassan something that is sadly lacking in Amir himself.

Alas, this unilateral rivalry reaches its climax at a local kite-fighting tournament, when Amir suffers the shame of witnessing Hassan's superior moral fibre. Amir, who has always benefited from Hassan's loyalty, fails to reciprocate when his young friend is beaten cruelly by a gang of local thugs. A minor event in the scheme of things perhaps, but it takes on greater significance as the country descends into chaos.

Although clearly a work of fiction, much of the story mirrors the timeline of Hosseini's own life. Born in Kabul on 4 March 1965, he is the eldest of five. His background was initially a privileged one; his mother was a secondary school teacher of history and Farsi, while his father was a diplomat with the Afghan Foreign Ministry. This, of course, meant foreign travel and the young Khaled was only five when the family moved to Tehran, Iran. When the family returned to Kabul in 1973, Afghanistan had become a republic. In 1976, they were dispatched once again, this time to Paris, naïve to the events that would soon prevent their return and change their fortunes forever.

On 28 April 1978, the world witnessed the Saur Revolution in which the communist People's Democratic Party of Afghanistan seized power. This was followed swiftly by the imbroglio of a Soviet invasion and an occupation that would have jeopardized the safety of the Hosseini family. In 1980, they were granted political asylum in the United States and moved to San Jose in California.

Always of a literary disposition, Hosseini had read novels and poetry widely as a child, sometimes in Persian and sometimes in English. As such, he had little difficulty adapting to the American education system and graduated from Independence High School in 1984. He went on to study biology at Santa Clara University and, following the conferral of his bachelor's degree, he enrolled in the School of Medicine at the University of California, San Diego. He was awarded his medical degree in 1993 and embarked upon his residency at Cedars-Sinai Hospital, Los Angeles. He practiced medicine until 2004.

Hosseini began writing *The Kite Runner* in March 2001 and clearly based it on his experience of Afghanistan as a child. Nevertheless, when he returned to Afghanistan in 2003 for the first time since his arrival in the United States, he found a suppressed and war-ravaged country that he hardly recognised even from his own fiction. The Wazir Akbar Khan district of his childhood bore no resemblance to what it had been prior to the arrival of the Soviets. Hosseini speaks fondly about his younger years and claims no heroism in his survival; where money and privilege did not save him from the Soviets and the Taliban, luck was largely responsible. *Time* magazine once reported his remarking that he felt some shame at not suffering to the same degree as many of his countrymen. Perhaps this sentiment underpins his desire to write, namely the opportunity bring the plight of Afghanistan to the attention of the world through fiction.

This is certainly plausible in the context of Hosseini's humanitarian activity since his retirement from medicine. In 2006, he became a goodwill envoy for the United Nations High Commission for Refugees (UNHCR). Subsequently, he established the Khaled Hosseini Foundation whose mission is to offer humanitarian assistance to those in need in Afghanistan. When not busy with humanitarian work, he lives in Northern California with his wife and two children.

The Kite Runner became an overnight success when it was first published in May 2003. This is little wonder for such a tenderly written tale of redemption that cannot fail to move the reader. Its sense of restitution is achieved perhaps through the timely repetition of phrases, not least when Hassan pledges loyalty to his childhood friend with the words "for you, a thousand times over". It is especially poignant when Amir repeats the phrase to Hassan's son some thirty years later.

In 2007, the book was adapted for the silver screen by Marc Forster, and starred the author in a cameo appearance. It was subsequently a Golden Globe nominee for best foreign language film of 2007, while the same year saw the publication of a second novel entitled A *Thousand Splendid Suns*. Also set in Afghanistan, the novel has a similar theme to its predecessor, although the protagonists in this case are two women. Reviews upon publication were every bit as positive as those of *The Kite Runner*.

In the end, Khaled Hosseini is the perfect example of a modern physician-writer who successfully gave up medicine to apply himself to writing. His achievement in this regard is remarkable and perhaps matched only by his devotion to humanitarian causes. But as the reader waits with baited breath for his next novel to come along, it is with slight regret that one wonders whether Hosseini has already penned his masterpiece. Such books come along only once in a generation. And few books have captured the public imagination quite like *The Kite Runner*.

Weaving Tense Yarns

No book about physician-writers would be complete without a mention of the medical thriller genre. Beyond Michael Crichton, several prominent authors continue to grip the reader with intricately plotted tales of action and suspense. Most of these stories are not simply a based on the daily affairs of some hospital or clinic, but are rather the exploration of an ethical question posed by misguided scientists' hunger for knowledge or desire to save humanity. The narrative voice is often that of an isolated and hardworking junior doctor who struggles against the odds to expose an injustice or prevent some catastrophe. Of course, this is not always the case.

To find one example, we need look no further than our own shores. When Paul Carson published his first medical thriller *Scalpel* in 1997, its success rivalled anything the American thriller writers had to offer. The novel was an instant *Irish*

Times bestseller and spent seventeen weeks in the number one spot. The story is that of Dean Lynch, a psychologically damaged surgeon who sets out on a killing spree. Although gritty and well-paced from the outset, the book is unlike many in its genre in that it does not attempt to grapple with any substantial ethical issues. But then, *Scalpel* was published at a time when doctors in Ireland were still seen as morally incorruptible; there was sufficient thrill in the very idea that someone in such a position of power and trust could go about committing murder with alacrity. Perhaps subsequent events have shown that life sometimes imitates art.

There is a second reason Carson's gripping debut is a little unconventional. *Scalpel* is really two novels in one volume because the sub-plot (involving the kidnapping of a baby) almost never merges with its main counterpart. The parallel stories simply happen among two sets of people who seem vaguely to know each other. Alas, sometimes a brilliant idea can be harder to execute. Carson's subsequent offerings have certainly been better structured without losing any of the raw edge clearly evident in his debut. The encores have also tended to fit more neatly into the genre, with explorations of medical ethics central to their themes. In his third novel, *Final Duty* (2000), for example, an Irish doctor based in Chicago must protect his family and his reputation from a scorned pharmaceutical giant.

Carson was born in 1949 and grew up in Newcastle, Northern Ireland. He studied medicine at Trinity College Dublin, from where he graduated in 1975, before spending some eight years as a family practitioner in the Barossa Valley, South Australia. He returned to Ireland in 1984 and established a general practice clinic in Stillorgan, south County Dublin, where he has developed renowned expertise in treating asthma and other allergies in children. During the course of his career, he has written numerous articles in various medical journals, in addition to five specialist health books and two storybooks aimed at children. To date, he has published five thrillers that also include *Cold Steel* (1998), *Ambush* (2003) and *Betrayal* (2005). He is married with two children.

If Paul Carson's first medical thriller caused a stir in Ireland, the same can certainly be said globally about Tess Gerritsen's *Harvest*. The book, first published in 1996, centres on the sinister discoveries of Dr Abby DiMatteo, a second year surgical student on an elite cardiothoracic team. Abby is the archetypal medical thriller protagonist; she is a talented and dedicated doctor whose curiosity gets the better of her until, finally, she is forced to jeopardise her career in order to make the right ethical decision.

The premise of *Harvest* is that children are being trafficked from outside the United States so that their organs can be transplanted by illicit surgeons into wealthy recipients. A highly original idea at the time, it germinated from a disturbing dinner conversation the author once had with a retired policeman who had, at the time, recently travelled to Russia. Seemingly, the policeman had learned from his Russian counterparts that children were vanishing from the streets of Moscow only to find themselves sold as organ donors in developing countries.

Although Gerritsen had previously published nine romantic suspense novels, she entered a new stratum with her debut medical thriller. *Harvest* was met with critical acclaim and appeared in the thirteenth position on the *New York Times* bestseller list. It launched a career that has subsequently seen the publication of over a dozen medical and crime thrillers. Many of these have featured recurring protagonists, such as homicide detective Jane Rizzoli and medical examiner Maura Isles.

Gerritsen was born on 12 June 1953 in San Diego, California. Her parents were of Chinese origin and, although Gerritsen showed an early inclination to become a writer, her parents encouraged her to aim for the safer career choice of medicine. In this regard, she graduated from Stanford University in 1975 with a degree in anthropology and went on to enrol in medicine at the University of California, San Francisco. She earned her medical degree in 1979 and began working as a physician in Honolulu, Hawaii. Famously, Gerritsen penned her first novel – the romantic suspense yarn *Call After Midnight* – while on maternity leave in 1987. It was published the same year.

Since her debut, Gerritsen's books have been translated into forty different languages, sold more than twenty-five million copies and appeared both regularly and prominently on the *New York Times* bestseller list. She has since left medicine to work full time at her writing. She lives in Maine with her husband and two children.

Long before either Carson or Gerritsen put pen to paper however, Michael Palmer and Robin Cook were each writing medical thrillers with an ethical edge to them. Palmer is most famous for his fourth thriller, *Extreme Measures* (1991), subsequently made into a film starring Hugh Grant and Gene Hackman. The plot centres on a neurologist's discovery that his esteemed colleagues are performing spinal experiments on homeless people without consent in an effort to find a cure for paralysis. As with Gerritsen's *Harvest*, the novel fleshes out the core ethical dilemma of the degree to which individuals should be expected to pay for milestones in medical advancement.

Palmer was born in Springfield, Massachusetts on 9 October 1942 and studied pre-med (with Russian as his minor) at Wesleyan University, Connecticut. Not only does Palmer profess to never having set out to be a writer, but he also admits his English professor was somewhat disparaging about his ability to write. Had the same professor changed his mind and read some of Palmer's novels, he might have been a little disconcerted to find one of Palmer's villains was named after him. While still at Wesleyan, Palmer took classes in topics as diverse as eastern literature and the writer Edgar Allen Poe, while he also kept himself occupied reading escapist thrillers by Alistair MacLean, Eric Ambler and Robert Ludlum.

Palmer studied medicine at Case Western Reserve University, Cleveland and subsequently trained in internal medicine at Boston City and Massachusetts General Hospitals. After a brief stint in military service, he initially practiced internal medicine before embarking on a career in emergency medicine. He spent some twenty years as a medical practitioner before finally retiring to concentrate on his writing.

His first published novel was *The Sisterhood* (1982), a thriller that tackles the ethical issues inherent in euthanasia. He has penned sixteen further medical thrillers to date, the most recent being *Oath of Office* (2012). His books have been translated into thirty-five different languages and have spent considerable time on the *New York Times* bestseller list. Palmer stated in his website that he was inspired to take up writing after he read the medical thriller *Coma* (1977) by Robin Cook. The latter was just two years ahead of Palmer at Wesleyan University and also trained alongside him at Massachusetts General Hospital. As such, we arrive at perhaps the most influential medical thriller writer alive today.

Robin Cook was born on 4 May 1940 in Brooklyn, New York and grew up in Queens and New Jersey. From high school onwards, his interests were sufficiently wide ranging to include architecture, archaeology, literature and sports. At Wesleyan University, he majored in chemistry but still achieved a distinction in the subject of government. He went on to study medicine at the Columbia University College of Physicians and Surgeons and, upon graduation, began his training as a surgical resident. Shortly after, he was drafted into the Navy and, as such, he spent some time aboard the USS *Kamehameha* in the South Pacific. He was eventually discharged at the rank of Lieutenant Commander and, after completing a residency in ophthalmology, he went on to practice privately in the field.

He also reserved some of his time for teaching residents at Harvard Medical School, alongside work at the Massachusetts Eye and Ear Infirmary.

Like Michael Crichton, Cook has successfully combined science and biotechnology fiction with the medical thriller genre. Like many other thriller writers, his tales are cautionary ones involving diverse ethical dilemmas related to, for example, the pharmaceutical industry, organ transplantation, stem cell research, genetic engineering and public policy paradoxes. He has published some thirty novels, the most recent of which is *Death Benefit* (2011). Most of his novels have appeared on the *New York Times* bestseller list and have been translated into forty or more different languages. He has sold almost one hundred million copies of his books to date, a feat among medical thriller writers matched only by Michael Crichton.

As we can see, the medical thriller genre is clearly alive and kicking. Formulaic it may be, but readers seem unable to satisfy their hunger for gripping narratives featuring ethically driven and hardworking doctors who somehow feel obliged to save the world. And as Crichton, Carson, Gerritsen, Palmer and Cook have all shown, who better to make our pulses race than a physician with a penchant for weaving tense yarns.

Summing Up

Abba Roth is a successful accountant who has dedicated his life to the firm of Priebe, Emond and Farmer. Married with three children, conservative, obsessional and introspective, he has been passed over for promotion on at least one occasion and seems lost in a maze of middle management. Still, Roth has a plan. A self-funded weekend retreat playing baseball with business executives is certain to land him that elusive and lucrative contract, thus turning around his corporate fortunes, earning him the gratitude of his firm and finally delivering to him the holy grail of partnership. But there is, of course, a catch. First he must overcome his jealousy of the prospective client, a successful and charismatic entrepreneur whom Roth once counted as a childhood friend.

Here we have the premise of Ethan Canin's novella *The Accountant* (1993), first published in *Esquire* and subsequently included in a volume of short pieces under the title *The Palace Thief* (1994). Even when writing about the world of commerce, it seems medicine is never far from Canin's mind; Roth values almost everything in monetary terms and counts doctors among those he perceives as high earners and therefore worth soliciting. When surprised on one occasion by the cost of hiring a vet to treat his daughter's horse, he remarks that, "Up until that time I had thought there were no professionals more expensive than a physician." Even the amateur baseball enthusiasts he randomly encounters on his weekend excursion turn out to be a team of vacationing radiologists.

Canin's frequent reference to the medical profession is, of course, no coincidence. Born in Ann Arbor, Michigan on 19 July 1960, he spent his early years in Iowa City and enjoyed a rather peripatetic childhood until his family finally settled in San Francisco. He studied English at Stanford University and followed this up with a Master of Fine Arts degree, which he received in 1984. Within a few years, he was at Harvard Medical School, from where he graduated at the ripe old age of thirty. He then began his residency at the University of California, San Francisco.

Canin has cited more than one reason why doctors make good writers and vice versa. With a longstanding ambition to write professionally, he published his first book of short stories entitled *Emperor of the Air* as early as 1988. Alas, fearing the impecuniousness of a literary calling, he had hedged his bets and was already, by that time, a medical student at Harvard. Such a decision paid dividends to his writing; he once remarked of medicine: "It's like being a soldier. You've seen great and terrible things". But he would eventually give up medicine completely in favour of teaching creative writing. His novels include *Blue River* (1992), *For Kings and Planets* (1999), *Carry Me Across the Water* (2001) and *America America* (2009). Much of his work has been filmed and he has been the recipient of several literary awards, including the California Book Award and Gold Medal in Literature.

Ethan Canin is just one of many contemporary fiction writers who began their working lives as doctors. Two Irish physician-writers of note are Juliet Bressan, a general practitioner and author of novels such as *Snow White Turtle Doves* (2008) and *Entanglement* (2009), and Séamus Sweeney, a psychiatrist whose story "The Driver" won the 2010 Molly Keane Short Story Award. Equally entrancing is Sweeney's short story "Dublin Can Be Heaven" (2011), a haunting tale of espionage and revenge in the aftermath of World War II.

Internationally, prominent contemporary writers as yet unmentioned include Daniel Mason, an American medical student in 2002 when he published his debut novel *The Piano Tuner*. Also noteworthy are Chris Adrian, an American paediatric oncologist and author of *The Children's Hospital* (2006), John Murray, an Australian whose collection *A Few Short Notes on Tropical Butterflies* (2003) is based on his experiences as a doctor in Africa, and Kevin Patterson, a Canadian doctor whose memoir *The Water In Between* (2001) was cited as a *New York Times* "Notable Book".

We could go on *ad infinitum*; the list of physician-writers is seemingly endless, but Part Two of *Fiction & Physicians* beckons, namely the half that offers a taste of the various vivid fictional doctors who have captured our imaginations. Perhaps these characters are all the more impressive when we consider that their creators were not for the most part doctors. But perhaps a little objectivity adds an extra layer of colour.

Part Two

FICTION ABOUT DOCTORS

Chapter Six

Incompetent and Ambitious
Fictional Physicians

THE TITLE OF "DOCTOR" SEEMS to lend prestige to fictional characters, particularly in the classic novels of the eighteenth and nineteenth centuries. But beyond this, as we begin delving into the world of medical fiction by non-doctors, it becomes evident that the portrayal of physicians in literature is not always flattering. More often than not, their unmasked incompetence is used to add comic relief to novels with Realist themes. This can be seen in, for example, Gustave Flaubert's Dr Charles Bovary. Similarly, incompetence has been used to add spice to satirical novels, as in the case of Dr Slop in Laurence Sterne's *The Life and Opinions of Tristram Shandy, Gentleman*.

In Gothic novels such as Mary Shelley's *Frankenstein, or The Modern Prometheus* and Robert Louis Stevenson's *The Strange Case of Dr Jekyll and Mr Hyde*, incompetence colludes with greed and ambition to produce disastrous results. This is especially true in terms of the moral implications of scientific advancement simply to satisfy a thirst for knowledge. Sometimes incompetence and ambition are personified to work side by side. Look no further than Dr John Seward and Professor Abraham Van Helsing, who represent a Watson and Holmes style duo as they track down and tackle the nefarious Count

Dracula. So, from Realism to satire and Gothic Romanticism, classic literature is filled with flawed fictional physicians.

Sloppy Medicine

There can be few things more amusing than a writer feigning incompetence in describing a doctor feigning expertise. The perfect example is Laurence Sterne's inimitable Dr Slop, the physician and "man-midwife" in *The Life and Opinions of Tristram Shandy, Gentleman*. The eponymous narrator invites us to imagine "a little squat, uncourtly figure of a Doctor Slop, of about four feet and a half perpendicular height, with a breath of back, and a sesquipedality of belly, which might have done honour to a serjeant in the horse-guards". If the opening description inspires little confidence, the events that follow do little to ameliorate such a perception. Indeed, the very name of "Slop" conjures up images of a blundering quack.

Irreverent, satirical, farcical, chaotic, digressive and strangely postmodern in its themes, Tristram Shandy was first published in nine volumes between 1759 and 1767. Sterne was clearly influenced by the forefathers of his genre, authors such as François Rabelais and Miguel de Cervantes. While its exuberance and coarse humour are Rabelaisian to the core, the novel echoes *Don Quixote* by serving up a protagonist who constantly sets out to regale readers with complex anecdotes but then repeatedly interrupts himself with non sequiturs. Often the narrator will regress to examine the cause of every minute incident, and then further pause to examine the cause of that cause, until a seemingly infinite search for causality renders the flow of the story non-existent. Indeed, so frustrated is Tristram in his attempts to make any progress, he amusingly takes stock about a third of the way through the book:

> *I am this month one whole year older than I was this time twelve-month; and having got, as you perceive, almost into the middle of my fourth volume – and no farther than to my first day's life – 'tis demonstrative that I have three hundred and*

sixty-four days more life to write just now, than when I first
set out; so that instead of advancing, . . . on the contrary, I am
just thrown so many volumes back . . .

The narrative meanders for some four hundred and fifty pages
until finally, failing utterly to reach any natural conclusion, it
simply stops. Some of the final scenes are set a full four years
before Tristram is born.

Such an approach to autobiographical literature was sublimely imaginative for the time. Sterne injected enormous creative energy into his novel, amusing and confusing his readers
with blank pages, marbled pages, funereally blackened paper,
missing chapters, empty chapters, out-of-sequence chapters, di-
agrams and misplaced dedications. How could the eighteenth-
century reader fail to be impressed? Much of the philosophical
world was still concerned with the age of reason and, similarly,
the literary fraternity was on the cusp the Realist movement
that would shortly evolve. While one natural counterpoint
would prove to be Romanticism and ultimately the emergence
of the Gothic novel, the other rebuff to Realism lay in satire.

It seems unlikely that *Tristram Shandy* is widely read today,
yet it recently garnered a new audience through a rather impressive adaptation for the silver screen. Michael Winterbot-
tom's *A Cock and Bull Story* (2006) starring Steve Coogan and
Rob Brydon was not a direct translation of the novel; given
the latter's erratic time sequencing, such an endeavour would
have been far too tall an order for any director. Instead, in a
truly self-referential style very much keeping with the novel's
theme, *A Cock and Bull Story* is a film about the making of a
film based on the novel. With a final sprinkling of irony, the
actors even refer to the novel at one point as being essentially
unfilmable.

In producing a work of fiction, Sterne clearly wrote about
what he knew. He was born on 24 November 1713 in Clonmel,
County Tipperary, the son of an infantryman but, more inter-

estingly, the great-grandson of Richard Sterne, Archbishop of York during the reign of James II. The young Laurence grew up in army barracks but was later educated in Halifax, Yorkshire and at Jesus College, Cambridge from where he graduated in 1736. He was ordained in 1738 and spent the subsequent twenty years as parson of Sutton-in-the-Forest, York. A man of diverse interests, he was also a Justice of the Peace and a part-time dairy farmer. It is little wonder the novel is so richly endowed with references not simply to medicine but also to war, religion and agriculture.

Despite Sterne's pious occupation, it is also easy to see in his lifestyle a hint of *Tristram Shandy's* coarseness. Sterne married Elizabeth Lumley in 1741 and was said to be happy with this union, but he nevertheless formed relationships with several other women who included the singer Cathérine Fourmantelle and a lady named Elizabeth Draper who was the wife of an East India Company official. Sterne's mistresses no doubt appreciated his literary talent, which is more than can be said for some of his critics. *Tristram Shandy* was dedicated to William Pitt the Elder (Prime Minister at the time), but the novel still received mixed reviews upon its publication. Horace Walpole referred to it as "a very insipid and tedious performance", while Samuel Richardson, Oliver Goldsmith and Dr Samuel Johnson all afforded it similarly negative reviews. Nevertheless, its commercial success allowed Sterne to follow it up with *A Sentimental Journey through France and Italy* (1768) and *Letters from Yorick to Eliza* (1775).

Sterne did not drink heavily and abhorred smoking, yet good health still eluded him. He contracted tuberculosis at a relatively young age and, from 1760, his breathing steadily declined. He moved to France in 1762 in search of a favourable climate and, following a brief return home, travelled similarly to Italy in 1765. In the end, he died of pleurisy on 18 March 1768, alone in his rented London lodgings except for his nurse.

He was buried in St George's burial ground but – as if to echo the chaos described in his work – his body was later stolen by grave-robbers and recognised as one of the cadavers at Cambridge University.

Perhaps this reference to anatomy is our cue to return to the imbroglio of Dr Slop. Tristram's mother, realising she has gone into labour, wisely sends for the old and trusted midwife. Alas Tristram's father – Walter – has different ideas and dispatches his servant Obadiah to fetch Dr Slop, who lives some eight miles away. Obadiah rides off on his horse but gets no further than "three-score yards from the stable-yard" before he collides with the good doctor, who just happens to be passing by, "coming slowly along, foot by foot, waddling thro' the dirt upon the vertebrae of a little diminutive pony". Walter and his brother Toby are naturally surprised to see Obadiah return so quickly with Dr Slop, but this saving of time is more than compensated for by the doctor's complete lack of urgency in dealing with the impending birth.

At first, Dr Slop is informed of the "sudden and unexpected arrival" and it becomes immediately apparent that he has "come forth unarmed" with his "new-invented forceps", his "crochet", his "squirt" and his various other "instruments of salvation and deliverance". Thus Obadiah is, once again, sent on horseback to retrieve the doctor's medical bag while Walter, Toby and Dr Slop expound on a vast array of irrelevant matters somewhat oblivious to labour pains ensuing elsewhere in the household. Topics meander from military terminology, to Walter's Theory of Economics, to Stevinus (a famous Flemish engineer who was actually named Simon Stevin), to how Stevinus's wind-propelled sailing chariot had seemingly travelled the country far and wide and was better than a horse, to a sermon by Parson Yorick that slips out of the volume by Stevinus. An argument ensues in which Dr Slop vigorously defends the Inquisition until finally he falls asleep because the sermon by Yorick is so boring.

Obadiah eventually returns with the medical bag but Walter suggests to Dr Slop that he need only remain on hand in case the midwife cannot cope. Dr Slop disagrees, citing significant recent improvements in obstetric knowledge and "the safe and expeditious extraction of the foetus". He does not have much faith in the midwife and neither, for that matter, does Walter who, it emerges, is obsessed with the foetus's *medulla oblongata*, which he believes to be the most important part of the brain. He fears its compression at the time of birth "as a pastry-cook generally rolls up in order to make a pye of" and urges his wife to consider a caesarean section. When she turns pale at the prospect, Dr Slop's new-invented forceps are called into action.

Or perhaps it is simply that the midwife has slipped and hurt her hip and thus cannot perform the delivery. Either way, it is unfortunate because Dr Slop presently experiences some difficulty accessing his medical instruments. Obadiah, it seems, has pulled the bag's drawstrings too tight and knotted them elaborately so that the increasingly flustered doctor cannot untie them no matter how loudly he curses. His temper rises as he struggles and is not soothed when he finally uses Walter's penknife to cut the drawstrings and slices his own thumb in the process. The bag now open, Dr Slop rummages for the forceps, retrieves them and accidentally pulls out a syringe at the same time. "Good God!" Toby remarks, ". . . are children brought into the world with a squirt?"

Dr Slop is not amused, especially when doubt is expressed over the safety of the new obstetric equipment. Determined to proceed regardless, he pauses to demonstrate the forceps on Toby's clenched fists but succeeds only in skinning his knuckles. By now, Walter is even more unnerved and suggests that the foetus might be better removed by the feet than by the head. But as Dr Slop and the midwife cannot agree whether it is the foetus's hip or his head that is actually showing, this does not really seem to matter. And finally, when Dr Slop succeeds in dragging out the baby using the forceps, everyone is distressed to see the infant's nose has been broken. Dr Slop is left with no option but to fashion a rudimentary rhinoplasty using cotton thread and a piece of whalebone from a maid's corset.

With all the chaos surrounding Tristram's birth, therefore, it is a wonder he survived to narrate the tale at all. And yet Dr Slop fits so easily into Sterne's novel, personifying many of its themes. Here we have one of the most comically incompetent doctors in literary history, a slovenly, choleric, chaotic and distractible procrastinator who strays well beyond his expertise. The end result is hilarious, just what the doctor ordered.

Bovary's Surgical Blunder

There's a line in a song by the band Supergrass that goes "you never learned to economise; you look around and before you know it's gone, turned to dust". The song is written about its eponymous Sad Girl and, listening to the lyrics, one cannot help but think Gaz Coombes and colleagues are singing about the spendthrift adulteress Madame Bovary. "Why on earth . . .?" you might ask. Perhaps the lyrics just seem to fit; but a more obvious clue lies in the title of the album from which the song is taken, namely *Road to Rouen*. This town in Normandy is the setting for *Madame Bovary* and the birthplace of Gustave Flaubert himself.

Also on the road to Rouen, if you like, is amateur Flaubert expert Geoffrey Braithwaite, the fictional subject of Julian Barnes's Booker Prize shortlisted novel *Flaubert's Parrot*. A retired English doctor visiting the various places in northern France associated with the famous nineteenth-century writer, Braithwaite sets out on a quest to identify which parrot (now the recipient of some expert taxidermy) truly sat on Flaubert's writing desk, and which (also recipients) are impostors notwithstanding claims of the various museums in which they are housed. Thus ensues a postmodern drama in which the real objective is the discovery of, not merely the truth behind the parrot, but rather that behind the French writer himself, an apparently futile exercise.

Still, we have a reasonable grasp of Flaubert's biography. Born in 1821, he was the son of Dr Achille Flaubert, the surgeon in charge of the Hotel-Dieu Hospital in Rouen. Young Gustave was educated at the College Royal in his home town but was expelled prior to his graduation. Undaunted, he went on to study law in Paris but his emerging epilepsy prevented his sitting his final examinations and, in the end, he failed to qualify at all. He lived with his elderly mother until well into his fifties and penned his masterpiece *Madame Bovary* in 1857, its central themes being those of adultery, suicide and personal debt. Other notable works included *Salammbô* (1862), *L'Éducation Sentimentale* (1869), and *La Tentation de St Antoine* (1874), which apparently took him twenty-five years to write.

Although Flaubert served as a lieutenant in the Franco Prussian War in the early eighteen-seventies and was awarded the *Légion d'Honneur*, it is perhaps more for his scandals that he is of interest. Like Madame Bovary, Flaubert descended heavily into debt and was declared bankrupt – mostly due to the overspending of his niece and her husband Ernest – forcing the writer to take a government post in order to pay off his creditors. Moreover, although he never married, he had several mistresses including the French poet and novelist Louise Colet (partly on whom the character of Madame Bovary is said to have been based) and an English publisher's wife named Eliza Schlesinger, eleven years Flaubert's senior. Most scandalous of all, however, was the publication of Flaubert's masterpiece, which resulted in the author's prosecution for immorality. In the end, he was acquitted along with his publisher and printer.

What was viewed then as scandalous could equally be seen today as progressive. Some commentators view *Madame Bovary* as the first example of the "sex and shopping" genre novels that were to become popular more than a century later. Certainly the description seems to fit: bored housewife in an unhappy marriage, utterly obsessed with money, seeks comfort in retail therapy amid a series of adulterous affairs. Sound familiar? More importantly, the novel is a comment on the utter powerlessness of women at the time. Locked into a marriage with a mediocre doctor whom she does not love, she is left with only two choices: engage in her illicit activities or do nothing at all. And when she tries the latter, she becomes depressed. At the time, Flaubert needed to create an antihero in *Madame Bovary* to gain the novel's moral acceptance in society. Nonetheless, several influential women, it is said, claimed they were the original model for the heroine.

Another theme touched upon in the book is, of course, medical malpractice. Midway through the story, Flaubert digresses to describe Charles Bovary's attempt to make medical history by performing an operation for *talipes equinovarus* – or club foot. "What do we risk?" Bovary asks his wife enthusiastically. "Merely consider (and he counted off on his fingers the advantages of this experiment): success almost certain, alleviation and rehabilitation for the patient, rapid and easy fame for the surgeon."

The unfortunate patient coerced into receiving treatment is Hippolyte, who serves food and drinks at the local pub, the Golden Lion. Madame Bovary is all in favour of the experiment, suddenly enraptured by her husband who, for once, may turn out to be a hero. "How satisfying for her to have coaxed him into taking a step that would enhance his reputation and increase his income." Indeed, everyone in town is caught up in the excitement of the experiment; even the unfortunate Hippolyte finally acquiesces to the inevitable. "The poor man gave in, for it was almost a conspiracy."

Needless to say, it all goes horribly wrong. Bovary makes an incision and cuts the appropriate tendon before fastening the leg in a home made frame, "a kind of box weighing about eight pounds, a lavish apparatus of wood and iron, leather and sheet-metal, nuts and screws". Left to recuperate, Hippolyte – initially pleased with the procedure – soon finds himself feverous, in pain, and finally in convulsions; as the frame is gingerly removed so that Bovary may examine his work, it becomes evident that gangrene has set in.

Flaubert, although not a doctor, came from a family of physicians and knew much of the language associated with the profession. Perhaps the idea for this literary scene came from his father, who had spent some time as an anatomy demonstrator to the surgeon Baron Guillaume Dupuytren (1777–1835), after whom a distinctive contracture of the hand is named. Bovary, of course, is not nearly so proficient and Hippolyte ends up having his leg amputated by a surgeon from Rouen.

So, from the vivid musings and longings of an utterly modern adulteress, to the gender issues beginning to emerge in western society, to the documentation of misguided medical practice in the nineteenth century, *Madame Bovary* is truly a masterpiece. Even the haunting realism of the heroine's suicide by arsenic poisoning is described with no holds barred. It has inspired writers and musicians in its wake, including Julian Barnes and possibly even Supergrass. Flaubert nearly went to prison for his work but perhaps it was worth the price.

Mister Frankenstein

If Drs Slop and Bovary were written into their respective stories only to provide comic relief, there are several other fictional physicians whose characteristics are central to the themes of novels. Think of the clichéd mad scientist who finds himself in hot water when his ambitious experiments go wrong. Alas, to begin this line of enquiry, it is necessary to stray marginally beyond our brief. One aim of *Fiction & Physicians* is to elicit the occasional enthusiastic response: "Wow, I never realised he (or she) was a doctor!" But with Victor Frankenstein, the reverse is the case; many don't seem to realise he is not.

At least this is the case if we choose to be rigid about how we classify a doctor. Over the past two centuries, Mary Shelley's *Frankenstein, or The Modern Prometheus* (1818) has been adapted time and time again for stage, film and television. The first stage adaptation was Richard Brinsley Peake's *Presumption; or the Fate of Frankenstein* (1823), while classic film adaptations include James Whale's *Frankenstein* (1931), his sequel *The Bride of Frankenstein* (1935), and Kenneth Branagh's *Mary Shelley's Frankenstein* (1994). Picture the monster and we typically see Boris Karloff with outstretched arms, a flat head and a bolt through his neck. Indeed, the legend has been twisted and reinvented so many times that many people still erroneously consider Frankenstein to be the name of the monster and not its creator. More importantly, several adaptations incorrectly refer to Frankenstein as a medical doctor – or even a baron.

According to the original text, he is neither. Having developed an interest in academia during childhood, he sets off for the University of Ingolstadt to study natural philosophy with a particular interest in chemistry. Yet his motivation is not dissimilar to that of a medical student in that he has a yearning for knowledge on how to preserve life. For example, he remarks enthusiastically, "Wealth was an inferior object, but what glory would attend the discovery if I could banish disease from the human frame and render man invulnerable to any but a violent death!"

Frankenstein's choice of subjects is also medical. He asserts that, "One of the phenomena which had peculiarly attracted my attention was the structure of the human frame, and, indeed, any animal endued with life." He goes on to reveal that he "determined thenceforth to apply myself more particularly to those branches of natural philosophy which relate to physiology". He furthermore becomes "acquainted with the science of anatomy" sufficiently to "prepare a frame for the reception of (animation), with all its intricacies of fibres, muscles, and veins . . . a work of inconceivable difficulty and labour", Finally, he learns to "observe the natural decay and corruption of the human body", a science otherwise known to us as pathology.

Frankenstein's work ethic might have suited a career in medicine, although his own health ultimately suffers as a result of his endeavours. He describes himself as "one doomed by slavery to toil in the mines, or any other unwholesome trade than an artist occupied by his favourite employment". The common assertion in cinema and television that Frankenstein is a medical doctor is not unreasonable therefore. In centuries gone by, medical training was a little more ad hoc than it is today and not all doctors – even the fictional ones – had medical degrees. Here, Shelley describes a young man as educated in medical matters as many real doctors of the late eighteenth century, even if he did eventually drop out of college.

Because, lest we forget, catastrophe strikes. Frankenstein is the classic cautionary tale built upon the traditions of the epistolary Gothic novel. As is usually the case, the protagonist only considers the moral implications of his endeavours after they are complete; by then, he is too exhausted to atone for them. As he describes, "It was already one in the morning; the rain pattered dismally against the panes, and my candle was nearly burnt out, when, by the glimmer of the half-extinguished light, I saw the dull yellow eye of the creature open; it breathed hard, and convulsive motion agitated its limbs".

Once the monster is born and has fled the nest, Frankenstein descends into madness. Shelley describes Frankenstein's psychiatric illness quite vividly, beginning with a grotesque nightmare in which he kisses his lover, only to find she transmogrifies suddenly into the corpse of his deceased mother. Frankenstein becomes manic, recalling "it was not joy only that possessed me; I felt my flesh tingle with excess of sensitiveness, and my pulse beat rapidly". He adds, "I was unable to remain for a single instant in the same place; I jumped over the chairs, clapped my hands, and laughed aloud". By the time he emerges from his "nervous fever" a tragic cascade of murder, deception and guilt has begun.

Like his monstrous creation, Frankenstein strikes a lonely figure albeit one whose isolation is largely self-imposed. His fatal flaw is that he considers knowledge the key to everything in life, and prizes it even more highly than maintaining a healthy relationship with his family. He attempts to play God, breathing life into an assembled corpse, but then cruelly abandons his creation like an orphan. The monster – essentially good natured until it encounters the cruelties of a harsh world – seeks affection like any child might do. But Frankenstein is repulsed and offers only rejection, lacking the maturity to take responsibility for what he has put upon this earth.

But then, Shelley's novel is rich with themes. The author explores the important social issues of the day, including societal alienation, the role of the nuclear family and the injustices of an antiquated legal system. *Frankenstein* was one of the earliest novels to explore the theme of "science gone wrong", something that would later preoccupy literary minds from Robert Louis Stevenson to the medical thriller writers we have seen. Also like Stevenson, Shelley explores the theme of the *doppelganger* or *alter-ego*, warning the reader of what will happen if that small element of evil within us all is personified and allowed to escape thus reaping havoc. Finally, Shelley implies in *Frankenstein* a fear of sexuality, not least through the explicit attempt to bypass normal sexual relations in the creation of a living being.

Few nineteenth century novels have had more influence on popular culture than *Frankenstein*, despite its author being only nineteen when she first wrote it. Originally published in 1818 and re-issued with corrections in 1831, the novel might never have reached the shelves at all were it not for the inclement summer of 1816. That year, Mary Shelley spent several months at the Villa Diodati by Lake Geneva, sharing ghost stories with her then-future husband Percy Shelley and their close friend Lord Byron. Amid the frivolity lay the seeds of one of the most successful Gothic novels of all time – even if we do sometimes forget that Frankenstein was not actually a doctor.

Dr Jekyll, Dr Lanyon and Mr Hyde

As a Gothic tale of medical misadventure, *Frankenstein* was just the first of many. Another fine example is *The Strange Case of Dr Jekyll and Mr Hyde* (1886) by Robert Louis Stevenson, a book that has enjoyed considerable commercial success, a vivid re-working for the West End stage and no fewer than four film adaptations. But with stage and screen versions alike lacking the novel's frightening believability (achieved in part, like its predecessors, through an epistolary style that uses letters, diaries, a casebook and several narrators), it is the original narrative and Stevenson's two fictional physicians that are of most interest to us here.

Jekyll and Hyde is not simply a parable of the fundamental struggle between good and evil; it is a blueprint for a thousand cautionary tales by the likes of Bram Stoker, Michael Crichton and others. Yet it builds upon a long tradition of supernatural horror that began with *Frankenstein*. We call these novels Gothic but strictly speaking they are not; they are Victorian ghost stories – or presumably, in *Frankenstein's* case, Georgian. The real Gothic novel dates back to the mid eighteenth century, when it represented an indulgence in fantasy that was a direct response to the prescribed reasoning of the Enlightenment period. The archetype was perhaps *Castle of Otranto* by Horace Walpole (1764), a novel set in Italy during the Middle Ages. Eighteenth-century Gothic novels characteristically used this era as a backdrop, unlike Victorian ghost stories like *Jekyll and Hyde* that tended to be set in contemporary times. Moreover, the latter were typically a reaction to excessive curiosity and materialism, often illustrating how not all scientific and medical advancement was necessarily good for society. Enter the mystery thriller and its veiled secrecy that epitomised Victorian society and we have the key ingredients of *Jekyll and Hyde*.

But for the sake of simplicity, we will continue to use the term Gothic in the broader sense, particularly as it is the characters that make a story. The first and most important is Dr Henry Jekyll, prosperous from birth and still wealthy to the tune of a quarter of a million pounds. He is single, well educated and has progressed smoothly through his medical career to date. Stevenson describes "a large, well-made, smooth-faced man of fifty, with something of a stylish cast perhaps, but every mark of capacity and kindness". Vague and economical, it is a description that leaves unanswered questions. What might Jekyll be hiding behind his "smooth-faced" exterior, mask-like with the fragility of a "cast"? Indeed, the mask motif is used throughout the novel, leaving us wondering if Jekyll – like many Victorian characters – has a share of secret guilty pleasures about which he feels intensely uncomfortable.

Far more destructive, however, is Jekyll's hypocrisy. The good and evil parts of him have been successfully spliced and, through this divided personality, he can act out his evil fantasies without guilt, shame or any sense of responsibility. At first, he enjoys the wicked indulgence of being Edward Hyde, knowing that he can revert back to Jekyll at will. It is a *modus operandi* infinitely more acceptable to him than existing as a whole person yet, deep down, he knows it is not acceptable to others. Indeed, his former colleague Dr Hastie Lanyon openly criticises his research as "unscientific balderdash".

The feeling is mutual. Jekyll scornfully refers to Lanyon as "an ignorant, blatant pedant". When we encounter Lanyon early in the story, he is very much in the prime of life, a "hearty, healthy, dapper, red-faced gentleman", whose pleasant demeanour is described as "somewhat theatrical to the eye". Like Jekyll, he is an eminent physician with a string of letters after his name, although perhaps more vain and superficial than his contemporary, and certainly more traditional in his views.

When we meet Lanyon for the second time, we see a terrified man close to his death. We learn that his greed for knowledge has led him to witness Hyde transmogrifying into Jekyll. So protected is Lanyon's past that the terrifying sight has shocked him utterly to the core, causing in him a "marked sinking of the pulse". Perhaps he recognises an evil in himself that he has hitherto rejected. Suddenly, he must face this evil or – like Jekyll – accept his own hypocrisy. If only he had simply walked away.

These two archetypal Victorian doctors fit very easily into a horror mystery that was cutting edge at the time it was published. To first-time readers in the eighteen-eighties, *Jekyll and Hyde* was a page turner right up until its twist at the very end. By now, of course, the plot is well known and thus little will be given away in its discussion. It opens with Jekyll's friend and lawyer Gabriel Utterson expressing to Richard Enfield – his cousin – some concern that Jekyll has been seen consorting with Mr Edward Hyde, a man he considers unsavoury. Enfield concurs, having recently witnessed the odious Mr Hyde trampling an eight year old girl on the street, seemingly without remorse. Moreover, he remarks that, when Hyde reluctantly agreed to pay compensation to the little girl's family, he was seen to withdraw the money from Jekyll's account. Already, we are curious about the unlikely relationship between Jekyll and Hyde.

Utterson knows that Jekyll has bequeathed a quarter of a million pounds to Hyde in his will and is concerned that blackmail may be afoot. He broaches the matter with Lanyon who, as we have said, is uncomfortable with the direction in which Jekyll has taken his research. Elsewhere, Hyde is witnessed murdering the elderly Sir Danvers Carew MP without provocation and the police immediately find evidence that Hyde is the culprit. Hyde suddenly becomes a difficult man to track down.

Jekyll, somewhat reclusive up to this point, is now on the social scene again but Utterson's curiosity is dissatisfied. He acquires handwriting samples from Jekyll and Hyde, seeks an expert comparison and is struck to learn how remarkably similar they appear. Now suspicious, he talks to Lanyon again and finds the doctor suddenly in very poor health. Lanyon entrusts the lawyer with a sealed letter and asks it not be opened until after Lanyon's death, an event that follows shortly after. As Jekyll becomes socially withdrawn again, Utterson takes a walk past his house and is shocked to witness the doctor through an upstairs window suddenly take on a look of terror. Utterson later finds himself summoned by Jekyll's manservant, convinced that his master has been murdered by Hyde. They rush to Jekyll's laboratory and break in, only to find Hyde on the brink of death from deliberate self-poisoning. There is no trace of Jekyll.

The twist finally comes as Lanyon's narrative is read. It turns out Jekyll begged his estranged colleague to collect a potion from the laboratory and deliver it to a messenger who would arrive at midnight. The messenger was, of course, Hyde, who proceeded to drink the potion that transformed him immediately into Jekyll, terrifying the unfortunate Lanyon to the core. Jekyll's posthumous casebook further reveals his research into the splitting of the personality by chemical means. Although he experimented successfully upon himself at first, events soon spiralled out of control with transformations occurring unprovoked. On one occasion, we are told, Jekyll went to bed and woke up next day as Hyde. On another, he changed suddenly while strolling through Regent's Park. And when Jekyll finally ran out of the potion, he decided there was only one solution.

Hyde, by definition, is an inherent part of Jekyll's character. Throughout the novel, Stevenson skilfully and sparingly describes him only in terms of his effect on other characters. Hyde provokes intense feelings of animosity, even hatred, and brings out the worst in whomever he encounters. For example, there is palpable anger in the crowd witnessing his trampling of the little girl. Even the doctor who assists at the scene, normally "about as emotional as a bagpipe", is "sick and white with the desire to kill him". When Hyde draws a hundred pounds from Jekyll's account, blackmail is everyone's immediate assumption. Even we, as readers, find it difficult to curb our animosity when Sir Danvers's murder is later described in such gruesome detail.

Jekyll's alter ego is constantly described with reference to a beast. In various encounters, he is observed to hiss "like a cornered snake", cry out loudly "like a rat" and move around "like a monkey". On one occasion he lets out "a dismal screech as of mere animal terror", while on another, Jekyll describes "the animal within me licking the chops of terror". But Hyde is a man of few words. Indeed, he is the only major character who fails to narrate at least part of the story.

Like most of the characters, he has many contradictions. He seems cold and callous, while also strangely frightened, a "murderous mixture of timidity and boldness". On one occasion, Lanyon describes him as a figure with a "remarkable combination of great muscular activity and great apparent debility of constitution". Nobody ever describes his facial features; the closest we get is Utterson's recollection of a face "having Satan's signature". Even the witnesses to the murder sketch a much better picture of the victim. All anyone else seems to say is that Hyde's clothes are too big and that they are repulsed by him. Or perhaps they are simply repulsed by the part of him that they can see in themselves.

And this, of course, is the novel's central theme. Hypocrisy is not confined to Jekyll; everyone encountering Hyde dislikes him intensely but cannot pinpoint why. It is not his appearance that offends them, but rather his inherent ability to bring out the worst in them. And when confronted with this truth about themselves, they become irrationally angry to the point of utter destruction; this is especially the case with our two fictional doctors.

But there are other prominent themes. As with *Frankenstein*, *Jekyll and Hyde* is very much about the doppelganger; even the minor characters contain inherent contradictions. The policeman at the murder scene is preoccupied with his "thoughts of professional ambition", while the old woman at Hyde's lodgings has "an evil face, smoothed by hypocrisy; but her manners were excellent". It is worth also noting the theme of secrecy, achieved not least through constant references to locked doors, barred windows, windowless rooms, thick fog, masked figures, and the fact that virtually everything appears to happen in the darkness and privacy of night. Perhaps such "suppression of the beast" inevitably leads to violence. Either way, the Victorians enjoy a good secret, especially if it leads to gossip or scandal.

And Stevenson was very much a product of the Victorian era. He was born in Edinburgh on 13 November 1850, the only child of a lighthouse engineer. He endured consistently poor health throughout his childhood and nearly died of gastric fever when he was just eight years old. One cannot help but think he knew what it was like to be an outcast, while he must have encountered countless doctors as a child. Educated at the Edinburgh Academy, he went on to enrol in engineering at Edinburgh University but did not complete the course. He travelled briefly to the Riviera and to Germany with his parents, before finally enrolling in law in 1871. He was called to the Bar in 1875 but never actually practiced as a lawyer.

Instead, he moved first to France and thereafter to New York. It was around this time that he met an American named Fanny Osbourne, a married mother-of-two who was ten years his senior. They courted illicitly and then married in San Francisco, shortly after her eventual divorce in 1880. Meanwhile, it was clear that Stevenson was destined to be a writer. He contributed to *Cornhill Magazine* as early as 1874 and, from then on, wrote prolifically, usually early in the morning and late at night. Much of his material is said to have come to him in his dreams, including the plot of *Jekyll and Hyde*. Its doppelganger theme was influenced by his fictionalised real-life tale of *Deacon Brodie*, a respectable Scottish businessman who led a gang of robbers by night. *Treasure Island* was said to have been be based on a game devised with his stepson Samuel. It originally appeared in 1881 as *The Sea-Cook* by "Captain George North" in the magazine *Young Folks*. Indeed, it was not until 1883 that it was published in one volume.

Additional works followed, including *The Body Snatcher* (1884), *Kidnapped* (1886) and *The Master of Ballantrae* (1889). Alas, Stevenson endured frequent bouts of serious illness as he hobbled into middle age. Trying to gain some symptomatic relief, he moved initially to Bournemouth in 1884 and then Samoa in 1889. Despite these interventions, not only did his breathing deteriorate, but he eventually developed scriveners' cramp and required an amanuensis in order to complete his work. He died quite suddenly of a brain haemorrhage on 3 December 1894, aged just forty-four. He was buried on the peak of Mount Vaea, with full ceremonial honour by the Samoan natives.

Although *Treasure Island* is Stevenson's best known work, *The Strange Case of Dr Jekyll and Mr Hyde* is undoubtedly his masterpiece. What could have motivated him to spin such an unusual yarn? Those unfamiliar with the timeline might cite the terror caused by the infamous Jack the Ripper, an as-yet unidentified man who murdered five women in Whitechapel, East London. But as these crimes took place in 1888, a full two years after the novel was published, one might more reasonably suggest that it was the novel that inspired the murders and not the other way round.

Certainly, the novel's themes were contemporary ideas that gripped Victorian society. A number of controversial philosophical theses were published around that time, not least Charles Darwin's *On the Origin of Species* (1859), which is directly relevant to Stevenson's theme of the beast that exists in man. The theme of repression is also a Victorian favourite, including that of sexual desires. All the major characters are austere single men enshrouded in secrecy. Beasts, after all, must be repressed or imprisoned – even those in men. It is easy to see how Stevenson might have been influenced by Jean-Martin Charcot's hypnosis demonstrations of 1885, or the seminal work *Psychopathia Sexualis* (1886) by Austro-German psychiatrist Richard von Krafft-Ebing.

Finally, while on the topic of psychiatry, we might take the opportunity to address a widespread myth that has existed since Swiss psychiatrist Eugen Bleuler first coined the term *schizophrenia* in 1911. As we shall see later, this psychotic illness is marked by delusions (false beliefs not the cultural norm yet held with conviction), hallucinations (seeing or hearing things that aren't there), disordered thought (a disruption in the logical sequence of thinking) and social withdrawal. It has absolutely nothing to do with the "split personality" described in Stevenson's novel; they are entirely separate entities. If Dr Jekyll has anything remotely psychiatric, it is *dissociative identity disorder*, an illness characterised by two or more distinct personalities within the same person.

But perhaps we should not take it too seriously. Robert Louis Stevenson was, after all, simply delving into a world of fantasy horror to thrill us in a manner rarely matched to this day. And as fictional physicians go, Dr Jekyll must be one of the most famous in literary history.

A Full Blood Count

Vampirism in popular culture has recently enjoyed somewhat of a revival. An obvious example is Lestat de Lioncourt, the principal protagonist in Anne Rice's *Interview with the Vampire* (1976) and its sequels collectively known as *The Vampire Chronicles*. So successful was the debut novel that, in 1994, Neil Jordan adapted it into a film starring Tom Cruise and Brad Pitt. And the resurgence of cultural vampirism does not end there. The television series *Buffy the Vampire Slayer* ran for seven seasons between 1997 and 2003, with its skilful use of the legend as an allegory for teenage growing pains. A similar theme runs through Stephenie Meyer's series of *Twilight* novels, also recently adapted for the silver screen. But perhaps the most impressive adaptation is that of the archetypal vampire himself in a film by Francis Ford Coppola, namely *Bram Stoker's Dracula* (1992).

Of course, when I say "archetypal" I refer to the original portrayal of a vampire in the manner we now tend to conceptualise automatically. Even in this regard, Stoker's novel was epistolary and so his vampire is described from the subjective angles of several different protagonists. A local zookeeper, for example, cites "a tall, thin chap, with a 'ook nose and a pointed beard, with a few white hairs runnin' through it" who "had a 'ard, cold look and red eyes". Jonathan Harker, the count's prisoner early in the story, gives a more detailed description of "a tall old man, clean shaven save for a long white moustache, and clad in black from head to foot, without a single speck of colour about him anywhere." Harker goes on to add:

> *His face was a strong . . . aquiline, with high bridge of the thin nose and peculiarly arched nostrils; with lofty domed forehead, and hair growing scantily round the temples, but profusely elsewhere. His eyebrows were very massive, almost*

meeting over the nose, and with bushy hair that seemed to curl in its own profusion. The mouth, so far as I could see it under the heavy moustache, was fixed and rather cruel-looking, with peculiarly sharp white teeth; these protruded over the lips, whose remarkable ruddiness showed astonishing vitality in a man of his years. For the rest, the ears were pale and at the tops extremely pointed; the chin was broad and strong, and the cheeks firm though thin. The general effect was one of extraordinary pallor.

Stoker's detailed visual portrayal of his otherwise rather elusive villain reflects the late nineteenth-century popularity of physiognomy, namely the interpretation of an individual's character by their outward appearance. Stoker, with his background in dramatics, pens his description almost like a set of detailed instructions to the wardrobe department of the Lyceum Theatre. It is little wonder such a vivid image has endured for over a century. Ask anyone who Dracula is and they will describe a pale-faced, superhuman sociopath with fangs and a lust for sucking blood from the carotid arteries of his naïve victims. Dracula casts no shadow and has no reflection in the mirror. He is elusive, transmogrifying himself into a bat or a wolf at will. Indeed, like Mr Hyde, he is seen throughout the novel almost entirely in terms of his effect on others.

But even Dracula is not the first vampire to be mentioned in the annals of literature. Johann von Goethe mentions such creatures in "The Bride of Corinth" (1797), while Lord Byron's poem "The Giaour" (1813) positively sends shivers down the reader's spine:

> *But first, on earth as Vampire sent,*
> *Thy corse shall from its tomb be rent,*
> *Then ghastly haunt thy native place,*
> *And suck the blood of all thy race.*

The first description of a vampire in English literature is generally thought to be in Samuel Taylor Coleridge's poem

"Christabel" (1816), but such early references are not confined to poetry. Alexandre Dumas's play *Le Vampire* (1851) is a case in point which, like the poems just mentioned, precedes *Dracula* by several decades.

Yet it is *Dracula* that has endured more prominently to this day, an impressive legacy for a lad from Clontarf in the outskirts of Dublin. Stoker was born on 8 November 1847, the son of a civil servant and the third eldest of seven children in a protestant, middle class family. Not unlike Robert Louis Stevenson, Stoker spent much of his childhood in a state of infirmity and was bedridden until the age of seven. Perhaps his frequent contact with doctors from a young age may explain why the theme of illness features so prominently in his fiction. After graduating from Trinity College Dublin, Stoker spent ten years as a civil servant in Dublin Castle. Around that time, he moonlighted as an amateur theatre critic and, in doing so, caught the attention of Sir Henry Irving, the most famous stage actor of the Victorian era. Stoker married Florence Balcombe in 1878 and moved to London to manage Irving's Lyceum Theatre. There, Stoker wrote much of his fiction and mingled with prominent figures such as Sir Arthur Conan Doyle, Alfred Lord Tennyson, Oscar Wilde and Mark Twain. Alas, when Irving died in 1905, Stoker found himself in impecunious circumstances as his own health began to fail. He passed away in 1912.

Stoker wrote thirteen novels between 1875 and 1911 but is still best known for *Dracula*. Surprisingly, perhaps, the book was not a critical success at the time. Some readers felt that various strands of the plot relied too much on coincidence. Equally, the epistolary Gothic novel that had been at its height when *Frankenstein* was published was falling out of fashion by the end of the nineteenth century. Yet, unlike many literary masterpieces of the era, *Dracula* has never since been out of print. In part, this is because its themes have endured – indeed, intensified – over the past century, but perhaps its appeal lies simply in it being a good old fashioned page turner.

Although the novel has several narrators, much of the story is told through the eyes of Dr John Seward, a young psychiatrist. Rather like Watson does for Holmes, Seward assists and records the endeavours of his old medical mentor, an erudite and mysterious adventurer named Professor Abraham Van Helsing. But let us first rewind to the beginning. Count Dracula wishes to migrate to England and Jonathan Harker, a newly-qualified solicitor whom we have already met, is dispatched to Transylvania to assist the count with his legal affairs. But all is not well at Castle Dracula and it becomes increasingly evident to Harker that his host possesses both sinister powers and malicious intent. Alas, he is too late in this realisation; Dracula sets off for England, leaving the incarcerated solicitor at the mercy of the other resident vampires. Although Harker makes a daring escape, this courage comes at a cost; he is exhausted by his ordeal and is admitted to a hospital in Budapest. Eventually, word of his ill health reaches his fiancée Mina Murray, who has been waiting patiently back in England. She travels at once to be with him and the two lovers are married upon her arrival.

Meanwhile, Mina's best friend Lucy Westenra, having just accepted one of her three marriage proposals, encounters Dracula as he reaches the port of Whitby, Yorkshire. Lucy quickly falls ill and Dr Seward is summoned discretely to offer aid. But Seward cannot make sense of Lucy's symptoms and he thus recruits his old mentor Professor Van Helsing. The professor uses crucifixes, garlic, blood transfusions and various other unorthodox tools of the trade, but is nevertheless unsuccessful in treating Lucy. She dies and becomes a vampire, and the two doctors spend the reminder of the story tracking down the count to save humanity from the scourge of vampirism.

Although Stoker never commented openly upon the themes of his novel, it is clear he must have had an interest in medicine and psychiatry. Through Seward, he comments on the pursuit of knowledge and echoes both Frankenstein and Dr Jekyll by asking "why not advance science in its most difficult and vital aspect – the knowledge of the brain?" As early as Chapter One, Harker notices the prevalence of goitre among the Czechs and Slovaks, while the practice of blood transfusion is an integral part of the plot, even though it was a relatively new procedure at the time. In this regard, the intimacy of swapping bodily fluids is emphasised. Seward gets a rush of excitement as he donates blood to Lucy and remarks that, "No man knows till he experiences it, what it is to feel his own life-blood drawn away into the veins of the woman he loves". Van Helsing silences him with a warning. "If our young lover should turn up unexpected," he says, referring to Lucy's fiancé, "... It would at once frighten him and enjealous him, too."

But then the theme of sexuality is shockingly present throughout. Stoker explores the concept of vampirism as a sexually transmitted disease spread by a predatory and parasitic vector that is cunning at adaptation. It is no coincidence that the author chooses two doctors as his main protagonists; it is their job to quarantine the spread before it becomes an epidemic. Sexually transmitted disease was common in Victorian society, as was prostitution, yet these public health issues often went unacknowledged such that, to many a fragile middle class reader, the raunchier descriptions in *Dracula* bordered on pornography.

Other prominent themes in the book include different gender roles, the fragility of civilisation and the concept of religion as an antidote to the supernatural. Madness is also a strong theme, as is the doppelganger or alter-ego – like in *Frankenstein* and *Jekyll and Hyde*.

When dealing with fictional madness, an equally fictional psychiatrist is always useful. We first meet Dr Seward in Chapter Five, shortly after Lucy has turned down his marriage proposal. Lucy nevertheless describes him as an excellent marriage prospect, "being handsome, well off, and of good birth. He is a doctor and really clever. Just fancy! He is only nine-and-twenty, and he has an immense lunatic asylum all under his own care". She goes on to remark that Seward is "one of the most resolute men I ever saw, and yet the most calm. He seems absolutely imperturbable. I can fancy what a wonderful power he must have over his patients. He has a curious habit of looking one straight in the face, as if trying to read one's thoughts". Stoker's belief in physiognomy is once more emphasised as he describes "the strong jaw and the good forehead".

Although measured in his suggestion of marriage, Seward is clearly self-conscious and prone to clumsiness. In summoning up the courage to propose, "he almost managed to sit down on his silk hat". Ostensibly, he takes the rebuttal well and, upon discovering Lucy is in love with another man, "he stood up, and he looked very strong and grave as he took both my hands in his and said he hoped I would be happy, and that if I ever wanted a friend I must count him one of my best".

But Seward is an introspective and somewhat sombre man. When low in spirits, he has a tendency to immerse himself in the study of his psychiatric patients, something in which he is certainly skilled and knowledgeable. Van Helsing confirms this when he says to Seward, "You were always a careful student, and your casebook was ever more full than the rest". Yet Seward is repeatedly emasculated, first in his role as Lucy's potential suitor and then in his role as her protector. He fails utterly in the latter, creating the need for several blood transfusions. As a conventional thinker, Seward is incapable of negotiating the twists and turns of Lucy's strange illness. Worse still, he verges on thinking his former tutor insane when the latter attempts to find creative remedies. Seward remarks that, "The professor's actions were certainly odd and not to be found in any pharmacopoeia that I ever heard of". It is only as the story evolves, that a change in Seward's character allows him to credit the alternative solution.

It is also worth mentioning Seward's darker side. Chloral hydrate was a popular recreational drug among the middle class of the late nineteenth century and the young doctor, it seems, is fond of a little indulgence. As he describes it, "I cannot but think of Lucy, and how different things might have been. If I don't sleep at once, chloral, the modern Morpheus – $C_2HCl_3O-H_2O$! I must be careful not to let it grow into a habit."

But let us reserve the last judgement for the real hero. In Chapter Nine, Seward first describes Professor Abraham Van Helsing, his old tutor and a metaphysician from Amsterdam "who knows as much about obscure diseases as any one in the world". Like Sherlock Holmes, Van Helsing is nothing less than brilliant. According to Seward, "He is a seemingly arbitrary man, but this is because he knows what he is talking about better than any one else. He is a philosopher . . . and one of the most advanced scientists of the day; and he has . . . an absolutely open mind". Van Helsing, moreover, possesses "iron nerve, a temper of the ice-brook, an indomitable resolution, self-command and toleration exalted from virtues to blessings, and the kindliest and truest heart that beats".

Such an accolade is echoed later in Mina's detailed description of the professor's appearance. Physiognomy reigns supreme once more:

> *I rose and bowed, and he came towards me; a man of medium height, strongly built, with his shoulders set back over a broad, deep chest and a neck well balanced on the trunk as the head is on the neck. The poise of the head strikes one at once as indicative of thought and power; the head is noble, well-sized, broad, and large behind the ears. The face is clean-shaven, shows a hard, square chin, a large, resolute, mobile mouth, a good-sized nose, rather straight, but with quick, sensitive nostrils, that seem to broaden as the big, bushy brows come down and the mouth tightens. The forehead is broad and fine, rising at*

first almost straight and then sloping back above two bumps or ridges wide apart; such a forehead that the reddish hair cannot possibly tumble over it, but falls naturally back and to the sides. Big, dark blue eyes are set widely apart, and are quick and tender or stern with the man's moods.

Despite his striking demeanour, Van Helsing is not without his shortcomings. When Lucy falls ill again after some initial success with her treatment, Seward witnesses Van Helsing losing his nerve for the first time. Accordingly, he "raised his hands over his head in a sort of mute despair, and then beat his palms together in a helpless way; finally he sat down on a chair, and putting his hands before his face, began to sob, with loud, dry sobs that seemed to come from the very racking of his heart". But he recovers quickly. As he himself asserts, "We learn from failure, not from success!" He represents everything that Seward is not, with his optimism, creativity, humour, experience, wisdom and manliness. While both doctors display humanity, Van Helsing's is more altruistic and greater in measure.

But, for the most part, Van Helsing mirrors Dracula. While both men are strong, Van Helsing is as ethereal as Dracula is diabolical. The former is rarely narrator and the latter never, so both remain mysterious; yet Van Helsing is as safe as Dracula is dangerous. Both men are foreign, yet Van Helsing is exotic while Dracula is the object of our xenophobia. Finally, when Van Helsing leads the other men in a quest to destroy Dracula, he is druid-like with powers that extend well beyond those of an ordinary doctor. His prowess casts him in the same light as the count himself.

And so, Stoker serves up a tale of two doctors very different from one another, yet united as they battle a common enemy that threatens humanity like an infectious disease on the verge of pandemic. But perhaps we should count ourselves lucky that Professor Van Helsing's ambition so easily compensates for Dr Seward's initial incompetence.

Chapter Seven

Heroic Fictional Physicians

DESPITE THEIR COMPLEXITY, modern fictional doctors are a little more virtuous than those described in the classics. In line with the emerging philosophy of existentialism in the nineteenth and twentieth centuries, they struggle with adversity we can relate to – loss, foreboding, crime, political tyranny, war, disease and death. Examples include the fearful Mr Henry Perowne in Ian McEwan's *Saturday*, the introspective Dr Yuri Zhivago in Boris Pasternak's classic, and the overwhelmed Dr Bernard Rieux in Albert Camus's *The Plague*. Dr Frank Eloff represents the cynical hero in Damon Galgut's *The Good Doctor*, while even the utterly selfish Doc Daneeka displays touching bravery in Joseph Heller's *Catch-22*. But perhaps most amusing are the real nineteenth-century doctors fictionalised as crime fighters in more-modern yarns. Who would have supposed such bravery existed in your average literary physician?

The Real Literary Detectives

If the shelves of my local bookshop are to be believed, most nineteenth century literary figures were super-sleuths in their time. Indeed, any prominent child of the Victorian era was seemingly a nonentity if they hadn't solved a murder or two. Oscar Wilde, Sir Arthur Conan Doyle, Sigmund Freud, Carl Jung, Sandor Ferenczi, Henry Wadsworth Longfellow and

Oliver Wendell Holmes Sr – all were at it, busily making as-tute observations as they examined clues that had hitherto con-founded the local constabulary.

A perfect example is Gyles Brandreth's *Oscar Wilde and the Candlelight Murders*, in which the discovery of a sixteen year old boy lying dead in an upstairs room entices the famous nine-teenth century writer to become an amateur detective, albeit temporarily. The story is set in 1889, a time when Wilde is enjoying the pinnacle of his success. Such is his celebrity that he is granted unique access to all levels of late Victorian soci-ety from the drawing rooms of the rich and powerful to the backstreets of the criminal underclass. To add a little spice, our hero teams up with a slightly more believable accomplice in the shape of Sir Arthur Conan Doyle and, between them, they set out to solve a string of bizarre and inexplicable killings; Wilde uses his singular genius, sharp wit and astute powers of obser-vation, while Doyle lends to the proceedings a much needed air of gravitas.

As we have seen, Doyle also puts his powers of deduction to the test in Julian Barnes's novel *Arthur and George*. Based on true events, the story initially contrasts the circumstances of its two eponymous heroes. Doyle is the son of an alcoholic from a run down area of Edinburgh, while George Edalji is the son of the Indian born vicar of a small village in Staffordshire. Doyle is destined for fame, while his counterpart becomes an obscure Birmingham based solicitor specialising in the intri-cacies of railway law. Their paths cross in 1907 when Doyle intervenes in a miscarriage of justice. He campaigns for Edalji's innocence of the "Great Wyrley Outrages", a curious event in which horses and livestock are slashed and maimed. Thus en-sues a milestone in the establishment of the Court of Appeal in English law – a story that might easily have been written for Doyle's most famous creation, Sherlock Holmes.

But Wilde and Doyle are not the only literary figures to be portrayed as fictional detectives. Recall Matthew Pearl's *The Dante Club*, which tells the tale of a number of brutal, bizarre and high profile killings. One such example is the murder of a State Supreme Court Judge, badly assaulted and then left in his garden to be eaten alive by maggots. A second victim is subsequently discovered buried upside-down with his feet set on fire, while a third is found sliced open exactly down the middle. Luckily, a small gathering of poets (in the process of translating *The Divine Comedy* from Italian to English) notice similarities between these murders and the various punishments dealt out in Dante's *Inferno*. As they set out to solve the murders in an effort to salvage Dante's reputation, the unlikely sleuthing skills of Henry Wadsworth Longfellow, Oliver Wendell Holmes Sr, and James Russell Lowell are thus put to the test.

But, when it comes to real life historical figures solving fictional crimes, it is Jed Rubenfeld's *The Interpretation of Murder* that ices the cake. Set in New York in 1909, the novel begins with Sigmund Freud, Carl Jung and Sandor Ferenczi arriving to deliver a series of lectures on the controversial subject of psychoanalysis. Within hours, they are attempting to crack the case of a brutal attack upon the seventeen year old daughter of a couple of high society Manhattans. The assault is seemingly so sadistic that the young girl is left with total amnesia for the event and an inability to speak. Thus Freud agrees to supervise protagonist Dr Stratham Younger's attempts at psychoanalysis in an effort to trace the perpetrator.

So, why have so many writers chosen real life medico-literary figures as their central characters? With the exception of the true story of *Arthur and George*, isn't it all just a little too implausible? Possibly so, but as we may be witnessing the inception of a new sub-genre (the marriage of historical biography and popular crime fiction), it becomes more credible when we note that most of the authors in this emerging trend are, in fact, scholars of the eminent figures about whom they write. And isn't any fictionalised account of celebrity super-sleuthing infinitely more exciting than a simple biography? Crime is a glamorous genre after all and, if the boring old Victorians can be put to work solving murders, all the better for the reader.

Presumably we haven't seen the last of it, not least because Brandreth continues to churn out sequels, beginning with *Oscar Wilde and the Ring of Death*. In the meantime, the mind boggles at what such authors will produce next. Emily Brontë and Napoleon III teaming up in the 1840s to solve a spate of gravity-inspired murders off the cliffs of Dover? I might make a note of that one . . .

The Fictional Physician-Writer

So far, we have discussed physician-writers and fictional physicians alike. Indeed, some real physician-writers have been successfully fictionalised, as proven in the examples we have just seen. But can there be any subject more worthy of our attention than a truly fictional physician-writer? In this category, Dr Yuri Zhivago epitomises the kind of medical protagonist who transcends his profession to symbolise something more fundamental. Yuri is not the typical doctor but he is the typical poet (if such a thing exists), introspective and humane, yet flawed to the degree that his very existence is incompatible with the sweeping changes of the Russian Revolution and subsequent Civil War.

Readers unfamiliar with the book may have seen the film. Directed by David Lean and starring Omar Sharif, *Doctor Zhivago* (1965) was so successful it garnered five Academy Awards and numerous other accolades besides. The film is over three hours in length and faithful to the basic plot, yet it sometimes struggles to convey the complexity of the original novel and its conflicted protagonist.

We first meet Yuri Zhivago as a young boy attending his mother's funeral around the turn of the twentieth century. Now orphaned, he is taken to Moscow to live with the Gromekos, friends of his parents. He is well provided for, and grows up to become an idealistic and deeply introspective poet and doctor whose views on humanity far outweigh his views on politics. He marries Tonya, the daughter of his foster parents but, although fond of her, he does not consider her the great love of his life. This will prove to be Lara, the beautiful wife of a revolutionary student named Pasha.

At the outset, Lara is having an illicit affair with her mother's lover Viktor Komarovsky, a well-connected and corrupt lawyer. Lara is only seventeen, but uses her sensuality with some skill to manipulate Komarovsky, who is clearly in love with her. Soon Lara's mother discovers the affair and is so devastated she attempts suicide. A doctor is summoned, who turns out to be none other than Yuri Zhivago; when he meets Lara for the first time, he is instantly besotted.

Meanwhile, the smell of revolution is in the air. World War I rages over Europe but the proletariat have little appetite for foreign conflict; indeed, they are so restless for domestic reform they threaten to volunteer simply for the chance to corrupt and weaken the Tsar's army. Amid the chaotic aftermath of the February Revolution, Lara and Yuri meet again when stationed together at a makeshift army hospital. They fall in love but are unable to express their feelings for one another. Instead, Yuri returns to his family in Moscow as they struggle to survive in a radically changed political landscape dominated by the Bolsheviks. Yuri's house has been commandeered and, worse still, his poetry is increasingly viewed as anti-communist. Enter the October Revolution, and Yuri must flee with his family to their estate near the Ural Mountains. On the way, Yuri inadvertently encounters Pasha – now General Strelnikov of the Red Army – and learns that Lara is now residing in the nearby town of Yuriatin. Yuri and Lara meet and finally consummate their relationship.

Needless to say, from here it all goes horribly wrong. On the road to visit his mistress one day, Yuri is ambushed by a band of guerrilla Bolsheviks and drafted as their doctor. By the time he manages to desert and return home with his health barely intact, he finds Tonya and the family have fled to France, leaving only Lara in their wake. Eventually Komarovsky reappears and reports that Pasha has fallen out of favour politically. Komarovsky remains well-connected and offers to smuggle Lara out of the country. As she is leaving, we learn that she is pregnant with Yuri's child.

Finally, Yuri returns alone to Moscow and becomes involved with another woman, but his exploits have ruined his health and he survives only a few more years. His funeral is well attended, not least by Lara who returns from exile in search of her daughter by Yuri. Lara is eventually arrested during Joseph Stalin's Great Purge and ultimately dies in the Gulag.

The themes of Pasternak's novel are very much inherent in the eponymous physician's character. In *Doctor Zhivago* all of the major characters are isolated, lonely and fearful, constantly longing for companionship as they traverse the country and beyond in search of some semblance of stability that might provide relief. Yuri's early loss of his mother is a crucial element of the story; he spends most of the novel yearning for female companionship that might fulfil the void left by the absence of a "mother figure". So strong is this need that it outweighs his instinct for loyalty and fidelity.

The theme of individuality is also a strong one. As we shall also see in George Orwell's character Winston Smith, Yuri is the ultimate free spirit whose ideals are entirely at odds with those of the Revolution. The Bolsheviks and the Communists prize the needs of society over those of the individual and are utterly intolerant of insurgents who fail to align themselves with the common ideology. Yet Yuri is emotional by nature and expresses himself through his poetry, placing himself in great danger. He is an icon of individuality that simply cannot survive in the new Soviet Union.

But perhaps such intolerance is symptomatic of the new regime's inherent weakness. While it may be ideologically sound, the people who enact it are largely portrayed as ignorant pseudo-intellectuals who recite the dogma of hackneyed Marxism. Greed and stupidity ultimately corrupt the communist ideal, causing far more damage than any of the transient villains in the story. Yuri, in contrast, is a true philosopher despite his political neutrality.

Boris Pasternak suffered in a similar way for his creative work. Indeed, his challenges as a writer were not unlike those of the physician Mikhail Bulgakov, whom we have mentioned. Pasternak was born in Moscow in 1890 and trained initially as a composer before deciding to concentrate instead on his writing. Rather like his most famous character, he was a prolific poet whose work was not always viewed kindly by Soviet Russia. He began working on *Doctor Zhivago* as early as 1920 but he made little effort to have it published until after Stalin's death and the cultural thaw that followed. The Soviet literary journal *Novy Mir* declined to publish the novel in serialised format because of its subtle criticisms of communism. Indeed, the manuscript might well have remained on the slush pile had not the Italian millionaire publisher Giangiacomo Feltrinelli arranged to have it smuggled out of Russia in 1957. The novel was later submitted to the Swedish Nobel Committee for its consideration and, on 23 October 1958, Boris Pasternak was declared the winner of that year's Nobel Prize for Literature.

Alas, such was the division between the Soviet Union and the West that Pasternak was obliged to turn down the Prize or risk being denied re-entry to Russia. Notwithstanding his polite refusal and a personal letter to President Nikita Khrushchev asserting his loyalty to Russia, Pasternak continued to be vilified by the Soviet press until his death from lung cancer in Peredelkino on 30 May 1960. His funeral was well attended, but *Doctor Zhivago* remained banned in the Soviet Union until 1988. The following year, Yevgeny Pasternak was finally allowed to visit Stockholm to collect his father's Nobel Medal.

The Catch

Not all heroic fictional physicians are quite as likeable as those we have met so far. A case in point is Dr "Doc" Daneeka in Joseph Heller's *Catch-22* who, although neither a villain nor an antihero, is nonetheless supremely and sublimely irritating. Readers familiar with the novel will recognise Doc Daneeka as the absurdly self-centred army surgeon who is persistently oblivious to the suffering of others, both friends and patients alike. But Daneeka's character is full of contradictions; he is heroic but he neither wants to be a hero nor considers himself one. Indeed, he mostly perceives himself as undeservedly unlucky. His standard opener is, "You think you've got troubles? What about me?" Yet, his problems are usually trivial in comparison to those of his contemporaries.

Heller's World War II novel, published in 1961, was the culmination of eight years' work. An absurdist masterpiece laced with wordplay and irony, it is set amid the 488th Bombardment Squadron on an American Army Air Corps base on Pianosa, a tiny island off the coast of Tuscany. Each day, dozens of airmen fly off on yet another seemingly pointless mission and some manage to return safely, pleased to cross another flight off their eternally rising quota, but fearful of doing it all again the following day.

There is a somewhat biographical element to the novel; Heller himself served as a bombardier during the war and logged over sixty missions. The story is convincingly real therefore, despite its satirically complex dialogue and its myriad of eccentric but sympathetic characters. In Heller's hell, any humour is a mere distraction transcended by pervasive fear.

No sooner are we introduced to Daneeka, than we are invited to view his former Staten Island office, with its waiting room containing "one of the finest suites of cheap furniture", everything paid for with credit or by greedy relatives unwise enough to invest in his practice. Or perhaps not; at first the war was good for business. "It was a godsend," Daneeka confesses solemnly to the principal protagonist, Yossarian. "Most of the other doctors were soon in the service, and things picked up overnight." Unfortunately, the draft board were not so keen to accept at face value Daneeka's assessment of himself as medically unfit for service. When they investigated the matter and found that Daneeka did not, in fact, have only one leg and crippling rheumatoid arthritis that rendered him bedbound, the good Doc was promptly "drafted and shipped to Pianosa as a flight surgeon, even though he was terrified of flying".

It is just as well, therefore, that Daneeka never has to fly. Yossarian generously enters his name repeatedly in the flight log, thus making it appear that the doctor is flying the necessary number of missions to warrant his eventual discharge from service. Alas, Yossarian's good deed is not reciprocated. Time and time again, he begs the doctor to take him off active duty on medical grounds but the doctor always declines, saying he has much more troubling issues to worry about. And thus Daneeka outlines for Yossarian the philosophy of catch-22. A man can only be relieved of duty if he is crazy but he must also ask his superiors specifically to be taken off duty. Unfortunately, once he does so, he has proven himself sane because it is a characteristic sign of rationality to express concern for one's own safety. With regard to further missions, therefore, "If he flew them he was crazy and didn't have to; but if he didn't want to he was sane and had to."

Daneeka's refusal to even contemplate excusing Yossarian from flying shows his ingratitude for the risks Yossarian has already taken in forging the doctor's flight log. But Daneeka ultimately redeems himself when called upon to act heroically. When the island base is heavily bombed, the doctor does not flee as others do; instead, he risks his own life by remaining on site and delivering emergency medical care to the wounded. Yes, one might argue he is simply motivated by the fear he might one day find himself in the same vulnerable position; but even if he is bargaining with the gods for his own salvation, he is still a good man to have around in an emergency.

Alas, it is his prevailing selfishness that finally proves his undoing. Yossarian continues to enter Daneeka's name in the flight log and, as the officers and men witness a desperate pilot crash his own plane, they soon realise that the good Doc is listed as having been on board. The fact that he is clearly alive and well makes little difference in the end. He is presumed dead and the appropriate compensation is paid out to Mrs Daneeka – sufficient to discourage the doctor's wife from entertaining the possibility that he may still be alive.

The moral of the story? If a hero cannot be nice, he should at least try to be likeable.

A Better Doctor

When it comes to recruiting new doctors, Frank Eloff is a difficult man to please. "The first time I saw him," Eloff confesses from the outset, "I thought, he won't last." It is a stylish opener and, in quality fiction, the opening line is everything. Without a baited hook to catch the reader, one might say a novel stands little chance of being read. It is easy to suppose that Damon Galgut knew this when he sat down to write *The Good Doctor*, whose first sentence conveys more intrigue to the reader than many a comparator's first paragraph or even first chapter.

He is Laurence Waters, a young, naïve, idealistic doctor who arrives to work at a dilapidated and failing rural hospital in post-apartheid South Africa. Perhaps inspired by the changed political climate or simply because of his youthful exuberance, Waters is as much a fountain of ideas as his name might suggest; he is a personified vision of how things in the hospital might work better. But Waters is not universally admired. The older, more weather beaten Eloff has already witnessed the Bantu homeland during its bloody political transformation and has little appetite for further change, particularly when the end result is no different from the corruption and violence that preceded it. A conflict of ideals seems inevitable until a burglary at the hospital suddenly throws the two men together as acquiescent allies. Alas, not even their unity can prevent a cascade of deadly and uncontrollable events.

The Good Doctor was nominated for the 2003 Man Booker Prize and the Commonwealth Writers Prize the same year. This is not surprising, given the vividness with which it captures the undercurrent of tension in a continent still experiencing the confused aftermath of colonialism. It is a good literary example of a chaotic backdrop mirroring the uncomfortable dynamic between two strong-willed but pioneering doctors. Waters is an idealist and Eloff is a cynic, yet both men are heroic in much the same way. They are certainly more alike than they care to admit.

Describing Huntington's Disease

Ian McEwan is no stranger to writing about medicine and psychiatry. An obvious example is *Enduring Love*, a novel about a young man with *de Clerambault's syndrome* upon which we will touch later. In the meantime, it is a more recent McEwan offering – *Saturday* – that has created the most significant stir within medical circles.

With the author's usual talent for lending humanity to complex science, *Saturday* tells the story of an incident involving a young man named Baxter who has Huntington's disease. The main protagonist is Henry Perowne, a neurosurgeon of note whose Midas touch has granted him a happy marriage, two well adjusted children, a job he enjoys, a large house in central London and a silver Mercedes S500 about which he feels slightly self conscious. Indeed, Perowne has more or less everything he has ever desired but alas, like anyone in such a position, he also has the uneasy sense he is about to lose it all.

The book is set on Saturday 15 February 2003, a day in which a large protest march against the war in Iraq is taking place in London. Perowne's personal unease is mirrored by that of the city and the era, and becomes quickly more tangible when a minor car accident brings him face to face with Baxter. Perowne can immediately see in Baxter many of the early signs of Huntington's disease and observes that, "His face is alive with small tremors that never quite form into an expression. It is a muscular restlessness that will one day – this is Perowne's considered opinion – become athetoid, plagued by involuntary, uncontrollable movements."

"What is Huntington's?" you might easily ask. A neurological disease first described in 1872 in New England by George Huntington, it is known to occur in males and females equally, affecting around one in every twenty thousand people worldwide. It is genetic, more specifically *autosomal dominant*, meaning that only one parent need have it for their offspring to have a fifty per cent chance of inheriting it. The disease is characterised by a marked loss of nerve fibres and a compensatory increase in the brain's "insulation" (termed *gliosis*). These changes occur primarily in certain parts of the brain (mostly the *basal ganglia*) and are accompanied by a depletion of certain brain chemicals (or *neurotransmitters*).

If you recall your leaving certificate biology for a moment, you'll know that we all have strands of DNA woven into chromosomes. Huntington's disease is simply caused by the expansion of an unstable triplet repeat within a gene on chromosome four. This gene codes for the protein *huntingtin*, which becomes abnormal when the number of triplet repeats exceeds forty. The number of repeats varies within the disorder and can be as high as eighty or more, with a longer repeat resulting in an earlier onset and a greater severity of the illness in a phenomenon known as *genetic anticipation*. Such longer repeats are thought to be inherited from father to child.

So, how does the disease present clinically? From a literary perspective, McEwan gives an incisive description:

> *Between ten and twenty years to complete the course, from the first small alterations of character, tremors in the hands and face, emotional disturbance, including – most notably – sudden, uncontrollable alterations in mood, to the helpless jerky dance like movements, intellectual dilapidation, memory failure, agnosia, apraxia, dementia, total loss of muscular control, rigidity sometimes, nightmarish hallucinations and a meaningless end.*

The first symptoms of Huntington's disease usually occur in the forties, but may also emerge at as young as ten years of age. Clumsiness is often the first noticeable sign, followed by uncontrollable twitching involving the face, shoulders or fingers, which the individual may make some effort to disguise. From there, symptoms typically worsen to a generalised writhing movement (*chorea*), loss of balance (*ataxia*), inability to articulate words (*dysarthria*) and inability to swallow (*dysphagia*).

In as many as four out of every ten patients, personality changes may emerge several years before the onset of chorea. Changeable mood, irritability and aggression may all occur and, while depression is the commonest associated psychiatric problem, psychosis and dementia can also feature. Indeed, individuals who initially present to psychiatrists usually have depression, dementia or loss of temper.

Aficionados of the television series *House MD* will know that the character Dr Remy "Thirteen" Hadley has Huntington's disease. She does not have any obvious psychiatric symptoms but rather displays an occasional tremor and the sense of foreboding inherent in having to observe in patients the disability one is destined to acquire one's self. Initially she is not certain of her diagnosis (and, indeed, does not wish to know) until Dr Gregory House himself surreptitiously tests her genes and presents her rather cruelly with the findings.

So, how is Huntington's disease diagnosed in the real world? Clinical evaluation by a suitably qualified doctor is naturally important, with a good history and physical examination paramount. As with Dr Hadley, genetic testing may be used to confirm the diagnosis. The latter is sometimes used to identify carriers among relatives or to elicit a diagnosis in an unborn baby but, given the obvious ethical considerations, such testing is best limited to specialist centres with experienced geneticists, neurologists and other members of the suitably qualified. Meanwhile, a *magnetic resonance image* (MRI) of the brain can aid diagnosis, as can an *electroencephalogram* (EEG), namely an electrical readout of the brain's activity. Although treatments such as *tetrabenazine* (for chorea), antidepressants and antipsychotics can be useful, the treatment of Huntington's disease is often largely palliative. Long term planning is vital, given the likelihood that individuals will become increasingly dependent on their care-givers and relatives.

Huntington's disease mirrors Henry Perowne's sense of foreboding to perfection. So, while we await further discovery on this most tragic of diseases, we leave the final word to Ian McEwan. "This is how the brilliant machinery of being is undone by the tiniest of faulty cogs, the insidious whisper of ruin, a single bad idea lodged in every cell, on every chromosome four."

A *Plague* upon Your City

When discussing literary heroes of the medical variety, no list is complete without a word on the narrator of Albert Camus's philosophical novel *The Plague* (1947). As those who have read the novel will know, it is only at the end that we learn who the enigmatic narrator actually is; Dr Bernard Rieux keeps us in the dark throughout, such is his modesty. Rieux is described as thirty-five, dark skinned, black haired, and of average height. His wife has been ill for some time and resides elsewhere at a sanatorium, while Rieux continues to live and work dispassionately in the Algerian city of Oran.

As the title suggests, the city is gripped by a six-month outbreak of infectious disease, leading to mass fatality, hysteria and ultimately the quarantine of residents and visitors alike. Those who try to leave are shot dead. Rieux and a small group of medical colleagues are challenged in both the practical and the existential sense as they battle to save literally thousands of lives. Rieux is not the archetypal hero, yet he occupies this role throughout the story. It is he who first identifies the risk of plague, attempts to treat the first infected patients, and implores the authorities in vain to act immediately to prevent an epidemic. Undeterred by their complacency, Rieux heads the city's auxiliary hospital and works long hours lancing abscesses and administering serum to relieve the suffering of his patients.

They are not the only ones who suffer. Every day Rieux must visit newly infected patients in their homes and face the demoralising task of summoning an ambulance immediately to sequester the infirm from their families in case they too might become infected. Resigned to the knowledge that these loved ones will never see one another again, he becomes gradually hardened by his experiences. His attitude to work becomes increasingly pragmatic; he offers medical assistance not because of any devout religious faith or any perceived status of his own position, but simply because he has the skills and means to help. Rieux does not consider himself a hero, even if others might.

Albert Camus was born in Algeria in 1913 and is also the author of novels such as *The Outsider* (1942) and *The Fall* (1956). In 1957, he was awarded the Nobel Prize for Literature. He died in a road traffic accident just three years later. In the end, he remains best known for *The Plague*, a masterpiece generally viewed as an allegory of the German occupation of France during World War II. The novel leads us nicely to the next chapter, which explores the manner in which infectious disease has been inextricably linked with the evolution of literature through the centuries.

Chapter Eight

Fiction and Infection

FICTION IS STREWN WITH REFERENCES to infection. Several poets and novelists focus upon smallpox, for example; now deemed eradicated, it afflicted many a poor soul in seventeenth and eighteenth century Europe. Conversely, one might be forgiven for thinking syphilis was reserved for the most creative in society – Keats, Shelley, Byron and a few select others. Cholera and leprosy have also featured widely, often as the prevailing ailment in the challenging backdrop of some fictional doctor. We have just seen such an example in Albert Camus's *The Plague*. Similarly, how better to depict suffering in a character than through his or her affliction with an untreatable infectious disease?

In this chapter, it is worth pausing briefly to examine the clinical features of these contagious diseases that have proved so fascinating. They are almost like characters themselves and each, like any fateful protagonist, must ultimately meet its nemesis. For some, this is vaccination or improved sanitation, but for others it is the advent of antibiotics. Either way, the infection often has the starring role.

The Age of Smallpox

There can be few infectious illnesses that have not, at some point, appeared in *House MD*, a television series to which we have already referred. In one episode, a teenager emerges from a deep sea dive with a sealed glass jar purloined from a shipwreck. The jar is subsequently shattered and its contents – we are initially led to believe – infect the unfortunate young woman with smallpox. As always, various dangerous investigations and unnecessary treatments ensue while House and his team attempt to uncover the real diagnosis. Finally, a translation of the long deceased captain's log (along with the absence of some cardinal symptoms) allows the doctors to diagnose, not smallpox, but instead the more benign *rickettsialpox*. The young woman is treated and thus permitted to go home.

This is far from the first fictional reference to smallpox. Indeed, it is difficult to imagine such a terrifying and disfiguring disease not becoming enmeshed in literary culture; so widespread was the illness in the seventeenth and eighteenth centuries that some commentators have suggested the "Age of Smallpox" might be a more apt name for the "Age of Reason". It is ironic that a society craving logic and order should be intermittently reduced to chaos by so earthy an infectious illness. Smallpox inspired both fear and fascination and this is reflected strongly in the poetry of the era, not least that of the Englishman John Dryden.

Dryden's first published poem was an elegy entitled "Upon the Death of Lord Hastings". The poem, which first appeared in print in 1649, was inspired by the untimely death of one of Dryden's old school friends. Henry Lord Hastings contracted the illness at the tender age of nineteen and died on the eve of the day he would have had his wedding. Perhaps most poetically, Dryden addresses the stigma of disfigurement by comparing the pock-marked appearance of Hastings's corpse to a constellation of stars in the night sky.

But then, one of the characteristic features of smallpox poetry is the direct manner in which the illness is described. For the royal physician Martin Lluelyn, it was witnessing a prominent and excruciating death from the illness in 1660 that inspired him to pen some rather graphic lines about its signs and symptoms. "An Elegie on the Death of the Most Illustrious Prince, Henry Duke of Gloucester" gives us a haunting taste of what it must have been like to suffer with smallpox:

> *The sharp disquiets of an aching brain,*
> *A heart in sunder torne, yet whole to pain.*
> *Eyes darting forth dimme fires, instead of sight;*
> *At once made see, and injur'd by the Light;*
> *Faint pulse; and tongue to thirsty cinders dry'd:*
> *When the reliefe of thirst must be deny'd.*
> *The Bowels parcht, limbs in tormenting throwes*
> *To coole their heat, while heat from cooling growes.*
> *Slumbers which wandering phansies keep awake,*
> *And sense not lead by objects, but mistake.*

Of course, writers were no more immune from smallpox than any other member of society. The poet and essayist Jane Bowdler was rendered permanently disabled after surviving the illness in 1759. Recall also that the physician-writer Oliver Goldsmith was heavily pock-marked after his brush with mortality. Although the American writer Mark Twain never suffered from smallpox as far as we know, he spared a thought for those who did. In Chapter Sixteen of *The Adventures of Huckleberry Finn*, the eponymous hero rafts down the Mississippi River with an escaped slave named Jim, hoping to convey the latter to a jurisdiction in which he might obtain his freedom. Alas, they encounter a skiff and two armed slave hunters, but the quick-thinking Huck avoids trouble by allowing the three bounty hunters to infer his only on-board companion to be his smallpox-ridden father. The men are suitably dissuaded from pursuing the matter any further.

In real life, smallpox has never been too far from the media headlines. In the so-called age of terror, smallpox is among a cluster of severe infectious diseases that are a source of concern to many governments. Although the illness officially exists only in the United States Centres for Disease Control and in a Russian secure storage laboratory, its potential use in biological warfare has led many governments to take special measures to ensure public safety. When all is said and done, Martin Lluelyn's description of the illness is disturbingly true.

Smallpox is caused by the *variola* virus passed from person to person by direct contact and has an incubation period of eight to eighteen days. Initial symptoms are sudden in onset and include a high fever, headache, vomiting and severe aching pains. On day three, the fever usually subsides and a rash appears on the face, then spreading to the trunk and extremities. This rash is initially smooth (*macular*), but then becomes raised (*papular*) with vesicles that soon become infected (*pustular*). At this stage, the fever may return, frequently resulting in sudden confusion (or *delirium*). Both fever and rash typically abate on day twelve, but the unfortunate individual remains infectious to others until the vesicles finally dry out, at which point scabs are formed and then shed, leaving a legacy of pitted scars. Complications include inflamed kidneys, pneumonia and death.

The successful amelioration of smallpox began with Edward Jenner, an accomplished physician, naturalist, musician and advocate of evidence based medicine. He was born in 1749 and spent his formative years in Gloucestershire, in the west of England. At the age of fourteen, he was apprenticed to the Bristol surgeon Daniel Ludlow, before moving to London in 1770 to become a house officer at the prestigious St George's Hospital. It was here that Jenner met the physician John Hunter, who became his lifelong tutor and friend.

In 1773, following a short spell an army surgeon, Jenner returned to his native town of Berkley, where he was to spend the rest of his career as a general practitioner. At this point, he had no formal qualifications, examinations or theses to his credit, but his training was no less distinguished than that of most of his peers and predecessors. Moreover, he was later conferred with MDs by the University of Oxford and that of St. Andrew's.

Having been a member of a medical society near Bristol, Jenner went on to help establish similar group more locally and, to this gathering, he contributed a number of original papers on diseases of the heart. He was also a dedicated naturalist and a member of the Royal Society and, in this capacity, was the scientist largely responsible for arranging the botanical specimens collected by Dr Daniel Solander, the Swedish naturalist on Captain Cook's first voyage to the pacific. John Hunter supervised many of Jenner's scientific experiments; when the latter would conjecture on various scientific possibilities, his tutor would ask: "But why think? Why not try the experiment?"

So it was that Jenner began to research the relationship between smallpox and cowpox, a subject in which he had been interested since his early days as an apothecary's apprentice in the late 1760s. At this time, the killer disease was rapidly reaching its peak and causing up to four thousand deaths per annum in London, where it was most prevalent. Jenner was the first scientist to note that the carriers of cowpox, a harmless virus endemic among dairymaids, were apparently immune to smallpox. Cowpox was transmissible between patients and thus he hypothesised that inoculating even a small number of people with the harmless disease would confer immunity to smallpox upon a larger population.

On 14 May 1796, therefore, Jenner used scrapings from a cowpox rash on the finger of a dairymaid named Sarah Nelmes to inoculate a young boy, James Phipps, with the cowpox virus. On 1 July of the same year, he attempted to inoculate the boy with smallpox and, despite repeated attempts, was unsuccessful. In July 1798, Jenner published his case studies, entitled *An Inquiry in to the Causes and Effects of the Variolae Vaccinae, a Disease Discovered in some of the Western Counties of England, Particularly Gloucestershire, and Known by the Name of Cowpox.*

Alas, his plans for further research met with some difficulty because volunteers understandably were not forthcoming. Indeed, inoculation against smallpox only really took off when Henry Cline, an eminent British surgeon of the same era, began to employ the vaccine in some of his patients. The practice of vaccination – a term coined by Jenner from the Latin *vacca* (meaning "cow") soon became popular, despite the absence of a convincing scientific explanation of how it worked.

But vaccination was not a new idea. Indeed, inoculation for the purpose of disease prevention was an ancient practice which had originated in the Far East, had been introduced to England around 1720 and was well recognised by Jenner's time. Although serious side effects due to vaccination were not infrequent, the British government would ban all other prophylactic treatments for smallpox by 1840.

Despite this measure, smallpox continued to be a major public health issue for over a century. In 1967, when the World Health Organisation proposed its ten year smallpox eradication programme, ten to fifteen million new cases and two million deaths were still occurring annually in thirty-one different countries. The new WHO programme was so effective that the last naturally occurring case of smallpox was documented just ten years later in Somalia. The disease was declared eradicated by the World Health Assembly in 1980.

David Cronenberg once opined that, "A virus is only doing its job". The variola virus would have continued to be a major threat to public health, were it not for the dedicated work of Edward Jenner. To appreciate fully his research into a disease that was once endemic, we need only read the works of Dryden, Lluelyn, Goldsmith and Twain. Even the writers of *House MD* cannot resist a little haunting reminder.

Syphilis, the Celebrity Bug

The poet John Keats once remarked that, "In disease medical men guess: if they cannot ascertain a disease, they call it nervous". Within the various medical specialties, there are quite a few physical illnesses masked by psychiatric appearances. Not least of these is syphilis, to which Keats may well have dedicated his hypothesis. As a former doctor, the poet might have known that this intriguing venereal disease sometimes presents with psychiatric or neurological symptoms that are not preceded by obvious infectious signs. Syphilis has always been a disease that ultimately likes to stand out, both clinically and historically. So, what are its clinical features and why should it interest literary figures such as Keats?

If the reader will again permit a small amount of esoteric jargon, the organism in question is the *spirochete* bacterium *Treponema pallidum*, whose initial presentation is in the form of a painless nodule on the genitalia termed a *chancre*. The incubation period is anything from nine to ninety days, by which time the spirochete has already burrowed through the skin and spread around the body. Even without treatment, the chancre heals within weeks, leaving a scar.

Secondary syphilis occurs four to eight weeks later and typically involves symptoms such as fever, malaise, swollen lymph nodes, hair loss, ulcers that resemble snail tracks, and other abnormalities of the skin around the groin. Tertiary syphilis occurs two to twenty years afterwards and, by this time, the individual is non-infectious. This phase of the illness involves the occurrence of *gummas*, which are small nodules in the skin, bones and joints.

The final stage of the disease is termed quaternary syphilis and involves various cardiovascular, neurological and psychiatric complications. Prominent examples include an aneurysm of the aorta (the body's main artery) and *neurosyphilis*; the latter sometimes culminates in a phenomenon called *general paralysis of the insane*, comprised of dementia coupled with spastic weakness of the limbs. Other psychiatric complications can also present, most commonly depression, auditory hallucinations and grandiose delusions.

Syphilis is diagnosed in the laboratory using a technique called *dark ground microscopy* of chancre fluid, or by *serology* to identify antibodies in the blood. In addition to treatment with antibiotics, it is essential to trace sexual partners to avoid unnecessary spread. So, with the aforementioned esoteric jargon now complete, what about the more important cultural significance?

Syphilis has made a notable impact on European literature. In his poem "La Belle Dame Sans Merci", Keats makes more than a passing reference to both the disease and the desirable but deadly women who, he suggests, are responsible for spreading it. In the days before penicillin, syphilis was treated using mercury or prussic acid which, although supposedly quite effective, carried some nasty side effects. This is noteworthy because both Percy Shelley and Lord Byron are believed to have treated themselves with such a regime. Perhaps syphilis ultimately contributed to Byron's reputation as a man who was, according to Lady Caroline Lamb, "Mad, bad and dangerous to know".

The French writer Guy de Maupassant is thought to have contracted syphilis during his early twenties. Even from the saner days of his earliest short stories, he displayed a singular interest in the theme of madness. For example, in the short story "Who Knows?", the protagonist experiences bizarre delusions regarding the furniture in his house. In "A Queer Night in Paris", the main character walks the streets in a state of paranoid agitation. In "The Diary of a Madman", a judge commits murder in cold blood and then sentences an innocent man to death for the crime. Alas, in January 1892, tormented by madness, Maupassant attempted to slit his own throat and was committed to the private asylum of Dr Esprit Blanch in Paris, where he died the following year.

The Germans suffered as badly as the English and the French. The poetic dramatist Johann Wolfgang von Goethe is believed to have contracted syphilis while in his late twenties, shortly after the publication of his first play *The Lover's Caprice* (1767). The philosopher Friedrich Nietzsche, meanwhile, is thought to have spent the last twelve years of his life in an increasing state of syphilitic madness with delusions of grandiosity and wildly disordered thought.

Finally, we arrive at the Irish literary figures. Some experts have suggested that James Joyce owed his poor sight and unusual gait to the venereal disease, while Bram Stoker had syphilis when he died in 1912 at the age of sixty-four. It used to be widely suspected that Oscar Wilde died of syphilis. That is until November 2000, when Dr Ashley Robins and Professor Sean Sellars – the former a psychiatrist and the latter an *otologist*, both from the University of Cape Town – published an article in the *Lancet* asserting that Wilde died of a right sided *cholesteotoma* (a destructive growth of the ear). It would have been cold comfort to the literary genius as he lay in bed complaining about the wallpaper in his Parisian bedroom and insisting that, "One of us has got to go!"

As we can see, European literature was influenced in no small measure by syphilis. For some writers, it was merely a source of preoccupation while, for others, it was a cause of suffering and untimely demise. Neurosyphilis might even have added to the originality of their poetry or prose. So, as the incidence of syphilis continues to rise in Ireland, we may take some solace in presuming that the future of creative writing at least looks promising.

The Symptoms of Love and Cholera

In his novel *Love in the Time of Cholera*, Gabriel García Márquez makes an interesting comparison between two illnesses. With a detailed medical history, he suggests, it is easy to establish repeatedly that love and cholera share the same cluster of symptoms. A little far fetched, perhaps, but the physician in Márquez's novel is utterly convinced by the clinical findings in his love struck patient. The latter displays a weakened pulse, hoarse breathing, a pale complexion and perspiration, a syndrome like that seen in those close to death. It could so easily be cholera.

The tale is set in an unnamed Caribbean seaport at the turn of the twentieth century. The author recalls the commoner symptoms of cholera and the manner in which Dr Juvinal Urbino goes to great lengths to avoid an epidemic. The sagacious physician even improves the region's sanitation by arranging for the construction of an aqueduct and a sewerage system. Evidently ahead of his time, Dr Urbino's most remarkable achievement lies simply in acknowledging the need for clean water.

Although Dr Urbino does not die from cholera, not all literary protagonists are quite as lucky. In Thomas Mann's novella *Death in Venice* (1912), an eminent middle-aged author named Gustav von Aschenbach travels to the great Italian city and, from a distance, falls in love with an adolescent boy. Mann draws a parallel between the immorality of Aschenbach's passion and the increasing prevalence of cholera within the city. Aschenbach's lustful distraction leads him to ignore discreet notices posted by a Health Department in denial, vaguely warning citizens that a contagious disease is afoot and that shellfish should be avoided. Even the strong odour of disinfectant does not seem to deter our anti-hero. In the end, such an oversight allows the epidemic to claim his life.

Kitty Garstin, on the other hand, is acutely aware of the dangers of cholera. In Somerset Maugham's *The Painted Veil*

(1925), the beautiful but shallow young *débutante* acquiesces to a marriage proposal by Dr Walter Fane, an ostensibly dull and eccentric bacteriologist. The newlyweds move to Hong Kong where Kitty quickly tires of her husband and allows herself to be seduced by a handsome stranger. But Kitty has under-estimated Walter. He confronts her with her adultery and, on pain of a very public divorce, insists she accompany him to the Chinese interior in the midst of a widespread cholera epidemic. There, Kitty witnesses the good work of selfless French nuns who risk their own lives to soothe unspeakable suffering in pa-tients and care for children orphaned by the disease. Dr Walter Fane is equally heroic, obsessed with saving as many lives as possible – ultimately to the detriment of his own. He succumbs to cholera, leaving a widow whose experiences of tragedy have led to a profound personal transformation and a longing for redemption. She returns home ready to atone.

Despite these twentieth-century literary examples, it was nonetheless the nineteenth century that stood out as the real era of cholera. It was an epoch marked by six great pandemics, all of which spread from the Ganges Delta where the disease was first recorded and has presumably existed since time im-memorial. But cholera has seen the world, from Africa to the Americas. A seventh pandemic arose in the 1960s and spread from Indonesia to most of Asia and Africa. More recently, chol-era was reported in Peru, where it rapidly spread throughout South and Central America and into Mexico. As a result, over one million cases and some ten thousand deaths were reported in the Western Hemisphere between January 1991 and July 1995. In 2010, Haiti was struck with an epidemic in the aftermath of a gargantuan earthquake. We can see, therefore, that cholera has been ubiquitous for quite some time with the result that only the most affluent of countries with adequate sanitation facilities have managed to avoid epidemics over the past century.

The causative bacterium is the *vibrio cholera*, a variety of *bacillus* with two main types, namely *classical* and *EI Tor*. The disease is spread from person to person via contaminated food and water. The bacteria adhere to the wall of the small intestine, an alkaline environment in which the flourishing organisms can produce a toxin that causes the bowels to fill with fluid containing various *electrolytes* such as *sodium, chloride, potassium* and *bicarbonate*. Most infected people have only mild symptoms of gastroenteritis; indeed, only around ten percent of those exposed to the illness actually develop clinical cholera. The remainder usually carry the bacteria for around ten days. Long term carriers are very rare.

When symptoms occur, their onset is usually sudden, with incubation periods of between six hours and five days. Such symptoms include explosive, copious and painless watery diarrhoea with a ricewater appearance. Indeed, up to twenty litres of fluid may be lost in a single day. A brief rise in temperature may also occur, as may projectile vomiting, muscle cramps and dehydration. In severe cases, fluid and electrolyte loss may be sufficient to cause *hypovolaemic shock* and kidney failure. Other remarkable phenomena include a curiously high pitched voice and a persistent clarity of the mind, almost until death.

As one might suspect, the diagnosis of cholera is simply made by isolation and identification of the causative bacterium in infected stools. Treatment involves rapid rehydration either orally or intravenously with a fluid containing suitable electrolytes. Some antibiotics have been shown to shorten the duration of the illness. Otherwise, cholera is generally self limiting and patients who survive the dehydration frequently recover remarkably quickly.

But as Dr Juvinal Urbino would have insisted, the best treatment for cholera is its prevention. Good sanitation with adequate sewerage disposal and the provision of clean water supplies is the most reliable way of preventing an epidemic.

But what should one do for the patient who presents with cholera when all the diagnostic tests prove negative? Simply follow the doctor's advice and assume the patient is in love.

Leprosy in Literature

In an earlier chapter, we touched upon William Somerset Maugham's novel *The Moon and Sixpence*. In it, Charles Strickland is a respectable middle aged Englishman who, without warning, abandons wife and children to devote himself to art in Paris. Strickland's subsequent complete rejection of Western civilisation brings him to Tahiti where he contracts leprosy and, after many draining years of illness, ultimately dies. Recall that the novel is based on the life of the French painter Paul Gauguin and is, in essence, the universal story of the tormented artist. In the eyes of Maugham, art cannot exist without suffering and the author uses leprosy as an icon to symbolise his point. Maugham's Strickland is obliged to suffer his mutilating disease in the same way Gauguin suffered for his art.

From a purely medical viewpoint, leprosy is little more than a tropical disease that affects the nerves and skin. But *The Moon and Sixpence* is an example of how such an ailment has featured prominently in the world of literature, where writers have used it to epitomise the human condition. The features of leprosy described in fiction relate primarily to the face, hands and feet. The loss of fingers and toes caused by trauma in the context of damage to the nerves and blood vessels gives rise to the clubbed appearance of the extremities. Characteristic facial features include thickening of the skin and earlobes, thinning of the eyebrows and flattening of the nose, and eventually lead to a so-called "leonine" expression.

Dr Coutras describes succinctly this aspect of the disease as he tries to convince Strickland of his affliction in *The Moon and Sixpence*. "Do you not see the change in your face?" he asks. "Do you not see the thickening of your features and a look –

how shall I describe it? – the books call it lion faced. *Mon pauvre ami*, must I tell you that you have a terrible disease?"

Leprosy exists mostly in poverty stricken regions of the tropics but is by no means restricted to fiction or obscure biblical references. Indeed, it affects approximately fifteen million people around the world, of whom only twenty per cent ever receive effective treatment. Theories regarding its origin have varied. Some have thought it hereditary, while others have believed it venereal. The eighteenth century Swedish naturalist Carolus Linnaeus blamed nematode contaminated fish, while the nineteenth century British physician Sir Andrew Balfour cited insect bites. Experts now believe the disease to be caused by a *bacillus* variety of bacterium similar to that causing tuberculosis; *Mycobacterium leprae*, as it is called, multiplies slowly but is highly infective. Although some varieties of the disease may progress rapidly, its incubation period is usually prolonged, typically lasting four to ten years.

Clinically, leprosy usually involves the skin and superficial nerves, with the individual's own immune response determining its severity. Initially, a transient rash occurs with a patchy loss of pigment or reddening of the skin. Common sites for such skin changes include the face, the limbs, the buttocks and the shoulders, with the presentation typically varying according to the type of leprosy. Dome shaped or oval *lesions* are commonest, with raised, reddened edges and coarse, whitened centres, often devoid of any sensation. As they develop, the lesions typically expand outwards while simultaneously healing at the centre, rendering them ring like.

In due course, certain nerves may gradually thicken, causing limbs to cease working efficiently. Particularly vulnerable are the *ulnar* nerve at the elbow, the *radial* and *median* nerves at the wrist, or the *popliteal* nerve behind the knee. Indeed, nerve *palsies* like *claw-hand* or *foot-drop* (they effectively are how they sound), without any skin involvement, may be the patient's first symptom. *Glove and stocking* anaesthesia (loss of sensation of an area of the skin covered by an imaginary glove or stocking) is also possible, as are problems with eyesight.

As we can see, therefore, leprosy is not a pleasant illness. Little wonder that, for millennia and throughout many civilisations, people have documented it extensively. The ancient Egyptians recorded leprosy among their slaves almost three and a half thousand years ago. It has been mentioned in the philosophy of Confucius and the remedies of the early Indian Vedic physicians, while the writings of both the Old and New Testaments make multiple references to the disease. Biblical accounts include structured systems for isolating lepers, although it is now suspected that many of those deemed "unclean" in this way might in fact have been misdiagnosed. Leprosy was also common in Europe during the Middle Ages and occurred in the Americas from the fifteenth century onwards. Its prevalence in the New World was partly because of the importation of infected slaves from Africa where the disease has always been endemic.

Perhaps unsurprisingly by now, leprosy has transpired to be the culpable ailment in at least two episodes of *House MD*. Clearly therefore, as a literary theme, the illness can be found in biblical passages, historic documents, contemporary novels and even a popular television series. Indeed, it has proved to be the most consistently alluring medical inspiration for writers and philosophers over the course of several thousand years. So, how could just one disease have this attraction?

The answer may lie in the fact that victims of leprosy were often ostracised. Many civilisations throughout history believed the disease to be a punishment from God, and would deliberately banish afflicted persons on religious or aesthetic grounds. In addition to enduring the horrendous physical symptoms of the disease therefore, lepers were frequently forced to lead solitary lives. Perhaps this is why the disease has become such an apt symbol of human isolation.

Graham Greene's character Querry is a case in point. In the novel *A Burnt-out Case*, Querry is a celebrated but disillusioned architect who abandons his vocation to journey into deepest Africa in search of escape from his worldly success and decadent lifestyle. Quite by accident, he stumbles upon a colony of lepers. Greene uses disfigurement to symbolise the burden placed on Querry by his past. Success is Querry's leprosy; it has mutilated him, leaving him burnt out, empty and in search of a cure. The novel opens with a variation of Descartes's *Cogito, ergo sum* – "I think, therefore I am". Greene writes of Querry that, "The cabin-passenger wrote in his diary a parody of Descartes: 'I feel discomfort, therefore I am alive,' then sat pen in hand with no more to record". Greene implies that suffering is inherent in existence; it is so inevitable that it requires no further explanation. It becomes an axiom.

The War against Infection

More than a few novels set during World War II pay homage to the then-recent discovery of penicillin. Louis de Bernières's novel *Captain Corelli's Mandolin* provides us with a good example. Set on the Greek island of Cephalonia, the story is essentially of a love affair between Captain Antonio Corelli, a young officer of the occupying Italian army, and Pelagia, the daughter Dr Iannis, the local doctor.

Dr Iannis is the most endearing of fictional physicians. Although self-taught and unlicensed, he has nevertheless earned the trust and respect of an entire community through decades of dedicated and humane service often paid for in kind with food and wine. Beneath his gruff exterior lies wisdom and tenderness. He is a kind father to Pelagia and sometimes imparts to her "some truths" based on his own youthful experiences. He spends much of his spare time attempting to write a complete history of his ancient island and its long list of bloody conflicts. In the process, he finds himself constantly frustrated by his inability to reconcile his own biases with the facts. Yet he is a man conscious of the cruel reality of political events, which is why he worries for his daughter as the threat of war looms large over the island.

The reference to antibiotics is made shortly after the novel's bloody climax when, barely surviving the September 1943 massacre of the Italian 33rd *Acqui* Infantry Division by the German army, the near-fatally injured captain is brought to Dr Iannis's house. "What am I supposed to do?" exclaims the physician, overwhelmed by the horrific injuries he must treat. "I am not qualified. I am not a proper surgeon. I have no gown, no cap, no gloves, none of the penicillin I've heard about . . ."

It is ironic that a war, an inherent destroyer of human life, should have been so expedient in the evolution of a medicine that has subsequently saved so many lives. There can be few who have not had at least one course of antibiotics; they are ubiquitous. Their discovery marked a turning point in medicine which, although serendipitous, required more than mere good fortune. Knowledge, innovation and determination were also necessary and Alexander Fleming possessed an ample measure of each.

Fleming was born in a remote part of Scotland in 1881, but moved to London with his brother at the age of fourteen. He completed his secondary education at the Polytechnic School in Regent Street and went on to work as a clerk for a shipping firm. Fortunately for us all, this job did not suit him; in 1900 when the Boer War broke out, he escaped from his uncongenial environment by joining a Scottish regiment. Alas, he never actually got to see the war; most of his time was spent shooting, swimming and playing water polo. Shortly after his discharge, he inherited a sum of money from an uncle and used this to finance his medical studies.

Fleming's medical career was not intricately planned. His excellent examination results would have gained him entry to any university he desired, but his scant knowledge of the three nearby medical schools led him to choose St Mary's because they had once been his opponents at water polo. In an equally impulsive move, he reversed his initial decision to specialise as a surgeon in favour of bacteriology because, it is said, the pursuit of the former would have meant his having to leave St Mary's. He was to remain at this infirmary for most of his career.

Fleming worked in the inoculation department, an autonomous and financially independent service within St Mary's. In 1909, when Paul Ehrlich, a German physician, developed a chemical treatment for syphilis called *salvarsan*, Fleming became one of the few physicians in London to administer it by the new technique of intravenous injection. Fleming also worked closely with Almroth Wright, a pioneer in vaccination and immunology and, when World War I broke out, he accompanied Wright to France to establish a hospital laboratory near the western front. While there, the two bacteriologists encountered soldiers with horrific and often fatal infections. At the time, most physicians had recently adopted Joseph Lister's protocols for antiseptic surgery, based on the deduction that, since germs caused infection and antiseptics killed germs, antiseptics must cure infection.

Wright and Fleming dismissed this concept, propounding that white blood cells (also known as *leucocytes*) were the best defence the body had against infection. They added that antiseptics were a hindrance to recovery because they killed leucocytes more rapidly than they killed germs. Washing with copious salty water (*saline*), they insisted, was a better measure. While in France, it occurred to Fleming that there might perhaps be an undiscovered salvarsan-like compound suitable for treating microbial infections without the harmful effects he saw in antiseptics.

He continued his research after the war and, in 1921, discovered *lysosyme*, an antibacterial enzyme occurring in many bodily fluids including tears and mucus. As was the case with leucocytes, lysosyme was a substance found naturally in the body, and this allowed Fleming to further his theory that infection was best treated by enhancing the body's own immune defences and not by chemical antiseptics. His greatest discovery, however, was yet to come.

Fleming was not a tidy man; his laboratory was constantly cluttered with various bacteriological experiments. One day in 1928, when he was tidying up some Petri dishes upon which he had been culturing *staphylococcus* bacteria, he noticed that one of the dishes contained the growth of some mould. Furthermore, he could see that the mould, which was subsequently found to be *Penicillium notatum*, would not allow the staphylococcus to grow in its vicinity.

Fleming initially published his findings in *The British Journal of Experimental Pathology* but excited little public interest. His enthusiasm waned as a result and it was not until the late 1930s that two eminent bacteriologists, Howard Florey and Ernst Chain, revisited Fleming's ideas and built upon his work. In 1941, spurred on by the infectious horrors of World War II, they successfully produced a clinical antibiotic. Fleming was knighted for his efforts in 1944. Just a year later, Fleming, Florey and Chain were jointly awarded the Nobel Prize for Medicine.

Louis Pasteur once opined that, "In the field of observation, chance favours only the prepared mind". Had the mysterious mould elected to grow on the Petri dish of a less innovative physician than Sir Alexander Fleming, infection and septicaemia would undoubtedly have claimed the lives of as many soldiers in World War II as in World War I. Indeed, it is difficult to exaggerate the importance if Fleming's discovery; it is hardly surprising that Dr Iannis complained so fervently of his lack of penicillin. Like Fleming, he recognised a revolutionary drug when he saw one.

Chapter Nine

Fiction and Paranoia

I F THERE IS A BRANCH OF MEDICINE that has inspired more works of fiction than any other, it is undoubtedly psychiatry. Think of all those novels and plays where paranoia is a key element of suspense, or where villains and anti-heroes alike are endowed with psychiatric explanations for their singular behaviour. Ian McEwan's Jed Parry and Patricia Highsmith's Tom Ripley are two vivid examples, while the incurable madness of King George III was fictionalised in the form of a stage play by Alan Bennett. All three characters translated easily to the silver screen with great success, but let us not forget that art mirrors life. To understand fully our morbid fascination with fictional psychiatry, we must first take a look at how paranoia in society drives us all.

Fear: Fiction or Fact?

The opening line of a famous song goes, "Please could you stop the noise, I'm trying to get some rest from all the unborn chicken voices in my head?" The tune in question is, of course, *Paranoid Android* by Radiohead, and a lyrical sentiment more than vaguely suggestive of a character grappling with mental illness or – at the very least – mental discomfiture. This is not surprising in the context of the band's body of work; Radiohead's lyrics consistently deal with the theme of postmodern angst and alienation. One might go so far as to call them spokespersons for the younger generation in an increasingly fragmented society.

Certainly this theme must resonate with at least a few lost souls; the band, after all, has sold over thirty million records to date and remains as popular as ever in its twenty-five year history. But why should it strike such a chord? Its message, surely, is not a new one. Indeed, writers from Emile Durkheim to George Orwell have, in their different ways, long since described the consequences of a societal fabric increasingly unwoven by the placement of individual interests ahead of the common good. More recently, Daniel and Jason Freeman have continued this theme in their book *Paranoia: The 21st Century Fear*. In it, the authors describe the consequences of a modern culture in which all trust has broken down.

So, where did it all go wrong? It was Durkheim, a French sociologist, who first coined the term *anomie* as he described a state of affairs in which social and moral norms were confused, unclear or even absent. Such a condition was, in his view, partly due to industrialisation and its role in dissolving the traditional restraints on society, particularly the teachings of religion. The end result was deviant behaviour. From a more modern perspective, therefore, one might expand on industrialisation by citing computer technology and the internet, bureaucracy and specialisation in the workplace, smaller and more fragmented family units, and countless other by-products of modern life. In this context, it is easy to see how Durkheim's anomic prophecy might easily have come true and, as social restraints are weakened and people feel increasingly insecure, thus rears the ugly head of mental illness or even suicide.

It is grim stuff indeed, but hardly unique to Durkheim. Who could forget the concepts of Newspeak, Big Brother and the Thought Police? George Orwell's *Nineteen Eighty-Four*, set in the futuristic super-state of Oceania, provides the supreme popular prediction of how the moral zeitgeist might change utterly in just a generation. The novel is set in Airstrip One (what was once called London), where cityscapes are dominated by posters of the ruling party's leader – Big Brother – and ubiquitous two-way television screens designed to intrude upon the private lives of every citizen. The people of Oceania are made up of three social classes: the elite Inner Party; the slightly less important Outer Party; and the Proles who comprise the majority of the population. Winston Smith, the protagonist, is a member of the Outer Party. He works at the Records Department of the Ministry of Truth, where his principal tasks include the rewriting of historical documents to ensure they comply with government policy, and the removal of all evidence that people labelled as "unpersons" ever existed.

But Winston is not a man of his time. Observing the squalid, socially isolated, disease ridden, post-apocalyptic landscape of an England ravaged by civil war, he turns his back on it and dabbles in *thoughtcrime* by writing in his journal dissenting opinions about the government. This is errant behaviour in a country where even children are indoctrinated into informing on their parents; if Winston is discovered, he will almost certainly be tortured and executed by the Thought Police. Were it not for a small bedroom alcove next to his telescreen (a secret storage place for his journal), he might already have met this fate.

Alas, what might have been a triumph of the human spirit is finally usurped when Winston makes the mistake of falling in love. Julia, a mechanic sent to repair the Ministry's novel-writing machine, passes Winston a note proclaiming "I love you". Thus a clandestine, romantic relationship ensues that provides the reader with a glimmer of hope. Perhaps this alien environment can be conquered after all by love, of all things. Sadly not. Winston and Julia are captured, interrogated, subjected to *electroshock* to cure them of their "insanity" and finally brainwashed into towing the Party line.

Clearly, in writing such a book as far back as 1948, Orwell had some reservations about the direction in which he felt democracy and society were going. He was not unlike Mikhail Bulgakov and Boris Pasternak in this regard. Important themes of the novel include nationalism, identity, sexual repression and, perhaps above all, censorship. The reader is filled with a sense of oppression and foreboding, as though there might be something vital the authorities are hiding. In short, if we are not paranoid yet, Orwell warns us we soon will be.

If Orwell's predictions appear extreme, try those of Aldous Huxley. In his novel *Brave New World*, Huxley writes about a utopian World State in the twenty-sixth century. Here, the principles of Henry Ford's assembly line are an integral part of daily life to such a degree that the original guru of the motor car is revered like a god. Indeed, homogeneity, predictability and the mass production and consumption of disposable consumer goods are all the order of the day. The latter even applies to human beings, with five pre-determined societal classes, namely the Alphas, Betas, Gammas, Deltas and Epsilons in descending order of intelligence and status. Created through Mendelian eugenics and selective breeding rather than genetic engineering per se (DNA was unheard of until two decades after the novel was published), class differentiation is further facilitated by recorded voices that repeat slogans during sleep. Everyone is seemingly happy with their lot.

Like *Nineteen Eighty-Four*, *Brave New World* stirred up considerable controversy and was ultimately banned in Ireland in 1932. But Huxley's concerns about the potential direction of our society were quite different to those of Orwell. The latter feared censorship, while the former feared apathy and triviality in the presence of too much irrelevant information. Huxley's fragmented and alienated society arises from banal hedonism and the absence of a common purpose; Orwell's arises from oppression. In a sense, they were both remarkably prophetic. It is easy to see, for example, the former Soviet states in Orwell's work. As for Huxley's, one wonders how far we would need to look for a permissive, pill popping, easily distracted culture centred on virtual reality and hedonism. Temple Bar?

Perhaps I am being a little paranoid; it is, after all, only fiction. Or is our society really as alienated as musicians, sociologists and writers would have us believe? If so, we should spare a thought for one of the books I alluded to earlier. In *Paranoia: The 21st Century Fear*, Daniel and Jason Freeman suggest we are living in a society that increasingly cultivates suspicion.

This raw sentiment has always existed. The authors, for example, cite Shakespeare's 1611 play *The Winter's Tale*, which describes the fictional paranoid rampages of King Leontes of Sicily. A description of paranoia by the English scholar Robert Burton in his 1621 book *Anatomy of Melancholy* provides another historical example. The very word itself was first coined by Hippocrates to describe a delirium experienced by people with a very high temperature. From a medical perspective, the word was revived almost two millennia later by the seventeenth-century French physician François Boissier de la Croix, who used it to convey the signs of dementia in his work of disease classification, *Nosologia Methodica*. Finally, the German psychiatrist Johann Heinroth extended the word's meaning to include delusions, paving the way for the more precise explanations provided later by Emil Kraepelin and Eugen Bleuler around the turn of the twentieth century.

According to the thesis of Freeman and Freeman, we were always relatively paranoid as a society but now the problem is worsening. Paranoia used to be a component of psychosis that required psychiatric treatment, but it has now become so generalised that its amelioration lies beyond the scope of just one profession. The difficulties arise partly out of our poor ability to judge risk, leading us to believe that road traffic accidents, murders, aeroplane crashes and terrorist attacks are a far greater threat than is really the case. This, we are told, is partly the fault of the media, who have traditionally sought dramatic headlines. Add to this, global urbanisation, mass migration, social inequality and the general fragmentation of our communities and, according to the authors, it is hardly surprising that we are all a little more paranoid than we used to be.

Still, at least with a healthy sense of foreboding, we are primed to enjoy our daily dose of fiction. Durkheim, Orwell, Huxley and even Shakespeare warned us about social alienation but, more importantly, they entertained us along the way. As for Freeman and Freeman, you could do worse than give their book a go if you fancy a good read. It may well spare you the torment and anguish of becoming a paranoid android.

George, by Bennett!

The British poet and playwright Alan Bennett is no stranger to writing about doctors, medical students and interesting medical illness. A case in point is his short story "The Greening of Mrs Donaldson", one half of a volume entitled *Smut: Two Unseemly Stories* (2011). Here, we have the humorous tale of sexual liberation in a middle aged and recently widowed landlady. Quite uncharacteristically, Mrs Donaldson agrees to accept certain voyeuristic opportunities from her impecunious lodgers in lieu of rent, partly out of an awkward inability to say no and partly out of simple curiosity. Unsurprisingly, it is not long before she garners for herself some notoriety.

So, where does medicine come into it? Apart from the fact that one of her promiscuous lodgers is a medical student, Mrs Donaldson has also recently begun working as a "simulated patient" at a nearby medical school. Daily, she must act out a range of aliments from duodenal ulcers to stroke, epilepsy, dementia, abnormal bereavement and others too numerous to mention. Bennett lists them out like the costumes in an actor's wardrobe, spending little time on their actual presentations but, instead, describing rather well the angst-ridden bumbling and occasional pseudo-confidence typically seen in the average first year medical student faced with a patient.

Certainly, faking medical illness is an occupation for which Mrs Donaldson shows considerable flair. At least, this is what we understand from the battle weary medical tutor Dr Ballantyne, a man on whom Mrs Donaldson's newfound reputation is not lost. As he attempts subtly to seduce her, it becomes gradually evident that the story has less to do with medicine and more to do with human nature. Or perhaps like many authors we have seen, Bennett simply feels there is little difference.

Also from a medical perspective, Bennett is noted for reviving the character Doctor Dolittle in a series of audio books based on the famous novels by Hugh Lofting. But then, Bennett's work over the past half century has been as eclectic as it has been prolific. Born in Leeds on 9 May 1934, he studied history at Oxford University and went on to collaborate with Peter Cook, Dudley Moore and Jonathan Miller in *Beyond the Fringe*, a piece of satirical comedy presented at the Edinburgh Festival of 1960. Since then, he has worked largely in television, to which his most famous contribution is the series *Talking Heads* (1987). He has written numerous stage plays including *The History Boys* (2004), which garnered many awards, and an adaptation of Kenneth Grahame's *The Wind in the Willows* (1990).

But Bennett's masterpiece – dipping its toe well and truly into the world of medicine – is a stage play entitled *The Madness of George III*, which premiered on 28 November 1991 at the Lyttleton Theatre in London. Directed by Nicholas Hytner, the production did very well and went on to tour the United Kingdom, America, Greece and Israel. Indeed, it was so well received that it was quickly adapted for the cinema by Bennett and Hytner under the slightly altered title of *The Madness of King George*. The film starred Nigel Hawthorne and Helen Mirren, and won three BAFTAs and an Academy Award. The latter was for Best Art Direction, but Bennett was also nominated for his own adapted screenplay.

Set in 1788, the story is that of King George III almost thirty years into his reign. Alas, all is not well at Windsor Castle. Readers may remember that Erasmus Darwin – grandfather of the evolutionary theorist Charles – was once invited to become the king's royal physician. It is a pity he declined, because most of the doctors with whom the king was lumbered as a result were seemingly incompetent. The first of these was Sir George Baker, then President of the Royal College of Physicians. Despite this accolade, his *senna* prescriptions – according to the story – did little to relieve his majesty's crampy abdominal pains.

Sir George remains reluctant to physically examine the king, proclaiming, "With any patient I undertake a physical examination only as a last resort; it is an intolerable intrusion on a gentleman's privacy". When he finally does so and detects a racing pulse, the best he can suggest is that, "A warm bath has a settling effect on the spirits". As for the actual diagnosis, Sir George conjectures that, "It may be that he has caught rheumatism in his legs and that it has flown to the stomach. Or gout, of course."

The king's problem soon evolves into a more persistent delirium with "ceaseless babbling and the spewing of obscenities" and the making of improper advances upon the Queen's Mistress of Robes, Lady Pembroke. His majesty rouses his valets at four in the morning and coaxes them to run through meadows in their nightclothes in a manner that mirrors the play's frequent references to *King Lear* and his catharsis on the heath. King George's pulse reaches one hundred and four and his urine turns blue, something in which his bombastic doctor fails to see any significance.

"Medicine is a science," Sir George declares. "It consists of observation! Whether a man's water is blue or not is neither here nor there!" Indeed, the physician proceeds to ignore all potentially relevant signs and symptoms in favour of a pointless insistence on bleeding the king. Other than physical restraint, he can provide little to ameliorate the king's delusions and somewhat embarrassing urges. As the king himself suggests to Sir George, "You couldn't cure a gammon ham".

But then how could we expect Sir George to treat successfully an illness that was not described until almost a century later? The ailment in question is *porphyria*, a rare inherited disorder caused by a failure of the body to metabolise correctly haemoglobin in the blood. Prominent features include the excretion of *porphyrins* and their associated breakdown products in the urine (turning it blue); sensitivity to sunlight (leading to inflammation or blisters); attacks of crampy abdominal pain; damage to the liver; inflammation of the nerves (*neuritis*); and – most importantly from our perspective – psychiatric disturbances such as the bizarre and persecutory delusions depicted in the play.

The king's royal physician falls from grace when the Prince of Wales eventually intervenes, insisting that "Sir George will in future be partnered by my own physician, Dr Warren". The latter feels strongly that the king "must be blistered on the back to draw the humours from the brain; and must be blistered on the legs to draw the humours to the lower extremities". Dr Warren, in turn, takes the liberty of consulting with the eminent physician Sir Lucas Pepys, who has "spent a lifetime in the study of the anfractuosities of the human understanding" and "would value an early view of one of His Majesty's motions". Finally, the king's health is placed in the hands of Dr Willis, who is "a homely provincial figure and looks less like a doctor – which he is – than a clergyman – which he also is". Dr Willis appears confident of curing the king of his ailment, although he is unsure what that ailment actually is.

King George III was a kindly, almost fatherly figure whose humanity is evident in the play, even when he barks orders and assertions at his subjects, ending every sentence with, "... what, what?" Yet the palpable fear that the king must have experienced as he rather insightfully lost contact with reality is depicted sensitively in a manner that, once again, indicates Bennett must have done his research. Certainly, he seems acutely aware of the nature of a delusion (as defined earlier in this book) and the standard psychiatric treatment available in Georgian England.

Bennett also captures the essence of the king rather well. George William Frederick of the house of Hanover was born at Norfolk House, St James's Square, London on 4 June 1738. He was the grandson George II, while his maternal grandfather was Frederick II, Duke of Saxe-Gotha. The young George was the first British monarch since Queen Anne to be both born and educated in England. Not considered, for some reason, to be academically gifted as a child, he garnered a reputation for his good nature and was tutored at home. He became King of England in 1760 after the death of his grandfather and reigned – at least technically – for almost sixty years, a long stint in English historical terms and surpassed only by those of Elizabeth II and Victoria.

His reign was such a lengthy one, indeed, that he was monarch during numerous significant historical events including the industrial revolution, the French Revolution, the rise and fall of Napoleon, the discovery of Australia and the Acts of Union between Great Britain and Ireland. He was also king during the American War of Independence and the subsequent foundation of the United States, a topic that vexed him considerably as alluded to repeatedly in the play.

King George was a well liked and well respected man. Horace Walpole once referred to him as "tall and full of dignity, his countenance florid and good-natured, his manner graceful and obliging". Dr Samuel Johnson, meanwhile, reflected upon "the finest gentleman I have ever seen". He took mistresses at a young age (while still the Prince of Wales he allegedly had several children by Hanna Lightfoot, the daughter of a tradesman), but later tried in vain to marry Lady Sarah Lennox and was prevented from doing so by George II. Destined instead to become his bride in 1761 was Sophia Charlotte, youngest daughter of Charles William Ferdinand, Duke of Mecklenburg-Strelitz. She bore the king fifteen children who included, most notably, George IV, William IV, Edward (the father of Queen Victoria) and Frederick, whose greatest claim to fame seems to be that he was supposedly the "Grand old Duke of York" referred to in the popular nursery rhyme.

Although not noted as a talented writer, George III did contribute to *The Annals of Agriculture* under a *nom de plume* and was a committed bibliophile. Indeed, he collected over 65,000 books that eventually ended up in the British Museum. His subjects sometimes referred to him affectionately as "Farmer George", but agriculture was only one of the king's many talents; he also engrossed himself in music (he liked Handel), shipping and mechanics. As such, he was a well educated man with broad interests.

Despite his gentlemanly nature, King George had his share of enemies, a few of whom went to great lengths to expedite his premature demise. In 1786, Margaret Nicholson attempted to stab the king outside St James's Palace while, in 1795, stones were thrown at his carriage, several of which hit him. In 1800, James Hadfield shot him twice outside the Theatre Royal and, three years later, an attempt by Colonel Despard to destroy the king's coach using cannon fire was intercepted only at the last moment.

But his undoing came largely from within. As is depicted in the play, the king's first episode of porphyria was as early as 1788 and led to parliamentary attempts to declare him unfit to rule and thus appoint his son (the future King George IV) as reagent. Although King George recovered from this initial episode, the illness was to afflict him intermittently for the remainder of his life. To compound matters, he developed a cataract in his right eye in 1804 and was rendered completely blind by the end of that decade. In 1811, his porphyria finally caught up with him and he was decreed permanently insane and incarcerated at Windsor Castle for the rest of his life. Around Christmas 1819, he endured a particularly long period of illness and subsequently fell into a coma. He died a month later at the age of eighty-one and was buried at St George's Chapel.

Beyond the madness, King George III is remembered as a gentlemanly and humane monarch. Alan Bennett's stage play and subsequent film do the king some justice in evoking such a complex man tortured by his illness. The playwright's background medical research is impeccable. But then, as we have said, he is no stranger to writing about doctors and interesting medical illness.

The Darker Side of Love

Love has always been a favourite topic among authors; nothing, apart from death itself, could be more universal. Through the archives of English literature, from *Wuthering Heights* to *Captain Corelli's Mandolin*, authors have taken every available opportunity to explore this powerful theme. But, while most writers prefer to concern themselves with love in the conventional sense (that in which the lovers in question are untroubled from a psychiatric perspective if not from a romantic one), Ian McEwan dares to differ with his novel *Enduring Love*.

> *Our love! First bathing me, then warming me through the (window) pane. I stood there, shoulders back, my arms hanging loosely at my sides, taking deep breaths. The old tears streaming. But the joy!*

These lines from McEwan's novel form part of a love letter written by the fictional character Jed Parry, a young and lonely born-again Christian who has pure *erotomania*. Parry directs his sentiments towards the book's narrator, Joseph Rose, with whom he has fallen suddenly and deeply in love. Although the two characters meet purely by chance during the opening chapter while participating in a futile attempt to avert a rather grotesque ballooning tragedy, what ensues is a cascade of events in which Parry hounds the somewhat bewildered Rose by phoning him at night and sending him explicit love letters. Rose and his wife Clarissa become increasingly alarmed by this unwanted attention, particularly when Parry's activities take a more sinister turn involving successive episodes of violence. Thus unfolds McEwan's eloquent exploration of a severe case of *de Clerambault's syndrome*.

We have, of course, spoken about McEwan already in relation to *Saturday*. No stranger to writing about love in its many guises, he studied English Literature at the Universities of Sussex and East Anglia and, while attending the latter, famously enrolled in a creative writing course taught by the novelists Malcolm Bradbury and Angus Wilson. McEwan's writing has won him much critical acclaim since he first took up his pen and began publishing short stories in the early 1970s. Winner of the 1976 Somerset Maugham Award and the 1987 Whitbread Prize for Fiction, he was also awarded the Booker Prize in 1998 for his novel *Amsterdam*. Just three years later, *Atonement* was also shortlisted for the much coveted award.

McEwan's attention to detail in portraying Jed Parry's delusional disorder is exceptional. An individual with de Clerambault's syndrome possesses strong erotic feelings towards another person (their *love object*) along with the erroneous, persistent and unfounded belief that the object reciprocates his or her love. This belief is usually, but not always, delusional while the love object is usually, but not always, a real person. The love object is often unaware of the situation and, unlike the case of Parry and Rose, the majority of cases involve heterosexual erotomania.

The onset of the de Clerambault's syndrome may be sudden or gradual while the love object is typically unattainable, usually of a higher social status and may, indeed, be already married. Although the patient frequently believes that the love object was responsible for initiating the relationship through secret signs and messages, the patient usually avoids making any contact with the love object and, even if given the opportunity to engage in a rendezvous, will often make excuses not to. Instead, the patient prefers to admire from a distance, sometimes writing love letters or buying gifts but never actually sending them. In such uncommon cases where a meeting does actually occur, the patient typically makes further rationalising excuses to explain the inevitable rejection that ensues.

As we can see, therefore, enough insight usually exists to afford the patient some discretion; indeed, the tightly knit delusional system often allows for relative preservation of a normal personality. Diagnosis, as a result, may be difficult for doctors to make and many cases go unrecognised. Others are only picked up because the unhappily rejected patient presents to a clinic with depressive symptoms and allows the delusional system to slip out inadvertently during a consultation. In some cases, paranoid schizophrenia and major mood disorders may lead to erotomanic delusions, as may learning disability and physical brain disorders.

As McEwan mentions in his book, it was in 1921 that French psychiatrist Gaetan Gatian de Clerambault first gave his name to this particular brand of erotomania, which he termed *les psychoses passionelles*. An early and famous case was that of a 53 year old French woman who held erotomanic delusions about King George V of England. She stalked him persistently from 1918 onwards, paying many visits to London and waiting patiently at the gates of Buckingham Palace. As she stood outside, tiny gestures made by the king, the twitching of curtains for example, would be interpreted by the woman as signals of his undying love. Moreover, she claimed that his love for her was common knowledge around London and that he had even exerted his royal influence to control her movement around the city.

The events depicted in *Enduring Love* are uncharacteristically dangerous. In reality, personal safety is rarely threatened, with serious problems usually limited to non-violent harassment of the love object or their spouse. Such persistent intrusiveness can nonetheless alarm a love object confused by a patient's accusations of duplicity. And of course, loose words can irreparably damage a reputation. This is particularly true in the context of a female patient whose personality may be otherwise intact claiming that a male figure of importance has displayed strong erotic feelings towards her. In the worst case scenario, severely aggressive behaviour may culminate in stalking, assault, kidnapping or even murder. Thankfully, this does not happen very often.

In the end, love remains one of the most written about themes in the English language; if you haven't experienced it, then at least you can read about it. For those who want a little extra, Ian McEwan's novel provides the reader with a brief but vivid portrait of the darker side of love.

The Paradoxical Mr Ripley

The psychopath has also made a popular protagonist in fiction. From Edgar Allan Poe to Stephen King, the archives of literature are filled with passages detailing the abhorrent acts of nefarious and notorious villains. Consider the Gothic novels we referred to earlier, or their more modern counterparts like Bret Easton Ellis's *American Psycho*. How many of us have sought the thrill of Thomas Harris's Hannibal Lecter sending shivers up our voyeuristic spines? As psychiatry's commonest contribution to popular fiction, the psychopath is the anti-hero we all love to hate.

But rarer in fiction – and infinitely more complex – is the non-dissocial serial killer, the most famous example of whom is Mr Tom Ripley. It is almost sixty years since our first introduction to Patricia Highsmith's charming anti-hero and, since then, *The Talented Mr Ripley* has come to be regarded as much more than just a crime novel.

Its author was born in Texas in 1921 and spent much of her adult life in Switzerland and France, no doubt surrounded by the kind of glamorous people and beautiful locations described in many of her books. She received early encouragement in her writing career when Alfred Hitchcock directed a film adaptation of her first novel *Strangers on a Train* (1950). Subsequently, Highsmith went on to publish more than twenty novels, including four Ripley sequels, but only really achieved worldwide fame a few years after her death when the late Anthony Minghella filmed his adaptation of *The Talented Mr Ripley* (1999), starring Matt Damon and Jude Law.

> He looked at Dickie. Was he dead? Tom crouched in the narrowing prow of the boat, watching Dickie for a sign of life. He was afraid to touch him, afraid to touch his chest or his wrist to feel a pulse.

The climactic scene occurs on a small boat off the coast of San Remo in Italy. As readers familiar with the novel will know, Tom Ripley has just committed his first murder using an oar to bludgeon to death his shallow and gregarious companion, Dickie Greenleaf. Thus begins Ripley's spree of villainy, in which he commits fraud, forgery and murder with impunity, often resorting to the impersonation of his first victim in order to evade capture by the apparently incompetent Italian police.

Why, therefore, is Ripley not a psychopath? Surely his deeds are so deplorable that any decent individual would have great difficulty sympathising with him. Even the rapacious, onomatopoeic texture of Ripley's name suggests violence. Alas, the reader is at worst ambivalent and at best openly sympathetic to Ripley's homicidal tendencies. Stranger still, as the plot thickens and the pages turn, the murderer dextrously charms the reader into openly rooting for him to evade capture.

How does Highsmith achieve this? Let us view it, for a moment, from a psychiatric perspective. Most of the villains depicted in the novels of Stevenson, Ellis, Harris and Poe have rather severe *dissocial* personality disorders. This is illustrated by their persistent unconcern for the feelings of others, a blatant disregard for social rules and obligations and the incapacity to experience guilt over their callous, cruel and odious aggression. Although morbidly fascinating, these psychopaths are never quite as easy to sympathise with as their unfortunate victims.

Conversely in the Ripley novels, the shallow and histrionic victims are mostly difficult to admire while their murderer has several important redeeming features. Although Ripley certainly has a severe and dangerous personality disorder, his traits are far more *emotionally unstable* than psychopathic per se. Admittedly, Ripley has a persistent disregard for certain social norms – like the expectation not to commit acts of murder, for example – but unlike his dissocial counterparts, our anti-hero frequently shows an obvious regard for the feelings of others including those of some of his victims. In addition, he displays a significant tolerance of frustration in certain key situations, the ability to profit from experience, and – most importantly – the capacity to experience guilt.

Ripley's weakness for murder and deceit is far more likely to be due to what is termed an emotionally unstable – or *borderline* – personality disorder. He is frequently impulsive, with an obvious tendency towards extreme outbursts. He turns close friends and relatives against each other (termed *splitting*), he is capricious in mood and he is prone to feelings of emptiness that he projects onto others around him. Indeed, Ripley's relationship with Dickie Greenleaf is intense and unstable, due partly to the murderer's chronic uncertainties about self-image and sexual preference, and due most significantly to his extreme and ultimately homicidal efforts to avoid abandonment.

Highsmith used considerable poetic licence in making her character's borderline personality disorder a reason to commit murder but, unlike most serial killers in fiction, Ripley has the singular ability to command our sympathy. He has a vulnerability with which all but the coldest of readers can identify. Ripley exists alone in a state of emptiness, with few real friends, no family and no role in the social circles he so desperately desires to be a part of. Who could remain unsympathetic to this?

Ripley, moreover, displays many admirable characteristics such as courage, intelligence, diligence, sensitivity, kindness and an appreciation of art and music. He is far more likeable than his callous, cruel, histrionic and materialistic victims, all of whom have the social advantages that our anti-hero was never afforded. And as Ripley rises up and takes the spoils he was hitherto denied, his charm seduces us to such a degree that we are even willing, as readers, to overlook a murder or two.

In the end, the real talent lies with Ms Highsmith. She has created a paradoxical but ruthless killer who nevertheless commands our loyal sympathy. In essence, Ripley is the perfect anti-hero: the charming rogue who succeeds in hiding his many weaknesses, including his penchant for murder.

Chapter Ten

Fictional Psychiatrists

PSYCHIATRISTS HAVE BEEN FAVOURED by novelists every bit as much as their patients. Two fine examples include Sebastian Barry's Dr Grene and Alastair Campbell's Martin Sturrock. Both are characters flawed to the point of being difficult to distinguish from those whom they treat. In a far more grotesque sense, the same is true of Thomas Harris's evil creation Hannibal Lecter. Sebastian Faulks's Dr Jacques Rebière and Dr Thomas Midwinter, meanwhile, provide a more historical perspective on the birth of psychiatry, juxtaposing the psychodynamic and biological viewpoints that diverged around the turn of the twentieth century. But by far the most vivid fictional psychiatrist is sketched for us by F. Scott Fitzgerald, whose protagonist Dick Diver secures his own fate when he makes the mistake of marrying his patient. It is a cautionary tale set amid the frivolity of the Jazz Age.

Trusting the Wrong Doctor

One of the most iconic culinary claims in cinematic history has to be Dr Hannibal Lecter's assertion that, "I ate his liver with some fava beans and a nice Chianti". We are then treated to the grating sound of air sucked through the cannibalistic psychiatrist's teeth, leaving us in no doubt that we are witnessing the darkest of psychopathic menace. Such is this spine tingling effect, that the portrayal of Hannibal Lecter in *The Silence of the Lambs* won Sir Anthony Hopkins an Academy Award in 1991 while, in 2003, the American Film Institute chose Lecter as its Number One Movie Villain.

But is Lecter really a psychopath? Could he, instead, be a *sociopath*? Is there a difference? In many ways, he is a difficult fictional character to diagnose. Arguably, the only certainty from the outset is that he is not taking a rather severe variety of antidepressant termed a *monoamine oxidase inhibitor* (MAOI). An idiosyncratic characteristic of this particular type of medication is that those prescribed it risk sudden and potentially harmful high blood pressure if they consume certain foods that include cheese, beans and pulses, liver, well hung game and certain varieties of alcohol including Chianti wine. If Lecter were prescribed an MAOI, the aforementioned eccentricities of his diet would almost certainly have brought about the altogether less spine tingling, so-called *cheese reaction*.

It all began with Thomas Harris's novel *Red Dragon*, first published in 1981. Lecter has a relatively minor role in the book, introduced to assist FBI agent Will Graham in apprehending an entirely different serial killer. Nicknamed the "Tooth Fairy", the latter's *modus operandi* involves murdering entire families and capturing the homicidal event on film for his later enjoyment as he labours under a genuine and systematic delusion. The book also recalls that it was Graham who originally captured Lecter, and that the dedicated but somewhat sombre agent nearly lost his own life in the process.

Lecter plays a larger supporting role in the Harris's 1988 sequel, *The Silence of the Lambs*. In a virtually identical plot, he assists trainee FBI agent Clarice Starling in profiling another serial killer who operates under the name "Buffalo Bill". Here, Lecter offers an insight into the killer's psychological motivation in return for details of Agent Starling's unhappy childhood. But it is only in the novels *Hannibal* (1999) and *Hanni-*

bal Rising (2006) that we gain a real glimpse of Lecter's own biographical background. In these two novels, he takes centre stage as both protagonist and anti-hero, showing us a highly cultured individual capable of being moved by music and art, of forming caring relationships, and of loyalty to specific people other than himself.

In true Harris style, the fictional childhood of Lecter is macabre. Born in 1933 into an aristocratic family in Lithuania, most members of his family are killed by the German and Soviet armies when they storm his estate in 1944, leaving only Lecter and his younger sister Mischa as survivors. Both are captured by Nazi deserters who proceed to murder and devour Mischa, leaving a traumatised Lecter with a fixation on cannibalism. While nonetheless intelligent (he trains in medicine at the Institut de Médicine St Marie, Paris and later at Johns Hopkins University Hospital, Baltimore), he is bent on revenge and sets out on a highly organised yet secret killing spree that will claim many lives and create many more fine dinners until his eventual capture decades later.

So, upon whom did Thomas Harris base his anti-hero? As Harris rarely gives interviews, this question has been left open to thirty years of speculation that amounts to little more than rumour. A librarian in Cleveland, Mississippi, for example, was once reputedly told by the author himself that Lecter is based on William Coyne, a local murderer who escaped from prison in the 1930s and proceeded on a cannibalistic rampage. Another candidate of note is Andrei Chikatilo, a Soviet murderer convicted of killing (and possibly devouring) fifty-three women and children in the 1970s and 1980s. Chikatilo's elder brother Stepan was allegedly once abducted and cannibalised by starving neighbours, although this was never confirmed. We can see the similarities to Lecter's biography but, in the end, Harris keeps us guessing.

Even in his early literary cameo in *Red Dragon*, Lecter strikes a chilling pose. We first encounter him lying on his cot with a copy of Alexandre Dumas's *Le Grand Dictionnaire de Cuisine* open upon his chest as if to illustrate immediately his love of French cooking. Lecter does not merely eat his victims; he feasts upon them. He is presented as a slight but lithe man with small white teeth and maroon eyes that "reflect the light redly in tiny points". Incarcerated at the Baltimore State Hospital for the Criminally Insane under the care of forensic psychiatrist Dr Frederick Chilton, Lecter, we are told, has killed at least nine people and maimed two others, one of whom is on a respirator while the other resides in a private psychiatric hospital in Denver. From his cell, Lecter reads avidly, corresponds by mail with "some of the most respected figures in psychiatry" and contributes academic articles to the *American Journal of Psychiatry*, the *Journal of Clinical Psychiatry* and the *General Archives*.

So what is Lecter's diagnosis, if any? Most importantly, his sanity is largely established from the outset. He does not suffer from obvious delusions, hallucinations or other symptoms suggestive of psychosis. Of course, when Lecter demands to know of Graham how the latter managed to apprehend him so easily, the agent confesses that it was not his own intelligence but rather Lecter's "disadvantages". Pressed upon the subject, Graham lists these shortcomings simply as "passion" and the rather subjective view that Lecter is "insane". The former may be true, but the latter certainly is not. It is later remarked that if Lecter were ever to be declared sane, he would be obliged to stand trial on nine counts of first degree murder. Clearly some legal advantages, therefore, in Lecter's reluctance to force the issue.

And not everyone doubts Lecter's sanity. A local police chief, for example, suggests that Lecter is "not crazy, in any common way we think of being crazy" but rather that he "did some hideous things because he enjoyed them" and can "function perfectly well when he wants to". When called upon to elaborate, the police chief asserts that "they say he's a socio-path because they don't know what else to call him". The po-lice chief lists Lecter's pertinent characteristics, namely that he lacks remorse or guilt and was sadistic to animals as a child. Conversely, Lecter lacks many other important elements, in that he "wasn't a drifter, he had no history of trouble with the law", he had some depth of character and sensitivity, and he was not "exploitive in small things, like most sociopaths are".

Perhaps the difficulty in diagnosis arises because of some confusion between the terms psychopath and sociopath, which are often used interchangeably. Any difference between the two seems to be somewhat historical, beginning in the early nineteenth century with what the French psychiatrist Philippe Pinel originally termed "mania without madness", and what the American physician Benjamin Rush later re-named "mor-al derangement". In 1941, the American psychiatrist Hervey Cleckley published *The Mask of Sanity* and proposed the notion of the psychopath, giving sixteen characteristics that included being manipulative, self-centred, shallow, impulsive and occa-sionally violent.

In 1952, the term *sociopathic personality* instead of psychopath was used in the original version of *The Diagnostic and Statistical Manual of Mental Disorders* (DSM). The latter is the American version of an agreed list of criteria required to make psychiatric diagnoses. Its updated sequel, the DSM-II, went on to replace this term with *antisocial personality disorder* in 1968. The crite-ria, at this point, had been refined to such a degree that many researchers considered them to be of little practical use. This led the Canadian psychologist Robert Hare to devise and revise the *Psychopathy Checklist* (PCL-R), which used twenty items to diagnose the psychopath proposed in the traditional sense by Cleckley some thirty years earlier. Again, such individuals are typically manipulative, self-centred, emotively shallow, impulsive and egocentric. They lack remorse, empathy and frustration tolerance, form only transient relationships, and persistently violate social norms before proceeding to blame others for these lapses.

This was perhaps the point at which the notions of psychopath and sociopath began subtly to differ. The modern DSM-IV criteria for antisocial personality disorder stipulate the need for a conduct disorder (essentially a documented history of bad behaviour) before the age of fifteen. Other characteristics include (a) a callous lack of concern for others, (b) consistently shallow and transient interpersonal relationships, (c) an irresponsible departure from social norms, (d) an impulsive and irritable nature lacking in goals or long term objectives, (e) a striking failure to feel guilt or remorse, and (f) the tendency to blame others instead of accepting responsibility for one's actions.

The notion of the sociopath – perhaps, someone with an antisocial personality disorder as described by researchers such as the behavioural geneticist Dr David Lykken – could be viewed as broader, in that not all individuals qualifying for that diagnosis would necessarily be psychopaths according to the PCL-R. Similarly, not all psychopaths would necessarily fulfil the DSM-IV criteria for antisocial personality disorder. In a sense, therefore, two similar diagnoses overlap but are not necessarily synonymous.

So, what is the difference? Some commentators have suggested that a sociopath has a greater moral code and is more capable of feeling guilt, building caring relationships and demonstrating loyalty – but only in a narrow context rather than to society in general. While a sociopath may superficially resemble a psychopath, he or she is more likely to experience personal remorse – however slight – over harm caused to people about whom they care. It is also thought that a sociopath may go to greater lengths to hide their distress and behaviour from certain people, while a psychopath will not bother. Finally, it is suggested that sociopaths are more the function of adverse or neglectful childhood environments, while psychopaths are more likely to be temperamentally abnormal from birth.

If (and I do mean *if*) the above is truly the case, then Hannibal Lecter as described in the novels is almost certainly a sociopath. He displays many psychopathic characteristics but, crucially, he charms intelligent people quite effectively and hides his condition well enough to allow him to complete his full training in psychiatry, be moved by fine art and music, empathise and care for Clarice Starling and – most importantly – practice psychiatry exceptionally well over a career that must have lasted at least twenty years. One might argue it is impossible to practise psychiatry at all without empathy.

This is why we find him so fascinating; like Thomas Ripley, he is a striking anti-hero. He successfully hides his darker side from an unsuspecting public for decades, almost flaunting his cannibalistic deeds while virtually everyone fails to notice. He is more intelligent, charismatic, perceptive, observant, cultured and educated than any of his adversaries. He has a clear moral code: he kills annoying middle aged men but never women or children and, indeed, on more than one occasion he actively protects Clarice Starling from other predatory threats within the plot. He helps vulnerable FBI agents catch the type of serial killers we really find it impossible to relate to and, most importantly, he entertains us, scaring and seducing us simultaneously.

It is easy to see, therefore, why we might forgive his idiosyncratic choice of menu.

Tracing the Human Condition

Readers may recall an earlier reference to Damon Galgut's *The Good Doctor*, cited as a good literary example of a chaotic backdrop that mirrors the uncomfortable dynamic between two pioneering doctors. An equally good example is in Sebastian

Faulks's novel *Human Traces*. The story is that of two ideologically divergent psychiatrists during the decades leading up to the climactic chaos of World War I. On the face of it, Dr Jacques Rebière and Dr Thomas Midwinter have a lot in common. They are the same age – both born around 1860 – and each feels strongly protective towards a vulnerable but profoundly influential older sibling. A more fundamental comparison lies, perhaps, in their shared curiosity about the workings of the human mind. Yet, they are destined to fall out over their differing views of what it means to be human.

Their contrasting backgrounds are striking from the outset. Jacques hails from a socially deprived rural community in Brittany, northern France. In the opening chapter, he is a lad of sixteen living with his father, an austere rent collector and small time property owner with vague social aspirations. The young Jacques has already been coerced into leaving school prematurely to work as a labourer for his father. Indeed, it falls to the local curé to notice in Jacques a flair for natural history, anatomical drawing and the dissection of frogs. The curé, a former medical student, takes the young man under his wing and instils in him a thirst for knowledge.

But Jacques has domestic issues to contend with. Jacques's natural mother died shortly after giving birth and, with no sketches or photographs available, nor any willingness among the older members of the household to share their memories, he has come to rely solely on his brother Olivier's scant recollections for any inkling of his clouded ancestry. All Jacques has really managed to piece together is that his mother may have been "moody or in some way difficult".

And time is running out because Olivier is increasingly unwell. Over the preceding years, we learn, he has "started to drift away from his family; it began when, previously a lively and sociable youth, he took to passing the evenings alone in his room studying the Bible and drawing up a chart of 'astral influences'". His father now locks him in the stable with the horse. His appearance has become dishevelled with "his hair uncut for more than a year, his dark beard reaching almost to his chest". He has grown paranoid and agitated, on one occasion demolishing the collection of jars and specimens that Jacques keeps in his bedroom. "These are my instructions," he insists. He is described harming himself, having "gauged a hole in his left forearm" because of a belief that spiders are laying eggs under his skin. And as if all this were not enough, Olivier appears to hallucinate, leaving his younger brother with "the feeling that, although there was no one else in the stable, it was not to him that Olivier was addressing his remarks".

It is with exceptional clarity that Faulks describes schizophrenia, not simply its signs and symptoms, but the reactions of relatives and friends to an illness that will not be named until some thirty-five years later when Swiss psychiatrist Eugen Bleuler finally coins the term. Jacques is unique among his family members in not rejecting his brother over the loss of his sanity. Indeed, Jacques's motivation is strong from the outset. He wishes to find a cure for his brother, perhaps in an effort to preserve a channel to the past and the mother he never knew.

Thomas Midwinter's upbringing is an altogether more privileged one. Also sixteen years of age at the beginning of the story, he lives comfortably with his family in Torrington House, Lincolnshire, a respectable domicile provided for by a longstanding agricultural business run by his father. But with larger overheads and smaller profit margins, Mr Midwinter is finding it harder to make ends meet. The family must survive with fewer and fewer servants as they reminisce about a time, long since past, when they had a butler to answer the front door. More disturbingly, Mr Midwinter is on the verge of marrying off his eighteen year old daughter Sonia in what is effectively a strategic business alliance.

Thomas is a romantic at heart who despairs of Sonia's disinclination to marry out of love. He shows no initial signs of wanting to study medicine. Instead (like so many of the doctors we have mentioned), he desires to read English literature, specifically poetry. Such an aspiration is met with disapproval by Mr Midwinter and the business associates he makes a strained effort to impress. But it is only at his sister's suggestion that Thomas eventually decides, "if they would not let him become a doctor of literature, then perhaps he should accept Sonia's parting present . . . and become a doctor of medicine". He notes quite rightly that "Keats, after all, had been apprenticed to an apothecary and qualified as a surgeon".

Strangely, it seems that Thomas has experienced his own share of psychosis. We learn early in the novel that he has been hallucinating, hearing the voice of "a narcoleptic man" who has "spoken to him regularly since childhood". This voice does not reflect his own thoughts, moreover. Instead, it is audible like the voice of his brother or sister, "outside him, not produced by the workings of his own brain but by that of another being". In part, the experience explains his opting for the evolving but impoverished field of psychiatry. As Thomas grows older, it will influence an entire theory on what marks out *Homo sapiens* as fundamentally human.

Thomas and Jacques meet by chance at the fashionable resort of Deauville, Normandy. They are but twenty years of age and still at medical school, yet they immediately discern in one another a shared fascination with the human mind. They sit up all night on the beach, passionately swapping their philosophies. When it is time to part, they agree to meet up again. Later, they become brothers-in-law and esteemed colleagues who establish a clinic together high up in the Alps. That is, until the degree of their enmeshment works ultimately to repel them. What a pity Galgut's Frank Eloff was not around to predict it.

Human Traces is intricately plotted and extensively researched if a little esoteric in parts, while it's descriptions of psychiatric illness are simply remarkable. We are provided with a vivid insight into the workings of a Dickensian lunatic asylum, with its grand classical façade and its six miles of corridors. Thomas – newly qualified in his mid-twenties – is taken under the wing of the charismatic Dr Faverill, "a man of science and learning, rather grandiloquent, filled with the optimism of our time". Yet, with two thousand patients in the asylum – rudimentarily classified under mania, melancholy, idiocy, cretinism, dementia or epilepsy – the doctors are clearly overwhelmed by the magnitude of the task. Most patients are reviewed medically only upon admission for the purpose of acquiring a label.

It will be sixty years or more before the advent of *lithium* or *chlorpromazine* and, as such, the only treatments available are toxic sedatives such as *hyoscine* and *paraldehyde*. Most receive little more than "a safe home, free food and lodging, ... tasks to perform in the grounds, the farm and the workshops" and, finally, "entertainments and distractions". On one occasion, Thomas witnesses the "bathing treatment of some male melancholics", which involves "their being kept in a bath at a temperature of between 92 and 96 degrees while cold water was intermittently poured upon their heads from a watering can". When Thomas finally enquires whether they have any more scientifically based treatment on offer, a colleague retorts, "We are an asylum not a hospital".

Thomas's raw experience of nineteenth-century psychiatry – with its brutal and pointless treatments behind closed doors – is contrasted sharply with the abject showmanship of Professor Jean-Martin Charcot. Charcot is professor of anatomical pathology at the Salpêtrière Hospital, Paris and will become a father figure in the study of neurology, hysteria and hypnosis. He is Jacque's mentor in much the same way as Faverill is

Thomas's; thus Faulks sows the seeds of our two protagonists' profoundly differing philosophies.

In the end, *Human Traces* is a gripping story of two doctors whose fiery paths cross during the birth of an entire profession. From an academic perspective, it pits psychoanalysis against biological psychiatry (a battle that still endures to this day); from a literary perspective, it is an epic journey filled with passion, friendship, loyalty and conflict, and a moving exploration of the inexorable passage of time. Like any good novel, it simply tells the truth.

The Rise and Fall of a Fictional Psychiatrist

Recession is not always a bad thing. Indeed, there is a school of thought that views it as a kind of societal detoxification after the excesses of a boom. From a literary viewpoint, Ireland's so-called Celtic tiger and our subsequent decline in fortunes are mirrored with remarkably good effect by the novels of Francis Scott Fitzgerald. Readers will, of course, be familiar with *The Great Gatsby*, for many years a firm leaving certificate favourite. With its theme of the impoverished soul amid the hedonistic Jazz Age, the novel warns us of how materialism corrupts and leaves ordinary people feeling empty as prosperity inevitably ebbs away. And let us be honest: Ireland in the Celtic tiger era was not dissimilar to America in the roaring twenties. Ireland of today (and perhaps tomorrow) might equally be compared to the bleak depression of the 1930s.

But Fitzgerald best helps us understand the cost of a frivolous existence in his novel *Tender is the Night*, a piece of literature particularly interesting from a psychiatric viewpoint. Its protagonist is Dick Diver, a handsome psychiatrist and psychotherapist of considerable talent and promise. He is a graduate of Yale, a former Oxford Rhodes Scholar and the holder of a medical degree from Johns Hopkins University. A man of respectable origins, he travels to Vienna during World War

I "under the impression that, if he did not make haste, the great Freud would eventually succumb to an aeroplane bomb". In due course, Diver is made a partner at a prestigious Zurich clinic frequented by the rich and famous. He partakes in the scientific discussions of the day and has published his first textbook of psychiatry by the age of thirty. And in his seemingly plentiful leisure time, he holidays on the French Riviera and scales boldly the dizzy heights of high society. His existence, in almost every sense, seems perfect.

Alas, Diver has an Achilles heel in the form of his wife Nicole. A former patient of the clinic in Zurich, she hails from the kind of old money that subsequently allows Diver to buy his way into private practice. Strangely, the questionable ethics of a doctor marrying a patient pail into insignificance next to the range of taboos violated during the course of the novel. Nicole, perhaps predisposed to mental illness by an incestuous relationship with her father, represents a literary example of someone with schizophrenia. In her wartime letters to young Diver (then a captain in the US army), she refers insightfully to her initial presentation, one that suggests social withdrawal or even *catatonia*. Much of the earlier correspondence implies disordered thoughts with some paranoia thrown in for good measure.

So what is it that attracts the high achieving Doctor Diver to the vulnerable and damaged Nicole in the first instance? Is their ill fated marriage a show of chivalry on his part, or some misplaced attempt to cure her? Whatever the reason, their union is accepted readily, especially by Franz Gregorovious – a medical colleague of sound pedigree whose grandfather "had instructed Kraepelin when psychiatry was just emerging from the darkness of all time". It is Franz who banishes any early disapproval of the marriage as he refers to Nicole's amorous inclinations as "a transference of the most fortuitous kind". Indeed, from that point onwards, Nicole shows some steady signs of recovery.

The story opens half way through their marriage, at the beachfront of an opulent hotel on the French Riviera. Rosemary Hoyt, a famous American film actress who is just turning eighteen, arrives with her mother and is instantly beguiled by the glamorous lifestyle of the Divers and their circle of socialites. Rosemary wastes no time in falling in love with the handsome psychiatrist, a state of affairs that does not escape the attention of Nicole. She befriends Rosemary nonetheless; perhaps it is her policy to keep her enemies closer than her so-called friends. Rosemary's love remains unrequited for some time; the Divers instead toy with her affections and invite her to Paris where she becomes more closely embroiled in their sinister affairs.

It is implied that Nicole has a brief psychotic breakdown in her bathroom during a party early in the story, but it is really Diver who begins to unravel from this point onwards. The good doctor is on hand, for example, to assist young Rosemary when she is alarmed to discover a black man named Jules Peterson lying murdered in her hotel bed. It is Diver who remorselessly disposes of the bloody corpse in case its discovery should threaten the reputation and career of the young Hollywood starlet. Diver's illicit lifestyle continues as he descends further into alcoholism, much like Fitzgerald did himself. The psychiatrist becomes involved in violent public altercations and, on one occasion while in Rome, is arrested by the police for public disorder. And inevitably, he succumbs to the seductions of Rosemary although she is barely half his age.

The affair, the alcoholism, the complaints and the ensuing chaos result Diver's colleagues mounting a hostile takeover of his partnership in the clinic. Then follows the final straw as Nicole has an affair of her own and proceeds to divorce her increasingly erratic husband. All the while, her mental health has steadily improved, as though the psychiatrist has succeeded in curing his most prized patient by trading his own sanity for hers.

Although much of Fitzgerald's work is autobiographical, *Tender is the Night* represents by far his richest example of fiction resembling fact. The late nineteen-twenties and early nineteen-thirties were turbulent times for the author. Frustrated by difficulty conceiving a novel that would live up to *The Great Gatsby*, Fitzgerald migrated with his wife Zelda Sayre from Europe to Hollywood. There, the author had an intense affair with a young actress named Lois Moran, upon whom Rosemary Hoyt is thought to have been based. In 1930, the Fitzgeralds travelled to Europe once more and it was in Switzerland that Zelda had her first protracted hospital admission with psychosis. Diagnosed with schizophrenia, she was eventually repatriated to a psychiatric facility in Baltimore where she resided until a hospital fire led to her rather gruesome and untimely death in 1948.

Having spent much of the earnings from his first three novels, Fitzgerald fell upon hard times in the early 1930s and was forced to borrow money from his agent. To compound matters, his father passed away in 1931, much like Diver's does in the novel. Indeed, the storyline is filled with numerous autobiographical references, but the clinching comparison lies in the overall theme. Diver's youthful potential ultimately remains unfulfilled and this was the perception the author had of his own achievements, namely the early critical and commercial success that he never quite managed to carry forward into middle age. Little wonder, perhaps, that Fitzgerald chose to borrow the book's title from "Ode to a Nightingale" by John Keats. Recall that the poem deals with life's ephemeral nature and how mortality pervades everything notwithstanding any youthful promise that may exist at the beginning. When Fitzgerald died of heart failure in 1940 at the age of just forty-four, he believed himself a failure.

Tender is the Night was first serialised in *Scribner's Magazine* in the spring of 1934. The subsequently published volume briefly featured in the bestseller list but failed to achieve the critical acclaim or substantial sales of its predecessor. Despite some positive and, indeed, sensitive reviews, Fitzgerald was disappointed with the negative manner in which the book was received generally. Mainstream America was, perhaps, unprepared for some of its more controversial themes. Or maybe readers did not wish to read about the excesses of the Jazz Age while they themselves were enduring an economic depression. Certainly, the critics disapproved of its confusing timeline and reliance on flashbacks; in due course Fitzgerald would concur and begin writing copious notes on how the book might be rewritten. Eleven years after the author's death, Malcolm Cowley – a literary critic and close friend – would publish a revised edition with a more chronological timeline that was in line with the author's suggested amendments.

Many of the themes explored in either version of the book are as relevant today as they ever were. The attractiveness of youth – along with its freedoms and its dangers – is pervasively explored across much of Fitzgerald's earlier work, not least in *The Great Gatsby* and *The Curious Case of Benjamin Button*. But *Tender is the Night* provides the darker perspective of a more mature author, one who has seen first hand the destructive power of materialistic hedonism. Youth was a fixation of the Jazz Age; to be young and attractive was a social advantage. While acknowledging this, Fitzgerald was not afraid to highlight taboo topics such as the vulnerability of young people to sexual abuse and incest.

But the novel is richly layered with other themes such as war, violence, murder and destruction. Fitzgerald makes reference to World War I, a time when Diver was unquestionably sober and respectable. Later, the protagonist descends into drunken street violence and complicity with murder. Theatrical showcasing represents another theme, while paternity is yet another, but perhaps the most important of all is that of mental illness and the fragile nature of one's sanity regardless of talent, wealth or promise. Diver the psychiatrist sets out to cure Nicole the patient, but she destroys him utterly in the process of regaining her own sanity.

Ask anybody about F. Scott Fitzgerald and they will probably cite *The Great Gatsby* as his masterpiece. But *Tender is the Night* is the novel he agonised over during the course of a decade or more. It is the novel he obsessed about from the time of its publication until his death. It is the novel into which he poured everything he possessed: his money, his marriage and all the traumatic events he experienced in real life. It is the novel whose protagonist personifies the entire era with which the author is indelibly associated. In essence, it is F. Scott Fitzgerald's true masterpiece, the novel he might never have deemed finished had he lived another fifty years. As we can see, not everything born of recession is necessarily bad.

Clear with a Hint of Grene

> The world begins anew with every birth, my father used to say. He forgot to say, with every death it ends. Or did not think he needed to. Because for a goodly part of his life he worked in a graveyard.

Thus begins Sebastian Barry's novel *The Secret Scripture*, a haunting tale of twentieth century psychiatry set against the inception of the Irish free-state. The story is that of Roseanne McNulty – or Roseanne Clear, as she prefers to be known – who, as she approaches her centenary, begins to write a surreptitious and very personal account of her life thus far, two thirds of which has been spent in Roscommon Regional Mental Hospital.

How did she come to reside there? She does not appear unwell. Indeed, for a woman of one hundred, she is in remarkably rude health. Yet, such is the patchy nature of Roseanne's memory, we wonder whether she is quite so certain of the facts in her own mind that she might tell them accurately. Either way, as she puts pen to paper, she peppers the alleged truth with moving non-sequiturs and beautiful irrelevancies, and hides the manuscript beneath the floorboards of the ancient, crumbling hospital whose origins nobody seems able to evoke.

But the timeless institution is shortly due for closure. Dr Grene, the hospital's chief psychiatrist, is charged with the task of assessing each patient in turn to decide who is suitable for release into that intangible utopia we term "the community", and who ought to be transferred to a modern, purpose built facility currently awaiting the arrival of its new clients. Until now, Roseanne has largely been ignored by the good doctor, by the profession and, indeed, by society. Her existence seems forgotten. But as Dr Grene trawls through the files, the reasons for Roseanne's incarceration become increasingly elusive; and, as he interviews her, a curious interaction ensues in which doctor and patient are juxtaposed. Perhaps she is saner than he.

Because, you see, Dr Grene has his own demons. Mourning the recent death of his wife, the perceived failure of his marriage and his lack of career success, he approaches retirement like a man seeking atonement. Roseanne McNulty becomes less a challenge than an obsession. Certainly, Dr Grene is a psychiatrist with neither talent nor a sense of vocation; he appears to know very little about medicine. Indeed, from the admittedly esoteric perspective of this reviewer, perhaps the only disappointment in the novel is that its protagonist is somewhat unbelievable as a modern psychiatrist. Perhaps he hails from a bygone era.

But beyond his mere occupation, his characterisation is hauntingly believable. He is an individual in crisis, far more so than Roseanne McNulty, whom you might expect to be the needier of the two. Dr Grene's search for the truth is the road to redemption; but, faced with crumbling records and conflicting accounts, he realises this is easier said than done. "We are like MI5 sometimes in this our profession of psychiatry," he surmises. "All information becomes sensitive, worrying and vulnerable, even sometimes I think the mere time of day."

Roseanne's own account begins with fond memories of her father and an ambitious physics experiment in which he attempts to prove to his daughter that feathers will fall from a tower at the same rate as a hammer. Roseanne watches from the ground as Joe Clear tries and fails to execute the experiment with success. This matters little to her; her love and admiration for him is beyond question. Little wonder, therefore, that he is portrayed as a well travelled, well educated, Presbyterian man with gentle disposition and a love of literature and operettas. "The sermons of John Donne he prized above all, but his veritable gospel was *Religio Medici* by Sir Thomas Browne, a book I still possess in all the flotsam and ruckus of my life, in a little battered volume."

The story darkens as Joe Clear becomes unwittingly involved in the disposal of the body of a young soldier shot in the "troubles". Inadvertently risking the life of the local parish priest Father Gaunt, he loses his job and is forced, through fear of hunger and destitution, to become the town rat catcher. No less tragic is Joe Clear's eventual demise – by murder or suicide depending on whose account you might believe. As Dr Grene reads the ragged files of Father Gaunt, he learns the official line that Joe Clear was once a politically involved member of the constabulary and a heavy drinker to boot.

And as Roseanne's account unfolds, her life almost becomes a personification of Ireland's turbulent history, from violation to emancipation. Even her keeper, it seems, is an Englishman. A woman destroyed by politics, psychiatric stigma and the misogyny of the Catholic Church, Roseanne hails from a psychotic pedigree. Her mother shows signs of psychiatric illness from an early point in the story; Cissy Clear's mental state deteriorates quietly in the background until her eventual commitment to an asylum. But she is not the only one. What of Joe Clear's sanity?

According to Roseanne, "He used to tell a curious story about Southampton, and as a child I received it as the gospel truth". An account is revealed of Joe taking a bed for the night with a local landlady during the travels of his youth. A restless night ensues, involving locked cellar doors and strange goings-on until, next day, he is told by a local shopkeeper that the house has been uninhabited for several years. Visual hallucinations or folklore? Roseanne, like the reader, is left wondering.

In the end, *The Secret Scripture* is a vivid, thought provoking and sometimes disturbing portrayal of twentieth century psychiatry. Exploring the themes of truth and fantasy, love and betrayal, and sin and redemption, it is a tale unravelled mellifluously and with intrigue that never fails to keep the reader fully involved. Highly recommended.

Better to Burn Out than Fade Away?

Flip over the back cover to glance at the headline and we are told that, "Martin Sturrock desperately needs a psychiatrist". The difficulty here, we are told, is that Sturrock already is one. Thus we gain a glimpse of the troubled life led by the protagonist in Alastair Campbell's impressive first novel *All in the Mind*. Praised in *The Times*, *The Irish Times*, *The Independent* and by numerous other reviewers, the author seems to have convinced the world that he is not a mere writer of diaries. He is a novelist.

A Cambridge graduate who went on to work for the Mirror Group, Campbell is probably better known as the Labour Party press secretary (or, rather, the "official government spokesman and director of communications and strategy") for the best part of a decade until 2003. Following his departure, he continued to act as a Labour advisor, particularly during their 2005 election campaign. More noteworthy was the publication of extracts from his diaries under the title *The Blair Years*, which became a Number One bestseller. It is an impressive résumé for the son of a vet from Yorkshire.

Campbell's journey into the psyche of the modern psychiatrist haunts the reader. The tale takes place over one weekend and explores Dr Sturrock's relationship with half a dozen patients booked into his Friday morning clinic. A diverse and eclectic group, they include a young woman disfigured by horrific burns, a Kosovan refugee recovering from a sexual assault, a young man with depression and a middle-aged member of parliament with alcohol dependency. Alas, Sturrock is rapidly becoming burnt out, finding it hard to unburden himself of the vicarious traumas that threaten his own piece of mind and that of his family.

Although convincing in character, the protagonist seems far from the archetypal psychiatrist. Surely there can be few in this profession who are quite so worn down by their daily duties that are rendered unable to communicate effectively with their own families? Fewer still, we assume, seek the illicit comforts of prostitution. But alas, we are dealing with fiction; a character does not need to be typical to be believable, while the ordinary does not necessarily make for exciting reading.

Like any contemporary novel, *All in the Mind* was not met with universal acclaim. Some reviewers criticised the plot as simplistic, while others suggested Campbell relies too much on cliché. Have such critics sorely missed the point? This novel is not just about a psychiatrist; it is the universal story of contemporary burnout and its effects on personal and family life. It does not really matter that the protagonist is a doctor (although the incidence of burnout is admittedly quite high within the medical profession). Campbell makes a meaningful effort to explore this theme in the form of a simple tale that is both moving and believable. It is well worth a read if you fancy taking a break.

And this brings us neatly back to where we started, namely Bewley's Café with a coffee and a good book. As we have seen, literature through the centuries has served as a lens through which the reader can view the worlds of medicine and psychiatry. Sometimes insights are provided by physician-writers but equally we encounter vivid fictional portraits of doctors or patients sketched by non-medical writers. In the end, *Fiction & Physicians* has provided merely a snapshot, dipping its toe tentatively into the sea of popular culture created by – and about – doctors. It might have been possible to proceed *ad infinitum* but, as mentioned at the outset, my favourite coffee emporium on Grafton Street has now downsized. I will first have to find somewhere else to sit and think.

References and Bibliography

Barnes, Julian. *Arthur and George* (2005). Jonathan Cape.

Barnes, Julian. *Flaubert's Parrot* (1984). Jonathan Cape.

Barry, Sebastian. *The Secret Scripture* (2008). Faber and Faber.

Bennett, Alan. *The Madness of George III* (1992). Faber and Faber.

Brandreth, Gyles. *Oscar Wilde and the Candlelight Murders* (2007). John Murray.

Bryant, Mark. *Private Lives* (1996). Cassell and Co.

Bulgakov, Mikhail. *The Heart of a Dog* (1968). Vintage.

Burton, Robert (Ed. Jackson, H). *The Anatomy of Melancholy* (1651, 2001). New York Review Books.

Cahill K, O'Brien W. *Tropical Medicine: A Clinical Text* (1989). Anniversary Press.

Campbell, Alastair. *All in the Mind* (2008). Arrow Books.

Camus, Albert. *The Plague* (1947). Penguin Classics.

Canin, Ethan. *The Palace Thief* (1994). Random House.

Carson, Paul. *Scalpel* (1997). Arrow Books.

Chekhov, Anton. *The Shooting Party* (1885). Penguin Classics.

Chekhov, Anton. *Ward Number Six and Other Stories* (2008). Oxford World's Classics.

Cleckley Hervey. *The Mask of Sanity* (1841, 1988). William Dolan.

Collins, Wilkie. *The Moonstone* (1868, 1992). Penguin Popular Classics.

Crichton, Michael. *A Case of Need* (1969). Arrow Books.

Crichton, Michael. *Jurassic Park* (1990). Arrow Books.

Crichton, Michael. *Prey* (2006). Arrow Books.

Crichton, Michael. *State of Fear* (2004). Arrow Books.

Crichton, Michael. *The Andromeda Strain* (1969). Arrow Books.

Crichton, Michael. *The Terminal Man* (1972). Arrow Books.

Crichton, Michael. *Timeline* (1999). Arrow Books.

Cronin, A.J. *The Citadel* (1937). Victor Gollancz.

Darwin, Charles. *On the Origin of Species: By Means of Natural Selection* (1859). Dover Publications Inc.

Doyle, Sir Arthur Conan. *A Study in Scarlett* (1887). Penguin.

DSM-IV: *Diagnostic and Statistical Manual of Mental Disorders* (4th Ed, 1994). American Psychiatric Association.

Faulks, Sebastian. *Human Traces* (2005). Hutchinson.

Fitzgerald, Francis Scott. *Tender is the Night* (1934). Vintage.

Flaubert, Gustave. *Madame Bovary* (1857). Penguin.

Foucault, Michel. *The History of Madness* (1961, 2009). Routledge.

Freeman D, Freeman J. *Paranoia: The 21st-Century Fear* (2008). Oxford University Press.

Galgut, Damon. *The Good Doctor* (2003). Atlantic Books.

Gelder M, Mayou R, Cowen P. *Shorter Oxford Textbook of Psychiatry* (4th Ed, 2001). Oxford University Press.

Gerritsen, Tess. *Harvest* (1996). Bantam.

Gibian, Peter. *Oliver Wendell Holmes and the Culture of Conversation*: Cambridge Studies in American Literature and Culture (2009). Cambridge University Press.

Goldsmith, Oliver. *The Vicar of Wakefield* (1766). Oxford World Classics.

Greene, Graham. *A Burnt-Out Case* (1960). Vintage.

Haddon, Mark. *The Curious Incident of the Dog in the Night-time* (2003). David Fickling Books.

Halley, Ned. *The Complete Prophecies of Nostradamus* (1999). Wordsworth Reference.

Hare R.D., Hart S.D., Harpur T.J. "Psychopathy and the DSM-IV criteria for antisocial personality disorder" (1991). *Journal of Abnormal Psychology*, 100(3):391-8.

Harris, Thomas. *Hannibal* (1999). Arrow Books.

Harris, Thomas. *Hannibal Rising* (2006). Arrow Books.

Harris, Thomas. *Red Dragon* (1981). Arrow Books.

Harris, Thomas. *The Silence of the Lambs* (1988). Arrow Books.

Hastings, Selina. *The Secret Lives of Somerset Maugham* (2010). John Murray.

Heller, Joseph. *Catch-22* (1961). Vintage.

Highsmith, Patricia. *The Talented Mr Ripley* (1955). Vintage.

Hosseini, Khaled. *The Kite Runner* (2003). Bloomsbury Publishing Plc.

Huxley, Aldous. *Brave New World* (1932). Vintage.

Keats, John. *The Complete Poems of John Keats* (1994). Wordsworth Editions.

Kerouac, Jack. *Doctor Sax* (1959). Flamingo.

Laing, R.D. *Knots* (1970). Vintage.

Laing, R.D. *The Divided Self* (1960). Penguin Classics.

Longmore M., Wilkinson I.B., Rajagopalan S. *Oxford Handbook of Clinical Medicine* (6th Ed, 2005). Oxford University Press.

Louis de Bernières. *Captain Corelli's Mandolin* (1993). Vintage.

Luria, Aleksandr. *The Mind and the Mnemonist: A Little Book about Vast Memory* (1986). Harvard University Press.

Lykken D.T. *The Antisocial Personalities* (1995). Lawrence Erlbaum Associates.

Mann, Thomas, *Death in Venice* (1912). Dover Publications.

Márquez, Gabriel García. *Love in the Time of Cholera* (1985). Penguin.

McEwan, Ian. *Enduring Love* (1997). Vintage.

McEwan, Ian. *Saturday* (2004). Jonathan Cape.

Milne, A.A. *The Red House Mystery* (1922). Vintage Classics.

O'Connor, Ulick. *Oliver St John Gogarty* (1964, 1981, 2000). O'Brien Press.

Orwell, George. *Nineteen Eighty-Four* (1949). Penguin.

Oyebode, Femi (Ed). *Mindreadings: Literature and Psychiatry* (2009). Royal College of Psychiatrists.

Pasternak, Boris. *Doctor Zhivago* (1957). Vintage.

Pearl, Matthew. *The Dante Club* (2004). Vintage.

Rabelais, François. *The Life of Gargantua and the Heroic Deeds of Pantagruel* (2010). Nabu Press.

Ramsland K. Forensic *Psychology of Criminal Minds.* (1st Ed, 2010). Berkley.

Richards, David G. *Georg Büchner's Woyzeck: A History of Its Criticism* (2001). Camden.

Robins A.H., Sellars S.L. "Oscar Wilde's terminal illness: reappraisal after a century" (2000). *Lancet*, 356(9244):1841-3.

Rubenfeld, Jed. *The Interpretation of Murder* (2006). Headline Review.

Sacks, Oliver. *Awakenings* (1973). Picador.

Sacks, Oliver. *The Man who Mistook His Wife for a Hat* (1985). Picador.

Schnitzler, Arthur. *Selected Short Fiction*, translated by Davies, J.M.Q. (1998). Angel Classics.

Shakespeare W., Orgel S. *The Oxford Shakespeare: Winter's Tale* (1611, 2008). Oxford Paperbacks.

Shelley, Mary. *Frankenstein, or The Modern Prometheus* (1818, 1831). Vintage.

Shuttleton, David E. *Smallpox and the Literary Imagination* (2007). Cambridge.

Somerset Maugham, William. *Cakes and Ale* (1919). William Heinemann.

Somerset Maugham, William. *Of Human Bondage* (1916). William Heinemann.

Somerset Maugham, William. *The Moon and Sixpence* (1930). William Heinemann.

Somerset Maugham, William. *The Painted Veil* (1925). William Heinemann.

Somerset Maugham, William. *The Razor's Edge* (1944). William Heinemann.

Somerset Maugham, William. *The Summing Up* (1938). William Heinemann.

Sterne, Laurence. *The Life and Opinions of Tristram Shandy, Gentleman* (1759-67). Wordsworth Editions.

Stevenson, Robert Louis. *The Strange Case of Dr Jekyll and Mr Hyde* (1886). Penguin Classics.

Stoker. Bram. *Dracula* (1897). Penguin Classics.

Storr, Anthony. *Freud* (Past Masters) (1989). Oxford Paperbacks.

Summerscale, Kate. *The Suspicions of Mr Whicher – or the Murder at Road Hill House* (2008). Bloomsbury Publishing Plc.

The Times Book of Quotations (2000). Harper Collins.

Twain, Mark. *The Adventures of Huckleberry Finn* (1885). Penguin Classics.

Uglow, Jenny. *The Lunar Men: The Friends who Made the Future* (2002). Faber and Faber.

Weir Mitchell, Silas. *The Autobiography of a Quack and the Case of George Dedlow* (2010). Filiquarian Publishing.

Williams, William Carlos (Ed. Rosenthal, M. L.). *The William Carlos Williams Reader* (1966). New Directions.

Wilson, Damon. *The Mammoth Book of Nostradamus and Other Prophets* (1999). Robinson Publishing.

World Health Organisation Statistical Information System (WHOSIS) and Global Health Observatory (GHO). See www.who.int/whosis and www.who.int/gho respectively.

Wright P., Stern J., Phelan M. *Core Psychiatry* (2000). W.B. Saunders.

Zola, Emile. *Germinal* (1885). Penguin Classics.

Glossary of Medical
and Psychiatric Terms

Agnosia – A disorder of the brain whereby the individual cannot interpret sensation, even though the senses are intact. In auditory agnosia, for example, the individual cannot place any meaning on sounds even though they can hear them.

Akinetic Mutism – A state of complete physical unresponsiveness, often as a result of damage to the base of the brain. The patient's eyes usually remain open and appear to follow movement. See also catatonia.

Aneurysm – A balloon like swelling in the wall of an artery.

Antipsychotics – Medications used primarily to treat psychosis (see below). Most examples inhibit the neurotransmitter dopamine (also see below). An example cited in this book is chlorpromazine.

Apraxia – A disorder of the brain that results in an individual's poor ability to perform skilled bodily movements.

Autosomal Dominant – Humans have 23 pairs of chromosomes, namely a sex linked pair (XX for females and XY for males) and 22 pairs of autosomes. When a disease is caused by a dominant gene on an autosome, it is termed autosomal dominant. Such a gene tends to express itself, if present.

Bacillus – A rod shaped variety of bacterium (see also vibrio and spirochete).

Basal Ganglia – A collection of several large grey masses embedded deep within the white matter of the brain. The primary function of the basal ganglia is to regulate (unconsciously) voluntary body movements.

Catatonia – A psychotic state whereby an individual becomes mute or rigid, or adopts fixed postures. See also akinetic mutism.

Cerebral Cortex – The most highly developed part of the brain, broadly responsible for logical thinking, sensation and the control the voluntary actions of the body. It is divided into two hemispheres and each hemisphere has four lobes, namely the frontal, parietal, temporal and occipital lobes (at the front, top, side and back of the cortex respectively).

Chagas Disease – A tropical illness present in rural parts of Central and South America, spread through the faeces of bloodsucking bugs. The faeces contains the pathogen Trypanosoma cruzi and enters the blood stream through scratches and wounds. The infection is currently treatable but can be fatal if left untreated.

Convulsion – An involuntary, rhythmical muscular contraction of the body and limbs, usually due to abnormal electrical activity in the brain. Also known as a seizure, it is a feature of epilepsy, among other ailments.

Dark Ground Microscopy – A scientific means of examining living cells through a microscope.

Delirium – A sudden onset brain disorder that involves the compromise of mental processes including disorientation, agitation, hallucinations and delusions. It can be caused by a variety of medical conditions such as infections, and is often reversible.

Delusion – A false belief held with immovable conviction that is at odds with cultural norms. Persecutory (or paranoid) delusions are among the commonest varieties, but delusions also include those of guilt, grandiosity, erotomania (de Clerambault's syndrome) and jealousy (the Othello syndrome). A delusion is an example of a psychotic symptom.

Dementia – A persistent and pervasive brain disorder that involves the compromise of mental processes marked by gradual deterioration. Features include loss of memory and reasoning ability, disorientation, change in personality and deterioration in self-care. Examples include Alzheimer's disease. Unlike delirium, dementia is irreversible.

Dissocial (or Antisocial) Personality Disorder – A personality disorder is a pervasive pattern of experience and behaviour that causes distress and adversely impacts an individual's social environment. Onset is usually in late childhood, while the symptoms cannot be due to an illness. There are roughly ten identified varieties of personality disorder. Someone with a dissocial personality disorder shows callous unconcern for the feelings of others, an inability to experience guilt, a disregard for social norms, an inability to maintain enduring relationships, a low tolerance of frustration and a marked tendency to blame others for deeds which bring them into conflict with society.

Dopamine – See neurotransmitter.

Electroencephalogram (EEG) – A type of brain scan that detects electrical activity so that it can be compared to the norm.

Electrolytes – A collective name for salts that exist everywhere within the body. They are generally taken into the body through food and removed via excretion of various bodily fluids. The kidneys help to keep their levels finely balanced. Examples include sodium and potassium.

Emotionally Unstable (or Borderline) Personality Disorder – A personality disorder is a pervasive pattern of experience and behaviour that causes distress and adversely impacts a person's social environment. Onset is usually in late childhood, while the symptoms cannot be due to an illness. There are roughly ten identified varieties of personality disorder. Someone with an emotionally unstable (or borderline) personality disorder displays chronic feelings of emptiness, an uncertainty about self-image, a tendency to become involved in intense and unstable relationships, excessive efforts to avoid abandonment, and recurrent threats or acts of self-harm, among other features.

Encephalitis Lethargica – A viral inflammation of the brain that reached epidemic proportions shortly after World War I. Symptoms include headache, drowsiness and tremor that eventually progress to coma, hence the nickname "sleepy sickness".

Enzyme – A protein catalyst found naturally in the body that speeds up the rate of a chemical reaction without, itself, being involved in that reaction.

Gastroenteritis – Inflammation of the lining of the gut, usually due to infection. Symptoms include abdominal cramps, vomiting, diarrhoea and high temperature.

General Paralysis of the Insane – A consequence of late stage (quaternary) syphilis comprised of dementia and spastic weakness of the limbs – and sometimes deafness, seizures and difficulty enunciating words (dysarthria). It is due to infection of the brain with neurosyphilis (see below) and, although it can sometimes be treated with penicillin, recovery is unlikely.

Haemoglobin – A substance found in red blood cells responsible for binding reversibly with oxygen and thus transporting it around the body. Heamoglobin gives red blood cells their colour and is composed of the pigment haem (which contains iron) and the protein globin.

Hallucination – A perception in the absence of a stimulus. Examples include hearing voices or seeing objects that are not really there (auditory and visual hallucinations respectively). A hallucination is an example of a psychotic symptom.

Hypovolaemic Shock – Collapse of the circulatory system due to insufficient blood (for example, due to bleeding or severe dehydration). Blood pressure becomes too low to supply the tissues and organs adequately. Symptoms include a cold sweat, a weak rapid pulse, irregular breathing and dilated pupils.

Incubation Period – The time lag between the exposure to an infection and the appearance of its first symptoms.

L-dopa (Levodopa) – A naturally occurring amino acid commonly used to treat the signs and symptoms of Parkinson's disease.

Lesion – An area of tissue with impaired function due to damage or disease.

Leucocytes – White blood cells containing a nucleus. They mostly fight infection.

Lithium – A naturally occurring salt, first used medicinally in 1948 by the Australian psychiatrist John Cade. It is still widely used primarily to treat mood disorders such as bipolar affective disorder.

Lymph Nodes – Filters within the lymphatic system, a system of vessels containing fluid that bathes the tissues and removes debris. Lymph nodes become swollen during infection.

Magnetic Resonance Image (MRI) – A type of radiology that allows internal body structures to be visualised when the atoms within cells are aligned using powerful magnets.

Medulla Oblongata – The base of the brain just above the spinal cord, essential for core physiological functions such as swallowing, breathing and regulation of the heart.

Negative Symptoms – A set of findings in schizophrenia whereby an individual becomes ambivalent about contact with family and friends, displays a paucity of facial expression, avoids conversing with others (sometimes to the point of mutism), and generally becomes withdrawn from society (for example, dropping out of work or education).

Neuroses – A collective term for anxiety related disorders.

Neurosyphilis – Syphilis affecting the nervous system. See also general paralysis of the insane.

Neurotransmitter – The brain is not merely electrical, but also chemical. While nerves themselves are electrical, there are gaps (termed synapses) between nerve-endings and these are bridged by chemicals collectively termed neurotransmitters, released from one nerve-ending to travel across the synapse to the next. Examples include dopamine and serotonin.

Otologist – An ear specialist.

Palliative – Treatment that temporarily relieves symptoms such as pain without actually curing the disease.

Parkinson's Disease – A disease marked by tremor, rigidity, poor gait and poverty of spontaneous movements. It is cause by a degeneration of those nerves that rely on the neurotransmitter dopamine.

Pleurisy – Inflammation of the covering of the lungs (pleura), often due to infections such as pneumonia. It is associated with pain upon breathing and a characteristic "rub" that is audible with a stethoscope.

Psychosis – A state in which an individual's thoughts become detached from reality. Common symptoms include delusions, hallucinations, disordered thought processes and what are termed negative symptoms (see above). Catatonia represents a less common symptom. The commonest psychotic illness is schizophrenia, while others include psychosis related to severe mania or depression, illicit drug misuse or physical illness.

Pulmonary – Related to the lungs.

Schizophrenia – The commonest form of psychotic illness, affecting one percent of people at some stage during their lives. See psychosis.

Senna – A laxative derived from the dried fruits of Cassia shrubs.

Serology – The study of blood serum, and particularly the degree to which it protects the body against disease.

Serotonin – See neurotransmitter.

Spirochete – A helical shaped variety of bacterium (see also vibrio and bacillus).

Talipes Equinovarus – Commonly known as club foot, the foot is turned downwards and inwards so that the individual must walk on the outer edge of its upper surface.

Vesicle – A small pinpoint blister containing clear fluid.

Vibrio – A comma shaped variety of bacterium (see also bacillus and spirochete).

Permissions

Excerpts by Edmund D. Pellegrino taken from *Medicine and Literature* edited by Enid Rhodes Peschel published by Neale Watson Academic Publications. Reprinted with kind permission.

Excerpt from "In Memory of Sigmund Freud" by W.H. Auden published by Random House Limited. Copyright © Curtis Brown Ltd. Reprinted by permission of Curtis Brown Limited.

Excerpts from *The Summing Up* and *The Moon and Sixpence* by William Somerset Maugham published by Vintage Books. Reprinted with the permission of A.P. Wyatt Limited on behalf of The Royal Literary Fund.

Excerpts from *The William Carlos Williams Reader* (1965) by William Carlos Williams and edited by M.L. Rosenthal, including a reprint of "The Red Wheelbarrow" by William Carlos Williams. Reprinted with the permission of Carcanet Press Limited.

Excerpts from *The Suspicions of Mr Whicher* by Kate Summerscale published by Bloomsbury Publishing Plc. Reproduced with kind permission. Copyright © Kate Summerscale, 2008 and Bloomsbury Publishing Plc.

Excerpts from *Catch-22* by Joseph Heller published by Vintage Books. Reproduced with permission of Curtis Brown Ltd, London on behalf of The Estate of Joseph Heller. Copyright © Joseph Heller, 1961.

Excerpts from *Saturday* by Ian McEwan published by Jonathan Cape. Reprinted by permission of The Random House Group Limited.

Excerpts from *The Citadel* by A. J. Cronin (copyright (c) A. J. Cronin, 1937) reprinted by kind permission of A. M. Heath & Co Ltd.

Excerpts from *Enduring Love* by Ian McEwan published by Vintage Books. Reprinted by permission of The Random House Group Limited.

Excerpts from *The Talented Mr Ripley* by Patricia Highsmith published by Vintage Books. Reprinted by permission of The Random House Group Limited.

Excerpts from *Red Dragon* by Thomas Harris published by Arrow Books. Reprinted by permission of The Random House Group Limited.

Excerpts from *Human Traces* by Sebastian Faulks published by Vintage Books. Reprinted by permission of The Random House Group Limited.

Excerpts from *The Madness of George III* by Alan Bennett and *The Secret Scripture* by Sebastian Barry published by Faber and Faber Limited. Reprinted in accordance with their fair usage policy (www.faber.co.uk/about/permissions-fair-dealing/).

The author has made considerable effort to acquire permissions to reprint the brief excerpts that appear in this book. Any quotations appearing in this book without explicit permission have been used in line with universal fair usage principals that apply to limited excerpts for the purposes of criticism or review. The author is pleased to address any inadvertent shortcomings in this regard.

Index

mc   11/13